Confronting Oppression, Restoring Justice
From Policy Analysis to Social Action
Katherine van Wormer

Council on Social Work Education Alexandria Virginia

*To marginalized people of the world who reach out past the boundaries of their own op-
pression to work for the liberation of others who are also oppressed, and to members of the
oppressor class who choose to give up privilege and become allies in the struggle.*

*This dedication is written in the belief that, as they say in treatment, "Alone I can't;
together we can."*

Copyright © 2004 by the Council on Social Work Education
All rights reserved. No part of this book may be reproduced or transmitted in any
manner whatsoever without the prior written permission of the publisher.

Reprinted 2005

Council on Social Work Education
1725 Duke Street, Suite 500
Alexandria, VA 22314-3457
www.cswe.org

Library of Congress Cataloging-in-Publication Data

Van Wormer, Katherine S.
  Confronting oppression, restoring justice : from policy analysis to social action / Katherine van Wormer.
      p. cm. -- (Advancing social work education)
Includes bibliographical references and index.
    ISBN 0-87293-106-4
    1. Social justice. 2. Social advocacy. 3. Oppression (Psychology) 4. Equality.
5. Social policy. I. Title. II. Series.
    HM671.V36 2004
    303.3'72--dc22
              2003027532

Printed in the United States of America

Contents

Foreword
by David G. Gil

Introducing a new work on social policy and social work practice involves viewing it in the context of the literature and history of the discipline, and locating its orientation and message on the field's intellectual, philosophical, and ideological map.

Dominant Themes of the Field's Literature

Many authors conceptualize social policy and social work as constructive responses to social and personal problems such as poverty, unemployment, injustice, discrimination, crime, violence, emotional ills, etc., that tend to be prevalent in many past and contemporary societies. A certain incidence of these and other problems is usually viewed by these writers as a "normal feature" of human societies. Policies and practice are meant to ameliorate and reduce the frequency of the problems, but not to prevent and eliminate them altogether.

While social policies and social work practice can indeed respond constructively to social and individual problems, the history of policy evolution and social work reveals that policies respond frequently to these problems in a neutral and even destructive manner. Social work practice, in spite of constructive intentions, often does not help people to solve their problems, but merely facilitates their adaptation to destructive existential realities. A study of history reveals also that coercively established social policies were actually the sources rather than the solution of social problems, and that social work practice, in spite of its ethical values, has often served to control victims of social problems and social injustice in the interest of dominant social groups, castes, and classes.

Writers on social policy and social work rarely ask whether human societies have always experienced the kind of social problems mentioned earlier; whether certain societies at different times and places did not experience such problems; and what has caused the emergence of social and personal problems in societies that were once free of them. Much writing on social policy and social work tends to disregard history and, therefore, does not raise these questions.

Many authors seem to consider social patterns of domination, exploitation, and hierarchy, and social and individual problems usually associated with these patterns, as constant aspects of human societies. They view these patterns as inherent in human nature in the sense of inevitability, rather than merely as one among different possible patterns inherent in human nature. They overlook historical evidence that these patterns were initiated and maintained through violent, coercive processes, some 10,000 years ago, following the transformation of relatively small, homogenous, nomadic tribes that lived by hunting and gathering into sedentary communities in larger societies who engaged in animal husbandry, agriculture, crafts, and trade. Over time, these societies became divided through internal conflicts into occupational and social castes and classes and they tended to expand their territories and populations into empires by warfare, conquest, colonization, and enslavement—the initial stages of patterns of domination, exploitation, and hierarchy.

Katherine van Wormer's Work

Professor van Wormer's new book derives from an alternative view of the nature of social and individual problems and of the function of social policy and social work. The book reflects a minority, "radical" tradition of the field that goes back to Jane Addams and the settlement movement of past centuries (Reisch & Andrews, 2001). Radical authors do not view social and individual problems as "normal features" of all human societies, but as usual consequences of societal patterns of domination, exploitation, and hierarchy, and of value systems stressing inequality and competition that sustain these patterns. They agree with non-radical writers that social policy and social work should respond as constructively as possible to problems intrinsic to prevailing social realities. However, they think that policy and practice ought to go beyond such inevitably limited responses within the established social system, and should pursue comprehensive transformations of destructive institutional realities into ways of life conducive to the well-being and full development of all people, everywhere. Moreover, they hold that in order to conform to the social justice principles of the "Code of Ethics" of social workers, policy and practice ought to advance the development of social, economic, political, and cultural systems assuring equal rights and responsibilities for everyone in all spheres of life.

In her book, van Wormer applies a radical perspective to clarifying the meanings of key concepts including oppression and its internalization, injustice, and social exclusion; social justice and restorative justice; and empowerment and critical consciousness. She then reviews biological, psychological, and sociological aspects of oppression and the impact of the dynamics of capitalist markets and culture on oppressive relations from local to global levels.

The book moves from theoretical perspectives to consideration of specific manifestations of oppression and social exclusion and their links to the values, ideology, and institutions of capitalism. Included among the manifestations she analyzes are gender-based oppression, personal victimization, economic and political oppression, racial and ethnic oppression, oppression based on disabilities, and oppression of children, youth, and aging people.

Important themes examined in the book include social-structurally focused vs. symptom-focused policy analysis; links between social work practice and political action for structural social change; empowerment and strength-based social work practice; social work practice and the human-rights perspective derived from the Universal Declaration of Human Rights; the futility of the "criminal justice" system and especially women's experiences in that system; the alternative concept and practice of "restorative justice"; and social change strategies involving dialogical communication aimed at the spreading of "critical consciousness" (Freire, 1970).

Van Wormer's book makes important contributions to a radical paradigm of social policy development and social work practice. It presents to the field an approach aimed at narrowing the gap between the social justice orientation of its Code of Ethics and the actual realities of the dominant policy and practice paradigm.

David G. Gil is professor, Heller School for Social Policy and Management, Brandeis University, Boston, Massachusetts.

Preface

The initial inspiration for this book, as often happens, came through the writing of another book. On the surface, the topic was different—addiction and addictions treatment, and this was more of a practice rather than a policy text. At least that's the way it started out. Essentially, *Addiction Treatment: A Strengths Perspective* made the case for helping people reduce the harm to themselves; the theoretical framework was a harm reduction as opposed to a zero tolerance approach. One thing that soon became apparent in the writing of this book, however, was how much of the harm being done was committed by the system itself. These harms related to the war on drugs, which has become a war on the drug users, and the relationship between personal oppression and the abuse of substances. The inequities in the system that would be obvious to even the most casual observer can be summed up in these terms: *The rich get treatment, and the poor get prison.*

I suspect that the damage done in the effort of drug use prevention by the state is more than equal to the damage done by the drug use itself. Take the zero tolerance concept in drug eradication as a case in point. Fought on foreign shores as well as on the home front, this war on drugs has taken a great toll in suffering on drug users, a toll disproportionately experienced by poor people and people of color. With the influx of drug users going to prison, there are today more than 2 million people behind bars, most of them minorities. In the midst of so much injustice (in the law itself) and oppression (in its enforcement), the challenge to the writer to present a harm reduction model was formidable.

A second realization that emerged in the writing of the addictions book is related to the first: Many people turn to drugs to escape oppression—oppression in the system and in their personal lives. Typical is the case of the gay runaway who lives on the streets, or the battered woman who has lost all sense of security and trust and who drinks to cope. More generally families mired in poverty may live in blighted communities where rents are cheap and drug use is rampant. As the single parent works overtime to compensate for low wages, the children are at high risk of exposure to drugs and violence. In addition to structural and interpersonal abuse is the harm inflicted upon people in the name of treatment. Consider the paradox from the author's standpoint—offering treatment guidelines from a strengths perspective for practitioners who work within an unjust and highly repressive system. Much of addictions treatment today, in fact, takes place within the walls of a jail or prison. Even in outpatient treatment centers, participation in demeaning practices, such as performing random, routine urinalysis checks on clients, typically was a part of the job description. The fact that few of the workers within the system seemed bothered by the paradox was as disturbing as the paradox itself.

The inspiration for *Confronting Oppression, Restoring Justice* was an outgrowth then, not of what was said in earlier writings, but of what was left unsaid. I am speaking here of the broader policy issues, those that go beyond treatment, beyond punitive laws, and into the area of social context. So it was that writing what started out as a practice book within one specialized setting led to grappling with ever higher abstractions, and that practice issues and matters of policy began to merge. In the end, advocacy for the *practice* of harm reduction would become advocacy for the *politics* of harm reduction.

For the present effort, I propose that we examine the twin forces of oppression and injustice and the manner in which the social structure promotes or sustains them. Let us look not only at policies themselves but also at the ideology behind the policies—the punishment rather than treatment of drug addicts, for example. Because every social system is full of contradictions, and the motives behind the shaping of policies are mixed, this venture will not be easy.

In the course of examining the system, I will draw on observations and experiences gleaned from working within the constraints of third-party reimbursement schemes and worse and from my investigations of the criminal justice system—from the courtroom to inside prison walls.

This book is informed, moreover, by the international experience of living and working in two foreign countries, one of which was more oppressive than the United States, Northern Ireland of the 1960s, and one of which was considerably less so, Norway of today. I should mention also my upbringing in the segregated Deep South as a member of the oppressor class, an upbringing to which I owe my horror of oppression and a personal awareness of how, in the unjust society, all classes of people pay in one way or another, forever. It is this horror and a certain fascination with bigotry and injustice and greed that have made the writing of this book less an academic exercise than a mission.

Is oppression inevitable? Perhaps. Still, the international variations are astounding. This is what analysis tells us. Policy analysis entails an examination of certain policies within the context of social norms. To know the social norms of a given society requires a stepping outside, the insight that comes from global awareness. Such an awareness leads us to contemplate how in one society doctors can prescribe heroin to help addicts avoid the street scene, a practical approach that would be unimaginable somewhere else. From a global perspective, we come to understand that interventions are acceptable to the degree that they blend into the fabric of the social structure, that they are consistent with the predominant values of that culture. More specifically, whereas the legacy of punitiveness and a fierce work ethic, archaic carry-overs from the Puritan "Founding Fathers," shape social welfare and criminal justice policies in the United States today, there are other approaches in other lands of which we should be aware. When I practiced alcoholism counseling in Norway, I was struck by the contrast between Norway and the United States in philosophy and attitude, a contrast that transcended the workplace and extended to areas such as child rearing and cradle-to-grave welfare programs. The advantage of living abroad or otherwise adopting an international perspective is in revealing the possibilities, in giving us pride in our own achievements, and in enriching our knowledge of other approaches, other visions. A global perspective is further required to comprehend the impact today of multinational economic structures on vulnerable populations everywhere.

At the dawn of the 21st century, the welfare state is in crisis. Much of the crisis stems from the transformation underway as we enter the age of the global economy. Let us start with the industrializing or "developing" nations. Here the pressures to reduce indebtedness to international banks or foreign powers are enormous. Two requirements imposed by the financial institutions are the production of cash crops and social welfare retrenchment. In industrialized economies as well, corporate interests favor cutbacks in spending for such social welfare programs as income maintenance, free healthcare, and subsidized housing while promoting such policies as free trade, managed health care, and privatization of services. The favored programs are all associated in one way or another with cheap labor. Economic forces conducive to a nation's industrial growth and competitiveness, in short, are not always conducive to the health of the individual citizens and families.

The impact of economic globalization is seen in the concentration of wealth at the upper echelons of society, an increasing gap between rich and poor, and the erosion of social and political supports at all levels. This impact is further evidenced in the depletion of natural resources, and the reliance on soup kitchens, food banks, and shelters for the homeless. The most salient aspect of this phenomenon is its universality.

Without an understanding of the impact of world capitalism, then, people will find it difficult to effect changes in policies to enhance the social life of their community. Much of the *oppression* we see in the world today is directly or indirectly related to forces in the wider economy. *Injustice* arises through inequalities in the distribution of resources and punishments. Injustice also arises through scapegoatism as some people, disturbed by economic insecurities, displace their aggression onto others. So how can the forces of good overcome the forces of oppression? That is among the questions that guide this work.

We cannot confront oppression and injustice without an awareness of the forces, including psychological factors, involved in their perpetuation. Nor can we create a countervailing force to this corporate power and arbitrary rule without thinking and organizing transnationally. "Think globally, act locally," as the environmentalists say.

To "act locally," policy makers, helping professionals, and advocates who care about poverty, oppression, and repression need to develop skills and abilities to enable them to step forward as change agents. Fortunately, they are not alone. The very information technology that bolsters the networking of corporate alliances and enhances the movement of centers of production from one part of the globe to another allows for grassroots collaboration to resist some of the most noxious of the economic trends. A new consciousness has arisen today, a consciousness of oppression and injustice. A large part of this consciousness, in fact, is a result of the communications revolution. Through Internet mobilization, regional teach-ins, and the alternative press, collective action is being taken on behalf of any number of deprived groups including "Third World" women, indigenous populations, and preservation of the physical environment. The new consciousness is promoting the protection of environmental and human resources. Challenges to some of the most unsavory aspects of global capitalism, perhaps, in response to the criticism, are coming from within the corporate leadership itself.

Tasks of This Book

The four major tasks of this book are (1) to provide a conceptual framework for understanding the nature of oppression and injustice; (2) to describe the skills of critical analysis needed to confront oppression and injustice; (3) to provide illustrations of successfully conceived and instituted programs; and (4) to forge a conceptual link between the oppression/injustice configuration and strategies of empowerment.

Oppression we can conceptualize as stemming from inequities in the power structure and the ideologies that serve to reinforce them. The first task or purpose of this book is to provide a context for the pursuit of policy making, to help readers develop skill in the critical analysis of social welfare policies and proposals. This context, one which has received little attention in social work policy analysis texts, let alone in the textbooks of related mental health disciplines, is enunciated in the National Association of Social Workers' (NASW) *Code of Ethics* (1996). As stipulated in Section 6.04(c): "Social workers should promote conditions that encourage respect for cultural and social diversity within the United States and globally. Social workers should promote policies and practices that demonstrate respect for difference, support the expansion of cultural knowledge and resources," etc. (See Chapter 1.)

Oppression. Injustice. Power. Empowerment. Innovation. The center point of any change effort is the notion of power. The very kind of economic benefits accorded to a constituency depends on its relationship to the power structure. Consider the generous economic incentives ("corporate welfare") for businesses and entrepreneurs and contrast this with the stigmatized, charity-type financial aid to poor families. Control of the mass media, of course, is crucial as a justification for the status quo. Ideology is shaped through the build-up of stories in the media (for example, "the crime wave," "welfare fraud") at the same time that attention is diverted away from the inequities in the system. And ideology shapes policy. But special interest groups such as social work professionals, can play the game, too, and inform the public through the media. Much of the clout of social work, incidentally, stems from media campaigns combined with political savvy. NASW is a formidable lobbying organization with more than 150,000 members. The political know-how represented by the membership is instilled in courses in social work such as one for which the present book is intended.

Apart from considerations of professional influence, the age-old question facing social workers is this: Working within the system or from the outside, how can we avoid participating in oppression? Or, working from the inside, how can we help the casualties of economic restructuring or the victims of structural or interpersonal violence? Here is where training in particular skills of writing up program proposals, lobbying persons in Congress, and using the Internet for grassroots actions come in. Attention to such policy-influencing efforts constitutes the second task of this book.

Despite the critical role that oppression and its counterpart injustice play within the shaping of the social welfare system, it is relatively rare for either practitioners or scholars to spend time investigating these twin phenomena. Attention may be paid to the social conditions of poor and other vulnerable people, and to progressive programs such as Head Start and home health care and prison aftercare, but little attention is given to a study of the context within which such programs appear; they may or may not be representative of the present social climate, in which case they are highly vulnerable to eradication. In order to effect positive social change, advocates need to focus more on the context of things, so that in anticipating the forces of resistance, they are better able to combat them. A study of the nature of oppression and injustice is in order.

Third is the presentation of exemplary programs and other initiatives. In this time of economic transformation and political turmoil, "visions of the possible"—innovative approaches to meeting people's needs, resolving conflicts, and restoring justice—assume a major importance. One such example that is presented in this volume is the social activism on behalf of and by poor people, the New Freedom Bus Riders of the Kensington Welfare Rights Union (described in Chapter 4). This and other initiatives related to social justice and human rights are described. The concept of empowerment is the link that ties this series of policy initiatives to the social policy agenda. Such initiatives sometimes start with grassroots organizing and lobbying and then are adopted by local government; most often, though, the momentum comes from state or national legislation and passes on down through the lower levels without input from the people themselves.

Research into program effectiveness, such as evidence of reduced crime rates or of client success in obtaining employment, can be pivotal in the promotion or continuation of an experimental project. Evidence of cost effectiveness can be a key deciding factor in the early stages of program development as well. Often, however, politics in conjunction with media hype is the deciding factor in the success or failure of a treatment innovation. Between treatment effectiveness and ideology, ideology commonly wins out, especially if media accounts portray the proposal as radical or as only of benefit to certain classes of people viewed as "other." Perhaps not surprisingly needle exchange programs, which were widely known to reduce the spread of AIDS contraction among drug addicts and their families, failed to obtain federal funding despite a wide backing for the bill in Congress. The opposition's moralistic stance carried the day. To counter such resistance and to mobilize public opinion, organizers must work with the media to share research findings concerning the program or proposal and evidence of cost benefits to taxpayers and cost-effectiveness to the state budget. Personal testimonials from program graduates (for example, of Head Start) can be especially persuasive in maintaining public support. This brings us to the fourth and final purpose of this book—to forge a conceptual link between the oppression/injustice configuration and strategies of empowerment that seek to alleviate these conditions. Preeminent among such strategies are those collectively known as restorative justice.

The intended audience for *Confronting Oppression, Restoring Justice* consists of frontline social welfare professionals, reformers, victim-assistance advocates, sociologists, and all other persons associated with the system's casualties. The subject matter of this book assumes a special relevance as globalization breeds both corporate political might and worldwide coalition building for social justice.

Structure of the Book

Forgive the long title. Aesthetics gave way to practicality in making this choice. The need was for a title that both proclaimed the problem and the solution in one neat phrase. The second need was to reveal the policy analysis focus of the book. Policy analysis, conceived here as a stepping stone on the journey to social action, entails the knowledge as well as the method involved in setting up alternative designs (for example, restorative justice formats) as a means of ensuring social justice. The title, *Confronting Oppression, Restoring Justice: From Policy Analysis to Social Action,* thus includes multiple key elements in a nutshell.

Oppression and injustice are linked, but not inextricably. For heuristic but mainly organizational reasons, I am focusing on matters most closely related to oppression in one section of the book and to social justice and injustice in the other section. Oppression as defined in this volume concerns domination and disempowerment. Part I explores the nature of oppression in terms of its consequences and proposed remedies. The first chapter sets forth the theoretical framework of the entire book; definition of key concepts related to oppression and injustice lays the groundwork for the anti-oppressive policy analysis to follow. Chapter 2 plunges into a holistic analysis of oppression, with attention paid uniquely to possible biological as well as psycho-social factors in dominance. The treatment of the world's marginalized populations through prejudicial ideologies culminating in racism, sexism, ageism and heterosexism, etc., is the subject of Chapter 3. The goal of Chapter 4 is to introduce models and principles of policy analysis for the purpose of effecting social change through initiatives that start at the ground level and move upwards. A unique contribution is the inclusion of an international framework of analysis. A focal point of this chapter is the presentation of personal narratives revealing highly charged experiences in overcoming or not overcoming oppression. Chapter 5 takes a closer look at the process of empowerment itself, a major goal of these initiatives and a proud tradition of social work practice.

Part II tackles the roots of injustice in our society. Injustice as defined here relates both to inequality and the coercive treatment of subordinate groups. What is the nature of injustice? How have various international bodies attempted to resist injustice? What are the human rights protections? What are the violations? These are among the questions addressed in chapter 6. This chapter examines the concept of social justice in a human rights framework, a subject followed up in the next chapter on international monitoring organizations and local initiatives. In Chapter 7, we take policy analysis one step further from where we left off in Chapter 4, drawing this time on David Gil's radical policy analysis design for a framework that can be applied to progressive social justice initiatives. Examples of successful grassroots activities and case studies of attempts to change social legislation are provided. Finally Chapter 8, in my opinion, is the highlight of the book. Restorative justice, a revolutionary but not new concept in conflict resolution, is presented here as an alternative to the adversarial model of justice. In keeping with the emphasis of the book on empowerment, this chapter and the book concludes with a juxtaposition of social work values and restorative principles. Topics covered range from family group conferencing to community and individual reparations.

From a general education standpoint, the study of oppression and injustice offers an opportunity for critical thinking on topics often infused with emotionalism and denial. Without a recognition that indeed many of the neoconservative policies introduced under the guise of economic progress or justice are, in fact, oppressive to large numbers of people, challenges to such policies and practices will not be effective. An understanding of the economic market extends from the macro level with global phenomena down through the system including all sorts of constraints at the state level (for example, managed health care) as well as client-centered initiatives at the local level. Human service workers, practitioners, and administrators who are dealing every day with oppressed people and victims of an unjust society have a moral imperative to provide practice based on social justice and to advocate for social change to alleviate some of the bureaucratic woes. In the lives of our clients, we need to remember that policy and practice are always intertwined.

I believe that, taken together, these chapters will enable social work practitioners to play an active transformative role for the 21st century. Based on the knowledge presented in the book, students and practitioners who complete a course in anti-oppressive policy analysis should become:

- Familiar with the dual nature of globalization—the opportunities as well as liabilities of living in an ever-shrinking world;
- Aware of the power in communication, both of the corporate media and alternative resources for research and political mobilizing available through the Internet;

- More aware of oppressive forces in the environment and the impact of racism, ageism, sexism, etc., which have a bearing on client perceptions and behavior;
- Able to systematically evaluate current policies and understand policy analysis as both an art and a science;
- Knowledgeable about the vested interests and ideologies behind proposals (such as for reductions in health care services for the indigent) or the promotion of means-tested benefits;
- Ready and willing to play a role in shaping policy initiatives to help meet people's needs; and
- Familiar with effective strategies for mobilizing support for policy change through legislative advocacy, skillful use of the media, publicizing research findings, and providing public testimony.

In a society where policies are shaped by values and norms consistent with the interests of the marketplace, education for politically effective mobilization of energy toward social reform is essential. Progress toward social justice requires direct involvement in the political arena. Preparation for that involvement comes with the evaluation of the socio-economic impact of change and the sharing of results. Our engagement in policy analysis can be reactive—geared to the prevention of proposed cutbacks in community services—or more ideally, proactive— designed within an empowerment framework with the aims of social justice and social security. The purpose of policy analysis, from the social work standpoint, is to promote and influence legislation that will benefit the poor and the crisis-ridden people who social workers represent. This, the social work imperative to fight oppression at individual and policy levels, often pits the profession's interests in strong social policies against political interests supporting a different agenda. This dilemma—how to reconcile individual needs and human rights with the interests of big business—is slated to be the key dilemma of the millennium era. At this moment in history, a great debate about economic dominance and oppression is being played out on the world stage. This book is conceived as a contribution to that debate.

Acknowledgments

Many individuals have contributed to this book. First, I'd like to thank members of the Council on Social Work Education Publications and Media Commission for their initial receptiveness to a proposal on the daunting topic of oppression and injustice. Thanks are also due to the reviewers of the manuscript for their helpful suggestions and guidance. Above all, my gratitude goes to Michael Monti, director of member programs, conferences, and publications, who moved this project through, from beginning to end, at remarkable speed.

The recent graduates who shared their moving consciousness-raising experiences deserve a special mention. On a technical note, I'd like to recognize my graduate student assistants, Carol Ann Hundley and Tina Smith, who handled the complexities of the computer and were able to turn convoluted longhand into a readable form.

Part One
Confronting Oppression

This book is designed to meet a specific need in social work education, a need addressed in both the NASW Code of Ethics and in Council on Social Work Education (CSWE) guidelines for professional education. This need is for a knowledge base in social and economic justice and the forces in oppression as a background for social policy practice.

Part I of this text—Chapters 1 through 5—moves from an examination of the nature of oppression to a discussion of the fundamentals of policy analysis as a way of resisting oppression to a consideration of the empowerment process in social work.

The major task of the first chapter is definitional—to offer a conceptualization of oppression and injustice and of their opposites, empowement and social justice. Think of Chapter 1, which is relatively abstract, as an attempt to lay the groundwork theoretically for the subsequent material relevant to our study of oppression and injustice. Much of the terminology introduced in this chapter, terms such as anti-oppressive practice, social exclusion, and restorative justice, are drawn from international sources. All these terms and the more familiar ones such as "social justice," for example, relate to social work practice and policy innovations. Succeeding chapters in this section analyze oppression in terms of biopsychosocial components (Chapter 2), social exclusion in today's world (Chapter 3), anti-oppressive policy analysis for social change (Chapter 4), and empowerment as a social work tradition (Chapter 5).

One
The Essence of Oppression

Never doubt that a small group of thoughtful committed citizens can change the world; indeed it's the only thing that ever has.

Margaret Mead (1901–1978)

Images of Oppression

Oppression takes many forms. It can occur when one race or group of people exploits and suppresses another race or ethnic group; it can affect whole families and classes of people who are economically oppressed by the system; it can occur within the family, taking the form of gender violence as well as child abuse and neglect. Membership in a disempowered group has personal as well as political ramifications. In his unforgettable memoir, McCourt (1996) takes us back to his humble Irish origins:

> People everywhere brag and whimper about the woes of their early years, but nothing can compare with the Irish version: The poverty; the shiftless loquacious alcoholic father; the pious defeated mother moaning by the fire; pompous priests; bullying schoolmasters; the English and the terrible things they did to us for eight hundred long years. (p. 11)

Angela's Ashes tells of ethnic hatred, adultism (mistreatment of children), and economic oppression in early 20th century Ireland. On the American continent, we see yesterday's oppression in the jolting words of bell hooks (1993):

> Black people are indeed wounded by forces of domination. Irrespective of our access to material privilege we are all wounded by white supremacy, racism, sexism, and a capitalist economic system that dooms us collectively to an underclass position. Such wounds do not manifest themselves only in material ways, they affect our psychological well-being... (p. 11)

> Just as the slaves had learned from their white masters the art of dissimulation, women learned that they could subvert male power over them by also withholding the truth. (p. 23)

To hooks, healing occurs through collective organization and personal testimony. Healing takes place within us as we speak the truth of our lives. Consistent with hooks' teachings, this chapter, like this book, is intended to break the silence, to help therapists, administrators, and, community organizers embark on a journey toward the truth. Part of that truth concerns the nature of economic oppression in the global society.

Just as economic forces in the global market shape ideology, so ideology shapes the economic structure. Some of this ideology, at least, serves to justify the inequality in society to the extent of blaming the recipients of aid. "What is the role of social work in this context?" ask Gutiérrez & Lewis (1999b). "How can we take an active role in confronting and immobilizing the forces that conspire to increase inequality while removing the tattered remnants of the safety net?" (p. xii).

An *empowerment* approach, the framework that is integral to social work, provides one avenue, as Gutiérrez and Lewis suggest, for responding to these challenges. Empowerment practice builds simultaneously by social and individual transformation. An empowerment approach, which is the guiding focus of this book, is the construct that most explicitly addresses power imbalances in the society.

The Professional Response to Oppression

While all the people-helping professions share more or less the same tasks—crisis intervention, mental health counseling, grief work, for example—it is in the clarification of its goals that social work distinguishes itself from the other human service professions (Figueira-McDonough, 1993). As stated in the National Association of Social Workers (NASW) Code of Ethics:

> The primary mission of the social work profession is to enhance human well-being and help meet the basic human needs of all people, with particular attention to the needs and empowerment of people who are vulnerable, oppressed, and living in poverty. A historic and defining feature of social work is the profession's focus on individual well-being in a social context and the well-being of society. (NASW, 1996, Preamble)

Because of its uniquely political emphasis, Popple and Leighninger (2001) refer to social work in the title of their book as the "policy-based profession." Similarly, the NASW Code of Ethics describes the focus of the profession as helping vulnerable and oppressed people, emphasizing respect for ethnic diversity in the United States and globally, and promoting social justice and social change. In the 1999 updated version of the *Code of Ethics*, Section 6, Social Worker's Ethical Responsibilities to the Broader Society, was expanded to include a global awareness. As stated in Standard 6.1 (Social Welfare):

> Social workers should promote the general welfare of society, from local to global levels, and the development of people, their communities, and their environments. Social workers should advocate for living conditions conducive to the fulfillment of basic human needs and should promote social, economic,

political, and cultural values and institutions that are compatible with the realization of social justice.

And with special relevance to this text, Standard 6.02 (Public Participation) states: "Social workers should facilitate informed participation by the public in shaping social policies and institutions."

The Canadian Association of Social Workers Code of Ethics (1994) states in Section 10 "Ethical Responsibilities for Social Change": "A social worker shall advocate change for the overall benefit of society, the environment, and the global community." And in Standard 10.6: "A social worker shall promote social justice."

In both Canada and the United States, national education policy statements follow the goals laid out in the profession's code of ethics and provide accreditation for academic programs. The Council on Social Work Education (CSWE, 2003) recently published *The Handbook of Accreditation Standards and Procedures* for U.S. departments and schools of social work. Among the purposes of social work education as spelled out in this newly revised document are these: alleviation of poverty, oppression, and other forms of social injustice; promotion of the breadth of knowledge and critical thinking; and preparation of social workers to recognize the global context of social work practice and to formulate and influence social policies and social services.

New to the accreditation standards is the change from the requirement to offer content on specific vulnerable populations such as racial, ethnic, and sexual minorities in favor of a more general approach. Standard 4.2 under Educational Policy states, "Programs integrate social and economic justice content grounded in an understanding of distributive justice, human and civil rights, and the global interconnections of oppression" (p. 35). The inclusion of course content on international issues in social welfare policy is also required.

The Canadian Association of Schools of Social Work (2000), similarly, ensures that the student acquire "preparation in transferable analysis of the multiple and intersecting bases of oppression, and related practice skills" (Section 3.4.3) and more specifically, "an understanding of oppression and healing of aboriginal peoples and implications for social policy and social work practice" (Section 5.10 L).

If we listen to Gil (1998), and if we agree with him that a major goal of social work education is to prepare students to work toward transforming "unjust and oppressive social economic, and political institutions into just and non-oppressive alternatives" (p. 1), then we need to embrace a framework for teaching and learning that relates personal troubles to societal oppression. Professional social work ethics and values require competence in policy advocacy and social change strategies. Empowerment practice follows a basic premise: Change the world, change yourself. This premise applies not only to the client but to the social worker as well who "becomes an ally." This brings us to the first definition in this discussion of terms related to oppression and injustice (one way or another) utilized throughout this book.

Key Concepts

Becoming an Ally

The definitive study on this topic is *Becoming an Ally: Breaking the Cycle of Oppression* by Canadian community development worker Bishop (1994*)*. An *ally* is defined in the glossary in these terms: "A member of an oppressor group who works to end a form of oppression which gives him or her privilege. For example, a white person who works to end racism, or a man who works to end sexism" (p. 126). An ally (from the Latin *to bind*) works to dismantle any form of oppression in which he or she receives the benefit (Ayvazian, 2001). A key role in allied behavior is making the invisible visible, as Ayvazian explains. Assuming the role of the ally benefits the role-taker in helping him or her overcome the sense of immobilization in an oppressive environment. Having an ally, in turn, facilitates the empowerment of persons targeted by oppression.

Few commentators think of it, but it is my observation from the civil rights movement, that active involvement in a movement to end oppression by members of the dominant group is a way of alleviating guilt. Segregation was an institution of perpetual cruelty—reminders were everywhere due to the "colored" and "White Only" signs. White privilege could become a heavy burden to bear. Becoming an ally or protesting helped alleviate this sense of complicity in an unjust system.

To become an ally in another's liberation, as Bishop (1994) suggests, one must be in the process of liberation from one's own oppression. To develop the inner strength needed to become an ally, as Bishop further informs us, we must work toward our own liberation, a process involving consciousness raising and healing at both individual and collective levels. The first step involved in becoming an ally is to understand the nature of oppression.

Oppression

Etymologically, the word "oppress" comes from the Latin *opprimere*, which means to press on or press against (Pearsall, 1998). As defined in *The Social Work Dictionary* (Barker, 2003), *oppression* is:

> The social act of placing severe restrictions on an individual, group, or institution. Typically, a government or political organization that is in power places these restrictions formally or covertly on oppressed groups so that they may be exploited and less able to compete with other social groups. The oppressed individual or group is devalued, exploited, and deprived of privileges by the individual or group who has more power. (pp. 306–307)

Some of the key words used in this definition—"power," " exploited," "deprived," "privileges"—are key variables related to oppression that will crop up again and again on the following pages of this book. Each notion is engrained in the institutional arrangements of racism, sexism, ethnocentrism, ableism, heterosexism, classism, and sectarianism (Appleby, Colon, & Hamilton, 2001). In each form of oppression—economic, racial, ethnic, sexual—a dominant group receives the unearned advantage or privilege, and a targeted group is denied the advantage (Ayvazian, 2001).

Oppression, loosely speaking, can be defined as inhumane or degrading treatment of a group or individual based on some defining characteristic (Dalrymple & Burke, 1995). Sometimes the meanings of words can best be known through their opposites. Societies are *non-oppressive*, notes Gil (1998), when all people are considered and treated as equals, and have equal rights and responsibilities concerning their land, resources, politics, and bodies, accordingly. Oppression, like non-oppression, is a word favored by social activists, and a central term of political discourse; it would not ordinarily be used by the mainstream and is inconsistent with the language of individualism that dominates U.S. politics (Young, 1990). In traditional usage, the word might be used to describe conditions in a foreign country such as North Korea or pre-occupied Iraq.

How is oppression kept in place? As Ayvazian indicates, oppression is kept in place by ideology or the propagation of doctrines that legitimize inequality or violence or the threat of violence. In the Deep South under segregation, the ideology of paternalism was highly effective in alleviating the guilt of a caste of people who prided themselves on taking care of members of an "inferior race." According to the ideology, "colored" people needed to be taken care of; servants were emotionally sort of like family members while financially they were more or less in bondage (see Dollard, 1998). Box 1.1 provides a rare glimpse into a world that is still in living memory. Elise Talmage (2001), the author of "The Dark Past," is an 81-year-old White woman (this author's mother) who grew up in New Orleans in the Depression era. In this poem, the poet's insights of today are juxtaposed with the voices of the past:

Box 1.1   The Dark Past

Were our sins so scarlet?
Were our virtues so few?
We remember, we remember
Yellow heads on warm black arms
"Doe doe lil baby
Doe doe lil baby"
Rocking and rocking to soothe little hurts
But did you hurt too and did we know?
Dark rich voices crooning low
Doe doe doe doe
And did we not pay a living wage?
It was ever so; it was ever so.

continues...

And were black babies left without a breast?
No voice to sing them "doe doe doe."
And did you crawl beneath the house
while white folks flushed?
And did we sow the seeds of hate?
Jim Crow Jim Crow
I remember, I remember
"Can I tote your books, Miss Leeze
Miss Leeze?"
They tried so hard to please.
I see their dusky daughters now
Passing by with haughty looks:
"We no longer remember
The songs that we sang"
"Listen, please listen; it went like this:
'Doe Doe lil baby
Doe Doe lil baby
Sleep on your mammy.'"
I cannot sing as once you sang.
Dark rich voices crooning low
Violet, Nicey, Many gone so long ago
So long ago
It hurts to know.
Our sins were scarlet
our virtues were few.

Reprinted with permission of Elise Talmage, Bowling Green, Kentucky.

Sometimes, as expressed in the above poem, both ideology and socialization are intertwined. Socialization within the family can play a dominant role in holding oppression in place. Power and privilege relationships, as hooks (1993) informs us, are played out in the home, often within a patriarchal setting. She herself experienced this form of disempowerment. In contrast to racist oppression experienced in society with the African American family operating as a buffer against the pain, sexist oppression is often first learned at home (Appleby, Colon, & Hamilton, 2001). Gender oppression involves denial of equality to individuals on the grounds of gender, for example, boys having privileges denied to girls (and vice versa). Gay/lesbian oppression is often played out in the family in the form of contempt for what is perceived as gender deviant behavior. In contrast to the case with other minority groups, with sexual minorities, the family is often not a buffer against discrimination from the outside, but a perpetrator of anti-gay/lesbian/transgender attitudes. The church, likewise, instead of offering solace, may condemn homosexuality as a sin. Some attempts at therapy have been ill-advised as well, and have actually compounded the social oppression of difference. Two promising developments in social work education are anti-oppressive practice and the empowerment perspective.

Anti-Oppressive Practice

Anti-oppressive practice or theory is a term widely used in all the English-speaking countries of the world except for the United States. According to this formulation, the assumption is that society is generally oppressive and that social workers must do their best to offset this. *Anti-oppressive practice* is about minimizing power differences in society and maximizing the rights to which all people are entitled (Dalrymple & Burke, 1995; Dominelli, 2002a). In her book *Anti-Oppressive Social Work Theory and Practice*, Dominelli perceives the context of social work practice within a globalizing economy. From this perspective, anti-oppressive social work is concerned about the deleterious effects that macro-level forces can have on people's daily lives.

How does the anti-oppressive formulation relate to empowerment theory? Payne (1997) likens anti-oppressive practice to an empowerment approach because of its attention to power differentials in worker/client relationships and the need to help clients gain control of their lives. Workers, as Payne suggests, can avoid oppressing (and thereby empower) clients through partnership, client choice, and seeking changes in the agency and wider systems that adversely affect clients. The term, anti-oppressive practice, as used in this book—*Confronting Oppression, Restoring Justice*—indicates an approach designed to reduce oppressive factors in the system; such an approach is necessarily anti-discriminatory and anti-racist.

The anti-oppressive concept is widely used in Canada. Al-Krenawi and Graham (2003), for example, utilize an anti-oppressive model of social work practice in their edited volume *Multicultural Social Work in Canada: Working with Diverse Ethno-Racial Communities*. At the University of Victoria, Canada, the mission statement reads: "The vision of the School of Social Work commits itself to social justice, anti-oppressive social work practices and to promoting critical inquiry... In particular, we endeavour to prepare First Nations social workers and child welfare practitioners, and we emphasize structural, feminist, First Nations and anti-oppressive analyses" (University of Victoria School of Social Work, 2003). To read a Canadian case study in which an anti-oppressive approach was used in helping a lesbian student successfully challenge a college's unjust practices, see Turner and Cheboud (2000). Social workers as mediators/advocates, according to these authors, must challenge oppressive social structures in concert with other groups in the struggle for political change.

The Empowerment Perspective

A closely related concept, and the one more favored by American social workers, is the empowerment perspective. The *empowerment perspective* encompasses the strengths approach in its focus on helping clients tap into their inner and cultural resources. It goes further, however, in focusing on oppression and power imbalances in the society. Empowering practice begins by acknowledging that structural injustices have prevented many individuals and groups from receiving the treatment and resources to which they are entitled. I have chosen the empowerment perspective as the guiding framework for this book both because of its familiarity and because of its relevance to issues of social justice and human rights. An empowerment approach responds to the individual's and group's experience of oppression (Saleebey, 2002).

Central to the empowerment approach is the concept of *power*, power not in the Weberian sense of the ability to coerce (refer to the later section on Power and Exploitation) but in the sense of liberation, of seizing control. Implicit in this concept, nevertheless, is an awareness that disadvantaged persons are threatened by powerful others in their lives. Their very economic hardships may stem from global forces over which they are powerless and may even be unaware. To Gutiérrez (1991), gaining a sense of personal power can be a first step in assuming personal responsibility for change; as an emotional force, this sense of personal power can move us from emotional apathy and despair to positive social action.

Empowerment practice, as Gutiérrez and Lewis (1999a) suggest, requires social workers to be agents of change, to help people gain or regain power in their lives. This is the goal of counseling at the interpersonal level. Oppressed individuals are not viewed as devoid of personal or moral strengths or resources: Help in tapping into those resources often is needed. McWhirter (1991) captures the essence of personal empowerment in her definition:

Empowerment is the process by which people, organizations, or groups who are powerless (a) become aware of the power dynamics at work in their life context, (b) develop the skills and capacity for gaining some reasonable control over their lives, (c) exercise this control without infringing upon rights of others, and (d) support the empowerment of others in their community. (p. 224)

At the societal level, the goal of empowerment practice, as Gutiérrez and Lewis (1999b) state, is social justice and a reduction of social inequality. Strengths-based practice, as Cowger (1998) argues, may involve partnerships between social workers and clients to influence the profession, social policy, and/or service delivery. But without collective action, "a strengths perspective doesn't have a chance against managed care and other recent changes in the delivery of social services that are now driven by market forces" (Cowger, 1998, p. 34).

In summary, empowerment is a key concept in social work practice and theory. Not only does it relate to counseling skills in helping people build on their inner strengths in overcoming adversity, but also, as formulated in the writings of Gutierrez and Lewis and others, it has important implications for challenging societal injustice.

Injustice

Commonly used throughout the social science literature, the term "injustice" is rarely defined in the text much less indexed in the books and articles. The exception is Gil's (1998) treatise, *Confronting Injustice and Oppression*. Injustice to Gil refers to:

> …coercively established and maintained inequalities, discrimination, and dehumanizing, development-inhibiting conditions of living (e.g., slavery, serfdom, and exploitative wage labor, unemployment, poverty, starvation, and homelessness; inadequate health care and education), imposed by dominant social groups, classes, and peoples upon dominated and exploited groups, classes and peoples. (p. 10)

What is the difference between injustice and oppression? According to *The American Heritage Dictionary of the English Language* (2000), *injustice* means "violation of another's rights or of what is right; lack of justice." This is the definition I favor for this book. Injustice relates to rights, especially legal rights. It generally is used within a societal context. Oppression, I see as more personal and less abstract, relating to the impact of mistreatment on people, for example, through family violence or harassment at work.

Finn and Jacobson (2003), in their writing on just practice, speak of "structural injustice" in reference to the increasing concentration of capital in the hands of the few. A context with which I am more familiar is that provided by Menninger (1966) in his landmark book, *The Crime of Punishment*. His opening chapter is memorably entitled "The Injustice of Justice." Unhappily, in practice, justice does not always entail fairness to all parties, as Menninger indicates. Instead, justice often denotes punishment and results in the very opposite of fair play. To take a contemporary example, with reference to terrorists involved in the Twin Towers airplane strikes, the call for justice seems to equate with a call for retaliation as, for example, in the article titled "Do We Seek Vengeance or Justice?" by Peterson (2001). It is another connotation of justice altogether, however, which is social work's concern.

Social Justice

The second of the six core values of social work, as spelled out in the NASW Code of Ethics (NASW, 1996), is social justice. As members of the profession, social workers have an obligation to promote social justice, or fair treatment of all people. But what is social justice? The word justice is derived from the Latin *jus*, which by classical times denoted right, especially legal right (Ayto, 1990). In the *Encyclopedia of Social Work*, Flynn (1995) defines *social justice* as the embodiment of fairness (reasonable treatment), equity (similar situations dealt with similarly), and equality in the distribution of societal resources. Throughout the social science literature, the term *social justice* has various shades of meanings. In social work literature, the usual meaning is the social rights of citizens of the social welfare state to have their needs met (Graham, Swift, & Delaney, 2000; Lee, 2001).

Healy (2001) similarly writes of distributive justice or principles relating to how scarce resources are allocated, whether based on merit or equality.

Distributive justice is of great concern to social welfare workers who daily see the impact of the system's attempt to distribute resources to the "deserving" poor while depriving the "undeserving" of help. Individuals with small children and disabilities generally will qualify for more financial aid than will able-bodied, childless adults. Individuals pursuing job training to "get off welfare" generally will be better treated than individuals unwilling to take such action. Consistent with the values of American society, the focus of this form of justice is on equal opportunity but not on equality.

Writing in *Justice and the Politics of Difference,* Young (1990) takes the position favored in this book. Instead of focusing on distribution of resources such as income, she contends, a concept of justice should begin with the concepts of domination and oppression. It is her belief that group differences should be acknowledged and affirmed, that sometimes recognizing particular rights for groups is the only way to promote their full participation in society. The aim of social justice to Young is to seek institutional remedy for cultural sources of oppression, the manifestations of which are seen in racism, sexism, homophobia, ableism, etc.

Schneider and Lester (2001) and Swenson (1998) concur: Social justice involves advocacy to end discrimination, oppression, poverty, and so forth. Social work advocates, as Schneider and Lester indicate, are involved frequently in pleading the cause of justice and combating injustices when client rights are at risk. Social justice practice, to Swenson, means working to increase client power relative to that of professionals and acknowledging and articulating the client's social realities, even to the extent of raising issues of socioeconomic status, race, and gender in the agency. Social justice activism indeed has a long but uneven history within the social work profession (see Reisch & Andrews, 2001).

I was fortunate to have the opportunity to provide input, as a member of the editorial board of *The Social Work Dictionary* (Barker, 2003). Now for the first time the term "social justice" is included along with injustice and economic justice. The definition of *social justice* is appropriately inclusive:

> An ideal condition in which all members of a society have the same basic rights, protection, opportunities, obligations, and social benefits. Implicit in this concept is the notion that historical inequalities should be acknowledged and remedied through specific measures. A key social work value, social justice entails advocacy to confront discrimination, oppression, and institutional inequities. (pp. 404–405)

What is social justice practice and does it apply to clinical social work? Swenson (1998) argues that it does. The overall goal of empowerment practice, as designated by Gutiérrez and Lewis (1999b), is social justice. The optimal form of social justice, in my opinion, can be found in the burgeoning movement called restorative justice.

Restorative Justice

Both an ideal principle—*belief* in the importance of providing justice to the offender, victim, and community—and a *method* of dispensing justice when a violation has been committed, *restorative justice* can be considered a form of social justice because of its fairness to all parties. Although this evolutionary development has important implications for social work practice because it works closely with victims and offenders, the social work literature has not devoted attention to restorative initiatives. The majority of these initiatives are geared to implementing much needed change within the halls of justice. The opposite of restorative justice is the traditional form of confrontational courtroom ritual in which one person emerges the victor and one the loser.

A highly effective means of settling disputes and providing for victim compensation, restorative justice offers a strong antidote to the political ranting and raving that seems to get votes. In bringing criminal and victim together to heal the wounds of violation, the campaign for restorative justice advocates alternative methods to incarceration when the offender's behavior can be controlled through close supervision. These methods include victim-offender reconciliation programs, victim-offender mediation, and community diversion programs. The impetus from these humanistic trends is enhanced by the victim's rights movement, which continues to gain strength and momentum across the country and which is at a threshold of a focus more on healing than on revenge. Meanwhile, forgiveness has become a hot research topic, which has received a lot of media attention. (A 2003 search of the web search engine Google [http://www.google.com] reveals more than 180,000 listings for "forgiveness research." Among the listings are The Stanford University Forgiveness Project and the Campaign for Forgiveness Research.) Through restorative justice, the effort is made to restore what the victim has lost, while at the same time requiring offenders to face up to the consequences of their act or acts and the personal pain caused to the victim, victim's family, the offender's family and the community.

The initiatives taking place, such as in the juvenile justice system, exemplify social change that has evolved through strong grassroots efforts. Another significant fact about restorative justice is how the idea has swept across the world, especially in English-speaking countries such as New Zealand, Australia, and Canada, where this approach is closely associated with indigenous populations. (Chapter 8 is devoted in its entirety to this progressive concept.)

Policy and Social Policy

One way to institute social justice in society and to lessen the extent of social exclusion and exploitation is through the shaping of governmental policy to those ends. Policy creates the world in which practice is accomplished (Graham, Swift, &

Delaney, 2000). Policy and practice are clearly intertwined. Jansson (2003) defines policy as a goal-driven "collective strategy that addresses social problems" (p. 11). Many collective strategies that are not policies, however, such as a movement for civil rights, address social policies. Conversely, some policies are not collectively formulated, may not address problems, and may even cause problems.

And so we turn to *The Social Work Dictionary* (Barker, 2003) for a clarification that is helpful. Barker distinguishes *policy* as that which guides an organization or government from *social policy* which guides the whole society and relates to cultural values. My interpretation of this difference is that social policy is the macro term: You would not say agency social policy; you would say agency policy. But you can have local or national policy as well. *Social policy* is defined by Barker as:

> The activities and principles of a society that guide the way it intervenes in and regulates relationships among individuals, groups, communities, and social institutions. These principles and activities are the result of the society's values and customs and largely determine the distribution of resources and level of well-being of its people. Thus, social policy includes plans and programs in education, health care, crime and corrections, economic security, and social welfare made by governments, voluntary organizations, and the people in general. It also includes social perspectives that result in society's rewards and constraints. (p. 405)

Combining these two definitions—the social action, goal-directed focus of Jansson with the less political definition provided by the social work dictionary, we can view social policy within the theory of social work, as Iatridis (1995) suggests, as both a field and a process. As a field, social policy focuses on societal concerns such as poverty. As a process, social policy involves a series of orderly steps in the formulation and implementation of programs to solve social problems. The two stages of the social policy process that are the most significant are policy analysis and implementation planning. These stages, as Iatridis indicates, correspond to the diagnosis and treatment stages of the clinical social work process.

Policy practice in social work, or practice concerned with policy changes in large systems, has its origins in the settlement house movement of the late 1800s. Participants in this movement, the most famous of which was Jane Addams, argued for making social change and policy reform central to the new profession of social work. The settlement house movement, which engaged in such activities as promoting factory legislation, adequate wages and limited working hours, better housing, sanitation, and providing free employment services, is often contrasted with the Charity Organization Society movement (Haynes & Mickelson, 2000) which promoted the provision of direct services and social casework as instrumental to the emerging profession of social work. The seeming polarization of these two approaches to helping the poor largely reflects the dual vision of the profession that is with us still. Yet, as most social workers would agree, each aspect of the helping process—political advocacy and the provision of direct services—is as essential as the other (see Iatridis, 1995).

Unintended Consequences

Policy is instituted based on certain expectations about outcome. Will poverty be alleviated? Will children get a better education? These are typical questions asked about a specific course of action. Ideally, to validate a course of action, pilot studies will be conducted and only then will nationwide policy changes be implemented. Otherwise, there may be consequences that may make the solution more of a problem than the original problem. The war on drugs is a case in point, and probably the war on terror, as time will tell. "First, do no harm" is a cautionary slogan of the medical and helping professions that we would do well to keep in mind.

Unintended consequences are not to be confused with latent or hidden functions. Latent functions often appear to be unintended but actually are not. The concept of latent functions is most famously described by Piven and Cloward (1993) in their conceptualization of "regulating the poor." That the public welfare system had latent or hidden functions in addition to the obvious manifest functions is their basic thesis. Prevention of poverty and providing a safety net—the rationales that figure so largely in traditional histories of social welfare—are the *manifest* functions of the public welfare system. Examples of *latent* functions are punishment of persons who do not work; social control of the poor and downtrodden; and prevention of civil unrest by unruly elements in the society. Unintended consequences of providing relief might include the breakup of families so that single mothers could qualify for help or the reluctance of individuals to seek work because of threatened loss of child care or health benefits if they were removed from the welfare rolls.

The criminal justice system, which operates ostensibly to protect society and punish offenders has both manifest functions as well as unintended negative consequences. Reiman (2000) provides an astute political analysis of this system in his book, *The Rich Get Richer and the Poor Get Prison*. Just because the rich and powerful benefit by the failure of corrections to "correct" people's behavior or to eradicate drug use (a failure revealed in the continuing high crime rate), does not, Reiman argues, mean that the privileged and powerful in our society are engaged in a conspiracy to deliberately make the system fail. His view is, more charitably, that the system has grown up piecemeal over time, "usually with the best of intentions" (p. 6). The unplanned overall result provides benefits to the elites in society, however, and therefore is not apt to be changed, because such benefits would be lost. For example, politicians can divert public discontent away from the rich and powerful and onto the losers of society by focusing on lower-class as opposed to white-collar crime. Thus, as Reiman's title indicates, the rich get richer, and the poor get prison.

From an international perspective, Bishop (1994) notes that the multinationals, the global corporate elites, and their political allies do not need a conspiracy to coordinate their efforts. They do not have to conspire because they have common interests and enjoy the same worldview. Collectively, they have the means to put vast resources into shaping the world the way they want.

World history is full of "the plans of mice and men gone awry" to paraphrase Robert Burns (1785). Virtually all wars are in this category. One thinks of World War I, the war to end all wars, and the war on drugs that has increased the price of drugs and therefore the profits in their sale. *Blowback* by Johnson (2003) is a best-selling book about the consequences of American foreign policy. The title *Blowback* refers to a CIA term for the unintended consequences of American intervention. Examples would be world distrust of American motives and terrorism.

In medical terminology, *iatrogenic* refers to the phenomenon where the treatment itself is the cause of the problem. As an example, take farming, where the use of pesticides led to a more virulent breed of insect which, in turn, led to the demand for ever more powerful pesticides. In mental health, the deinstitutionalization of mentally ill persons in the interest of human rights closed the mental wards; jails and prisons then became the new mental hospitals. In child welfare, a movement called *permanency planning*, which stressed the need to keep abused and neglected children in the home, resulted in the deaths of thousands of children known to have been in high-risk situations by child welfare authorities.

One of the most absurd instances of legal reform "gone awry" was associated with the women's movement for equality. When women correctional officers won the right to perform the same duties as men, a victory in terms of women's career advancement in correctional work, men were given comparable rights to perform strip searches of residents of women's institutions. Nearly every state, accordingly, has been plagued with lawsuits against correctional officers. International investigations have confirmed the reports of extensive sexual abuse of female inmates by male officers (Amnesty International, 1999; van Wormer, 2001). In this instance, the value of equality won out over common sense. In light of a proliferation of lawsuits, male officers increasingly are being curtailed in the duties that they perform in women's prisons (van Wormer, 2001). Sadly, the outcome could have been easily predicted through a study of the history of women's prisons when the prisons were male-run and the scandals commonplace.

Writing from a historical perspective in *That's Not What We Meant to Do: Reform and Its Unintended Consequences in Twentieth-Century America*, Gillon (2000) details some of the scientific and government spending follies of the last century. Among the examples he provides are, first from science, the use of antibiotics that helped spread and strengthen the bacteria they were intended to conquer, and the widespread planting of kudzu, the Japanese vine that promised to stem soil erosion yet which swallowed whole forests in the U.S. South. Secondly, from business, Gillon asks us to consider the introduction of the office computer that was expected to create a paperless office but which actually used more paper, not less. Finally, Gillon provides case studies of public welfare allotments, which he claims had a negative impact on work incentive; deinstitutionalization of mentally ill patients, many of whom ended up homeless or in prison; the abolition of affirmative action which led to a decrease in admissions of non-Asian minorities into some state universities; immigration policies producing an influx of unskilled workers and their relatives; and campaign finance reform, which because of loopholes has increased the contaminating influence of corporate money on lawmakers. What are the reasons for such fallacies? Gillon lists miscalculation due to poor planning, drastic changes based on media-generated moral indignation, a political culture hostile to state power, and just plain human error for the negative outcomes that plague the society.

The key lesson that we can learn from a review of the unanticipated negative impacts of social policies is a recognition that although there are no easy solutions to systemic problems, carefully developed, multidimensional policy analysis is essential to the creation of effective policies that endure. (Policy analysis is the subject of Chapter 4.) Sometimes a knowledge of history is all it takes to convince us that a policy that did not work before (for example, Prohibition) probably will fail once again under similar circumstances. Informed planning is therefore crucial; central to informed planning is critical thinking.

Critical Thinking

In the context of policy development, social justice can be pursued by means of constant critical scrutiny of existing social structures and knowledge about how power differentials and oppression characterize the experiences of various groups. The kind of critical thinking called for, as Gutiérrez and Lewis (1999b) indicate, is not mere factual knowledge concerning specific group characteristics, such as familiarity with certain Indian tribal customs, for example. No, the goal of what Gutierréz and Lewis refer to as "affective learning," embodies awareness of one's own prejudices and beliefs and of how one's worldview affects one's attitudes and behavior. Once we recognize how much our biases and presumptions (such as prioritizing occupational success over relationships) are culturally derived and relative, only then can we come to appreciate a worldview that is different from our own. And in knowing another culture, we can gain a sense of perspective about our own.

The goal of critical thinking is a generalized goal; it can be defined as the ability to put phenomena (whether problematic or just customary) in perspective. This goal is as applicable to the members of minority groups themselves (and realize that we are all members of various diverse categories) as to members of the mainstream population. To think critically, we need to be able to see parts of the whole—practitioners urge clients to partialize or break down problems into manageable parts. But we also must never lose sight of the whole (that is, the cultural rhythm or pattern) itself.

Two aspects of critical thinking delineated by Keefe (2003) are empathy and critical consciousness. Each social work skill complements the other along a continuum of individual to social change. We will discuss these attributes of critical thinking along with a third and closely related concept—cultural competence.

Empathy, the ability to put oneself in place of another, requires both cognitive and emotional responses to the client on the part of the worker. Awareness of the client's emotional state and of the impact of the social and cultural environment are essential. Only through empathy can a therapist work with a wife batterer or sexual offender and help such persons move away from such destructive behavior. Often understanding of and even empathy for the sorriest client may accrue from knowing his or her childhood histories.

An ethical dilemma can occur when the client's cultural values and behavior conflict with the social worker's personal and/or professional values. When this happens, as it commonly will, the social worker is enjoined to tap into all his or her inner resources so as to be able to work *with*, rather than *against*, the client's best interests. We will delve into such value and ethical dilemmas in Chapter 3.

Critical consciousness involves an understanding of the encompassing social-structural context of human problems. Larochelle and Campfens (1992) discuss the importance of inculcating student social workers with the ability to link the personal with the political in the tradition of C. Wright Mills' (1959) "sociological imagination." Several Canadian undergraduate university social work programs have developed an integrated approach gearing change efforts at both the personal and collective levels, according to Larochelle and Campfens. However, many other Canadian students and seasoned social workers fail to respond appropriately to the socioeconomic realities of their clientele. Larochelle and Campfens attribute this failing to the Canadian's exaggerated emphasis on individual responsibility and technocratic solutions when dealing with social problems. In the United States, the focus on minority courses has more often been on the minority group's worldview, on their unique characteristics, than on the world the minorities inhabit (Gutiérrez & Lewis, 1999b).

Another shortcoming in social work education that few have recognized is that while the training of social workers seems to prepare them too well regarding their limits in dealing with clients and their problems, there is little done to help social workers recognize the consequence of their silence, much less the possibilities of instituting change (Larochelle & Campfens, 1992).

In some parts of the world, including a few places in the United States, students of social work are uniting with members of grassroots organizations to work among the poorest and most needy groups of society. Today in Chile, for example, and throughout Latin America, schools of social work are training their students in a collectivist consciousness and learning by the practice of dialogue rather than the lecture format. The goal is individual and collective growth; the means is education designed to engage all participants in the process of personal and political transformation.

Feminist educator hooks (1994, p. 202) articulates Freieran premises in terms of "teaching/learning to transgress," and critical thinking as "the primary element allowing the possibility of change." This summarizes critical thinking. A related aspect is, of course, cultural competence, an indispensable ingredient for working in a multiculturally diverse and complex environment.

Cultural competence entails recognition of society's prejudices—ethnocentrism, sexism, classism, heterosexism, and racism—and of our own possession of many of these traits. As Ronnau (1994) enunciates, to fully appreciate cultural differences, self-awareness is a must. Social workers must recognize the influence of their own culture, family, and peers on how they think and act. Cultural competence requires continuous efforts to gain more knowledge about the client's culture— the norms, vocabulary, symbols, and strengths. Ronnau argues against the color blind and gender blind notions of many European-American social workers.

Color-Blind vs. Culturally Competent

Through accepting that significant differences do exist between people of different ethnic backgrounds, professionals are recognizing a person's wholeness and individuality. To tell a lesbian or gay person, "Just stay in the closet and you'll be all right," is to deny that person an important part of him- or herself. To tell an African American "we're all the same under the skin," is to deny the importance of race in society. Multicultural social work education exposes students to divergent thinking as they are forced to examine formerly taken-for-granted assumptions.

Affirmative action (a term introduced by President Kennedy in 1961) programs are strategies both for alleviating prejudice through encouraging equal status contact among people who are different and for compensating for what prejudice is ingrained in the society. In contrast to color-blind policies, which strive to overlook differences and treat everyone the same, policies of a proactive stance seek to increase diversity in the educational and professional communities.

Through affirmative action policies, members of historically deprived groups, including women, have made significant strides in gaining access to privileges that might otherwise not have been available to them. As often happens when progress is made, a backlash ensues. And so it is with affirmative action. Opponents of affirmative action argue that minorities are hurt more than helped by policies that lower the standards for their admission or hiring, that such policies only arouse resentment by White/Anglo males and that such preferential policies undermine the principles of equality and fair play.

Persuaded by such logic, some states such as Texas and California have retreated from their previous efforts toward educational integration. But such color blindness, notes Gillon (2000), may not be a practical option. Given the substantial decline in African American and Latina/Latino enrollments at the top universities in Texas and California, color blindness means effective exclusion today of persons of color from positions of influence, wealth, and power (Glazer, 1998). Still, many conservatives continue to profess a belief in color blindness, arguing that society has an obligation to guarantee every citizen the opportunity to compete as equals (Gillon, 2000). Liberals, in contrast, contend that the equal opportunity focus perpetuates inequalities because we are indeed not all equal. This book argues in agreement with Young (1990) that a conception of social justice that fails to seek institutional remedy for the cultural sources of oppression is inadequate.

A related issue to affirmative recognition of difference is recognition of the need for an educational focus that is ethnically sensitive. In the helping professions, cultural competence, which entails an appreciation for a variety of cultural values and practices, becomes more and more critical in the light of the increasingly global nature of all professional work. *Culturally competent practice* as set forth by Appleby, Colon, and Hamilton (2001) elicits an insider's view of the culture and is informed by the belief that the family as defined by each culture is primary. A recognition of the uniqueness of Anglo American values—individualism, nuclear family as primary, moralism, optimism, Protestant work ethic, and classism related to capitalism and of oppressive elements in North American society is a major component of cultural competence as is awareness of oppressive elements in other societies as well. Much of oppression is related to suppression of difference and stems from patriarchal social arrangements; this brings us to a discussion of gender.

Gender Neutral vs. Gender Specific

The same argument commonly heard in race-related discussion is also voiced on the issue of gender: "Why can't we just all be treated the same?" This is the gender-neutral stance, one with which most people would agree on the surface. Slogans like "equal pay for equal work," and the realization that protective legislation for women can be used to restrict women's freedom or career success remind us of the important feminist and social work ethic of impartiality in treatment. The risk in such a focus, however, is that it minimizes central aspects of people's lives and the differences among individuals.

This issue, whether to fight for special treatment for women as women or to restrict our efforts to a demand for uniformity in opportunities for men and women, has divided the feminist movement. The challenge is to reconcile the right of equality with a recognition of allowances for gender difference in areas (such as measurements of physical strength) where gender makes a difference.

In fact, the issue of whether to work toward policies providing parity of treatment versus special treatment can be reconciled by avoiding an either/or position and arguing for equality but not sameness. In the area of medical leave from work, women should expect to have equal access to time off for illness as men but their special needs, such as time for late pregnancy, childbirth, and recovery, should be met by means of gender-appropriate policies. In Scandinavia, for example, both parents are encouraged to take a period of leave for childcare responsibilities.

Where social group differences exist, and some groups are privileged while others are oppressed, the propensity to universalize, as Young (1990) argues, can reinforce that oppression.

Members of the privileged group, after all, are those who set the standards they can claim as neutral and impartial, their authoritative decisions, as Young further suggests, "often silence, ignore, and render deviant the abilities, needs and norms of others" (p. 116).

The backlash against affirmative action and women's "creeping equality" today is played out in the U.S. courtrooms in the form of what Chesney-Lind and Pollock (1994) term *equality with a vengeance*. As compassion takes a back seat in a punitive society, women connected to crime through family ties—mothers who protect their drug-dealing children, or wives and girlfriends of drug-using men, for example—are now subjected to harsh punishment alongside their menfolk (van Wormer, 2001). Today women's prisons are constructed architecturally according to the same designs used for medium-security men's prisons; the majority of correctional officers and administrators of women's prisons are now men. Gender-neutral sentencing policies have resulted in a growth rate in incarceration for female offenders that far exceeds the male rate of increase (Bureau of Justice Statistics, 2000). (The treatment of female offenders is one of the aspects of injustice explored in Chapter 6).

Within prison walls, there is a trend today, much stronger in Canada than in the United States, to provide gender-specific programming to inmates with addictions problems. Gender-specific programming utilizes a woman-centered approach to enhance empowerment of women. In addition to a substance abuse focus, work is done in the area of partner and child abuse, early childhood trauma, parenting, and other issues of primary concern for women. Needless to say, however, community-based treatment as opposed to treatment behind bars is the priority among proponents of woman-centered programming (Kassebaum, 1999; van Wormer, 2001) We turn now to three related concepts to the contemporary treatment of persons convicted of crime: social exclusion, power, and exploitation.

Social Exclusion

A European term originating in France in the 1970s that is useful in denoting the *relational* aspect of oppression is *social exclusion*. Social exclusion often refers to immigrant groups, persons who are usually unemployed and live in poverty and are not allowed to participate in opportunities available in the wider society (Healy, 2001). This term, as Healy indicates, can apply to the long-term unemployed, ex-offenders, and persons with mental or physical disabilities. The concept can be applied nationally or globally to indicate how whole nations are left out of trade or use of economic resources. At a meeting in early 2001, the European Union Council of Ministers formally adopted an action plan for combating poverty and social exclusion. The plan calls for better understanding of exclusion and national action of the member states (Council of Europe, 2001).

The concept of social exclusion goes beyond the mere words "social" and "exclusion" into the political realm. Embodied in this concept is a framework concerning political and economic process. The beauty of this formulation, as opposed to the pejorative earlier term, the *underclass*, is its placement of the onus on the people who are doing something to other people. The central tenet of the underclass or culture of poverty argument, in contrast, is that miserable conditions are self-induced—the poor do it to themselves (Byrne, 1999). Subscribers to this theoretical framework acknowledge the influence of global economic transformation on social cohesion at the national level. These impacts vary considerably across class and racial categories. The literature on social exclusion, as Mitchell (2000) notes, highlights the multi-dimensionality of disadvantage thereby broadening the focus from disadvantage on purely economic grounds to include marginalization through the denial of civil, political, and social rights of citizenship.

The opposite of social exclusion is *social inclusion*. "As an applied profession," notes Healy (2001), "social work will be particularly interested in the development of effective strategies toward social inclusion" (p. 274). The relevance of the social exclusion/inclusion framework for British social work is pursued by Barry and Hallett (1998) in their edited volume, *Social Exclusion and Social Work: Issues of Theory, Policy, and Practice*. Individual chapters (originally presentations at the University of Stirling) attend to the structural dimensions of social exclusion as the basis of race and ethnicity, offender status, and disability.

Power and Exploitation

The classic definition of power to the sociologist is that provided by Max Weber (1947): "*Power* is the probability that one actor within a social relationship will be in a position to carry out his own will despite resistance" (p. 152). Note the focus on relationship here; never is power just an attribute of one actor. As well, there is the implication in this formulation that noncompliance would be met with sanctions. We can take this definition one step further to infer that situations involving extreme power imbalances and the threat of negative consequences are associated with a sense of powerlessness on the part of the threatened party and, ultimately, the inability or lack of confidence to make choices about one's life or livelihood. Consider the subordination of women, for example, in a patriarchal family or within the family system. Such subordination is associated with low self-esteem, anxiety, and dependency in many cases (van Wormer, 2001).

Power is not merely an attribute of individuals and groups but a function of control over resources. From a global perspective, such control of resources is gained through domination of one sort or another. When power imbalances become extreme, exploitation of the weak by the strong is likely.

Two key elements of exploitation are *coercion* (to create inequalities) and *ideology* (to maintain inequalities). *Exploitation* is defined by Mullaly (1997) as "those social processes whereby the dominant group is able to accumulate and maintain status, power, and assets from the energy and labor expended by subordinate groups" (p. 146). To Young (1990), exploitation is viewed as a major category of oppression, one that is economically based. Exploitation may consist of harnessing the poor and foreign to do the dirty work of society or, at the macro level, of using poor nations as cheap sources of labor. The work that the have-nots do increases the power and status of the wealthy classes above them. In the working world, women often expend energy in time-consuming jobs to enhance the position of others, usually men who are released to carry out more important and rewarding work (Mullaly, 1997). Within a given nation, the determination of which groups will be subordinate and exploited by which other groups is often on the basis of race, class, and/or gender. In India it is by caste.

Economic dominance by the strong of the weak is especially pronounced internationally. The privileged nations of the Global North are in a position to extort resources from debt-ridden nations in the Global South. Dominelli (2002a) warns that the new economic ideology is guiding the planet into increasingly dangerous terrain of a predatory form of capitalism "which greedily ingests those who do not subscribe to its tenets" (p. 3).

Not only are people exploited for the sake of the capitalist system, but also the physical environment is exploited for the sake of immediate profits. Throughout the world, the destruction of vast areas of forest, the pollution of already scarce fresh water sources and of the air are among the consequences of shameless prioritizing of economic development over sustainable development. Bringing about environmental justice and alleviation of the other injustices related to exploitation requires a placing of global priorities ahead of national or corporate interests.

Worldview vs. World View

For creative, well-informed policy making on the local or global level, a multicultural worldview is paramount. The word *worldview* denotes a perspective as in "the European versus the American worldview" (related to gun ownership, for example). World view, on the other hand, is the goal to obtain a vision that gets beyond ethnocentrism, a vision that is truly global in scope. In my earlier book, *Social Welfare: A World View*, for example, the major objective was to critically examine social welfare issues from an international perspective. The comparative approach was chosen as the best way to reveal the uniqueness of U.S. ideology regarding human needs and structural attempts to address those needs. In this book, similarly, we will view the shaping of social welfare policy within the context of North American value dimensions and within the context of universal values. The United Nations' Universal Declaration on Human Rights will serve as the guide to internationally agreed-upon values by members of "the human family" (see Appendix). The world view adopted in this book will make available to us a breadth of vision for considering policy proposals for social change. Often a solution to a problem in one part of the world that seems to work, such as the restorative justice model, may be adopted and legally sanctioned elsewhere.

Basic Assumptions of the Book

At a time when social services are being downsized and even eliminated, involvement in the policy making process is essential. The kind of policy making we will be dealing with here is, of course, the shaping of policies to benefit *all* the people as opposed to the conservative notion that policies favoring the global corporations will produce a healthy economy that will benefit the masses. Other basic themes that are evident throughout the pages of this book are that:

- The global exchange of information concerning successful strategies is an essential mission of social work;
- In accordance with the dictum "knowledge is power," the starting point for progressive policy development is an understanding of the dynamics of oppression and injustice;
- Injustice and oppression are normal but not inevitable outcomes of power imbalances;
- Recognition of group differences and advocacy for ethnic-sensitive and gender-sensitive policies are essential to meeting the needs of vulnerable populations;
- An empowerment approach to emphasize community development and prevention over treatment after the situation has grown critical;
- "What goes around comes around"; oppression hurts the oppressors as well as the oppressed;
- Power is intoxicating and corrupting; power plays an important role in determining how differences are defined and which differences matter;
- Social injustice and perceived differences in race, class, gender, sexual orientation, etc., are linked;
- Reality is rarely dichotomous but more often exists on a continuum; and
- Finally, a critical perspective is needed and a healthy dose of what I call our "social work imagination" to tackle all forms of oppression through developing strategies that link individual and social change.

Summary and Conclusion

Anti-oppressive practice seeks to develop an understanding of both the totality of oppression and of its specific manifestations. To fulfill the social work profession's social justice mission for the 21st century, social workers need to analyze current policies in terms of their global and regional origins and ramifications. Concepts defined in this chapter are the rudiments of planning for social change, concepts like *becoming an ally, empowerment, critical thinking, social justice,* and *policy analysis.* Unlike social scientists and many other policy analysts, social workers often see firsthand the unintended consequences of social policies. Becoming politicized and organized, social workers can have a voice, albeit indirectly, in shaping policy. Cultural competence and empowerment counseling skills alone will not shape policy to reduce oppression. Confidence as well as competence is required, and the development of confidence comes with acquiring the tools to effectively challenge current practices. The opposite of the belief that you have a voice, that you can have input in influencing policy, is burnout.

In Kendall's (1989) description of the early visionaries of the profession is a message for today. "In embracing the necessity to join social reform with individual help," she wrote, "(the visionaries) long ago settled the question of whether social work should be equally concerned with therapeutic action and social action" (p. 30). For planning intervention policy and strategies, practitioners need to examine the causes of oppression and injustice. We now turn to this complex but intriguing subject.

Two
Understanding Oppression

Knowledge is power.

Francis Bacon

To be treated unequally, patronizingly, on the basis of inborn or acquired characteristics is to be oppressed. Sometimes the oppression is personal, sometimes pervasive across the culture extending to an almost unlimited number of interactions and activities in everyday life.

The truth to the vulnerable and deprived persons is so often palpably different from the truth to the person at the opposite end of the political spectrum. In essence, oppression is an act of destruction and/or exploitation that inflicts pain and loss to its victims. And as we will see in the following pages, members of the oppressor class, many of whom "march to the tune of a different drummer" are, in a real sense, victimized as well.

Oppression is about power, about control of resources, about hatred of those we have wronged because we would feel bad otherwise. Hence the tendency to blame victims for creating the conditions of their own demise. Oppression at the personal level, for example, of the slave by his or her master or of a woman by a battering spouse, has its parallel in the domination of whole tribes and ethnicities at the national level. Sometimes the tables are turned and the underdogs persecute the persecutors, oppressing individual members of the original oppressor group. So-called reverse racism is an example of this phenomenon. In the final analysis, in the judgment of historians of some future day, ethnic hatred, like wars, is generally regarded as cruel, often futile. In response to the seemingly senseless slaughter in Afghanistan, Gillespie (2002) ponders the essence of global inhumanity:

Catholics and Protestants terrorizing and killing each other in Northern Ireland, Indians and Pakistanis, Hindus and Muslims, Israelis and Palestinians, Hutus and Tutsis, all in their hideous dances of death. The Khmer Rouge slaughtering millions in Cambodia. So many killing fields, so few places on this planet where blood has not been shed again and again. Racism: political, social, or economic oppression; religious zealotry; ethnic animus; nationalism, old grievances and grudges passed down from generation to generation; dormant one minute, erupting the next. We kill each other, and the AIDS pandemic keeps expanding—tens of millions dead and dying—feeding on denial, inequity, and greed, human hope and misery; destroying families, crippling economies, transforming societies. (p. 1)

That social oppression occurs and is maintained at individual, institutional, and societal levels, all three, is an overriding assumption of this chapter. That self-awareness and sociological awareness are prerequisites for a true understanding of the nature of oppression is a second major assumption of this chapter and this book. Without some familiarity with the dynamics of oppression, attempts to develop a culturally competent social work (or other counseling) practice will be in vain.

Whereas Chapter 1 presented an introduction to the basic concepts of oppression, this chapter explores the bio-psycho-social-spiritual dimensions of oppression as a backdrop to an understanding of racism, sexism, heterosexism, and class privilege in modern society. As this chapter argues, it is not so much the particular characteristics of a group in question that generates prejudice as personal qualities in the "eye of the beholder." Some of these qualities may stem from innate tendencies; most are learned and culturally bound. In this chapter we will consider biological, psychological, and sociological theories to account for the existence of oppression. Then drawing on narrative reports we will look more intimately at the various levels of oppression in society. For relevance to the 21st century, attention is devoted to forces of domination and exploitation stemming from unleashed forces in the globalized free market economy. To what extent the personal is political and the political personal is revealed in the consciousness-raising narratives that highlight the theme of this portion of the book.

Biological Aspects of Oppression

At first glance, a consideration of biological factors in oppression will seem surprising. Gil (2001), for example, is emphatic on one point: "Being results of human choices and actions, domination, exploitation, and injustice... were never, nor are they now, inevitable" (p. 36).

And yet, biology is a crucial component in much that is human. Increasingly, brain studies clarify differences in male and female thought processes relating to such factors as communication and aggression (Black, 1999), while the addicted brain can be shown in magnetic resonance imaging (MRI) to look different from the non-addicted brain (Leshner, 1998). Other research with relevance for oppression of the weak by the strong are testosterone studies and observational reports of primate behavior (Wrangham & Peterson, 1996).

Thanks to the remarkable capabilities of MRI technology, scientists can now observe the inner workings of the brain. They are on the threshold of discoveries with implications for the kind of antisocial behavior associated with impulsive, forceful activities and exploitative attitudes and blaming of victims of exploitation. Twin studies conducted at the University of Southern California and brain studies done at the University of Iowa show correlations between the possession of certain biochemical characteristics and a diagnosis of antisocial personality (Barovick, 1999). In general, eight times as many men as women receive this label.

Aggressive behavior of a pathological sort, the kind evidenced in male-on-female battering, is linked to low levels of the neurotransmitter serotonin (Vines, 1999). Brain damage is another area of recent research activity. The impact of injuries to the prefrontal cortex is being studied as a factor in exploitative and aggressive behavior (Nash, 1999).

Research on prison inmates reveals that males and females with abnormally high levels of testosterone tended to have been convicted of violent crimes and to show high dominance and aggression toward other inmates (Dabbs & Dabbs, 2000). Evolutionists such as Wrangham and Peterson (1996), authors of the controversial bestseller, *Demonic Males: Apes and the Origins of Human Violence*, similarly look to biology to explain patterns of dominance. Emphasizing male dominance, these authors study predatory violence including rape and murder among chimpanzees and other apes, our closest living relatives. We need to study such violence, they suggest, as biological phenomena and to examine the role of the reality of such violence in the social lives of all members of the animal kingdom. Their findings have important implications for the study of oppression in human society in revealing the degree to which aggressive behavior, if goal oriented and calculated, can be rewarding in terms of the possession of power. Their conclusions are bolstered by ape studies in which male predators attack the weak, and females (of the chimpanzee variety) often bond with the predators. Is the frequency of male violence a mere artifact of physical strength?, they ask. For answers, they look to human society.

Examining data drawn from global crime statistics on same-sex murder (to eliminate the factor of male strength), Wrangham and Peterson found the statistics to be amazingly consistent. In all societies except for Denmark, the probability that a same-sex murder has been committed by a man, rather than a woman ranges from 92% to 100%. (In Denmark, all the female same-sex murders were cases of infanticide).

Kurzban and Leary (2001) argue from an evolutionary perspective likewise. Their focus is on social exclusion of individuals and groups who are devalued or stigmatized, in one way or another, by society. In strong contrast to writers such as Gil, Kurzban and Leary make the case for the biological basis of between-group competition and exploitation. From this perspective, social exclusion of "out groups" involves a set of distinct psychological systems designed by natural selection to enhance group survival. Human beings are adaptable in their avoidance of contact with persons who are undesirable in some way and have little to offer the group as a whole.

Whether or not we accept that there is a biological force behind interpersonal violence and oppression, we can certainly appreciate the role of biology in such aspects of social life as territorial conquest for access to vital resources—food, water, and oil. We can also appreciate the relevance of theories of the "survival of the fittest" in coming to see how some groups of people, including whole nations and classes, are able to acquire and maintain their power over others.

However strong is the biological component in human behavior, the nature versus nurture controversy is fallacious. There is no either/or in the real world. The person and environment are in constant and dynamic interaction. Nature *and* nurture, biology and culture, are intertwined. Interceding between biology and culture is the human psyche.

The Psychology of Oppression

The social work literature on teaching about women, people of color, and gays and lesbians has most often focused on the need for factual content on specific groups (Gutiérrez, Fredricksen, & Soifer, 1999). What are the rituals of a particular Indian tribe? What is the Hispanic concept of *la familia*? But as Gutiérrez et al. indicate, multicultural education needs to move beyond this know-the-culture approach into the realm of structural inequalities and oppression. I would carry this one step further and reword this sentiment slightly to say that we need to understand the mechanisms that allow for this structural oppression. The starting point is at the individual level with the psychology of oppression.

Related to psychology, three key elements of oppression are victim blaming, displaced aggression, and internalized oppression. Without these components, oppressors would be relatively impotent.

Blaming the Victim

If we stop to think about it, most of us will recognize our natural tendency to want to distance ourselves from victims by blaming the victims for creating the conditions leading to their own victimization. The homeless, the sick, the raped and assaulted—these are all persons apt to be held as at least partially responsible for their fate. Pervasive in the American psyche, blaming the victim as Ryan (1976) first described the phenomenon, is a generic process applied to almost every social problem in the United States. Workers in all branches of the social services need to know the rationale for this natural tendency—simply put, it makes us feel better—and to be aware of it in ourselves and others.

Victim blaming occurs when the downtrodden or underdogs of society are held responsible for creating their own distress. Because of the reciprocity involved, the victim tends to internalize the blame attached to his or her condition, and the negativity may become a self-fulfilling prophecy as we will see in the later section, "Internalized Oppression."

In a classic article in *Psychology Today*, "All the World Loathes a Loser," Lerner (1971) indicates our vulnerability to the suffering of other people. We are only vulnerable to the suffering of a hero. Condemning the victim (of crime, a disease, a relationship) is a response we create privately without awareness so as to maintain our sense of justice in the world. The seemingly natural tendency is to believe that the unfortunate victim somehow merited his or her fate (van Wormer, 1997).

So universal is the tendency to resent others who suffer, as we shield our-selves emotionally from their distress, that this phenomenon occurs between and within oppressed groups as well as among neutral observers. This fact is brought home to us in the following compelling passage from *Night* by Wiesel (1982). In this passage, Wiesel describes his complex emotions as a child witness to the beating of his father:

> I had watched the whole scene without moving, I kept quiet. In fact, I was thinking of how to get further away so that I would not be hit myself. What is more, any anger I felt at that moment was diverted, not against the Kapo, but against my father. I was angry with him, for not knowing how to avoid Idek's outbreak. That is what concentration camp life had made of me. (p. 52)

Pervasive in the American psyche, the phenomenon of blaming the victim is a generic process applied to almost every social problem in the United States (Ryan, 1976). Individual tendencies and cultural forces coalesce in placing the blame on those who bear the costs of capitalism, the class sometimes pejoratively referred to as the "underclass." (Today, the term *socially excluded persons* is used instead of underclass.) As a traditional ideology related to the work ethic, intellectual, scientific, and religious forces have all historically fed the mythology that hard work generates success. Consistent with the dictates of the Protestant work ethic on which the United States was founded, victims of the market economy are seen as victims of themselves. As in earlier times, new formulations of blaming are constantly appearing. Internal (genetic) differences among individuals and slovenly habits have been paraded out as the rationale for social inequality (see *The Bell Curve* by Herrnstein & Murray, 1994, for example). A new slant has been provided to the old claims that social welfare programs cause more problems than they solve, not in terms of their stinginess but in terms of their perceived generosity.

What is the opposite of victim blaming? Is it tolerance? Or support? In the help-ing professions, the opposite of blaming is *empathy*. Empathy is the ability to iden-tify with another person and through a leap of the imagination momentarily to view the world through the other's eyes (van Wormer, 1997). The Sioux prayer re-veals the difficulty in acquiring this virtue, "Oh great spirit keep me from judging a man until I've walked a mile in his moccasins." It is echoed in the harmonizing of a gospel hymn commonly sung in Bowling Green, Kentucky: "Do not accuse, condemn, or abuse, till you've walked in my shoes."

Closely related to the phenomenon of victim blaming is prejudice, defined here as an unjustified negative attitude toward a group of people and discrimination or the act of social exclusion that often accompanies the attitude of prejudice. Blam-ing poor and/or homeless people for creating the conditions that have led to their poverty effectively exonerates us from responsibility and excuses us from our failure to provide some sort of relief even in just admitting one's wrongs. At the personal and national levels, the process is the same.

In an interview in *World Press* taken from the Buenos Aires newspaper, *Pagina*, sociologist Cohen (2001) speaks of the denial mechanism with regard to crimes of the state:

> Today, the Turks continue to deny that between 1915 and 1917 they massacred nearly a million and a half Armenians. In France the great myth of the Resistance described a historic reality—that there were people who fought against the Nazi occupation—but it also covered up something unbearable: that there were also those who collaborated. The case of Israel is especially interesting because it's an open society. Information circulates, there is freedom in teaching, and there is a political opposition. However, at the same time, the mechanism of collective denial functions to astonishing extremes, such as the well known statement by Prime Minister Golda Meir on the violations of Arab's human rights. Turning things around, Golda Meir accused the victims of forcing those poor Israeli young men to commit horrible acts. (p. 47)

Guilt is an emotion, unpleasant in the extreme, which is often aroused on the part of oppressors. The most effective way to alleviate guilt feelings is as Canadian author Bishop (1994) suggests, "to become an ally," even to the point of turning our backs on our own people or traditions. Southern White people who participated in the U.S. Civil Rights Movement were in this mold. But guilt is a dangerous emotion as people obviously do not like to feel bad about themselves. Guilt, accordingly, is often played out as rejection, hatred of the "other." In a cruel twist of fate, members of the ruling class and the class below them sometimes lash out at the underdogs for causing their or their nation's distress. Thus one hears comments like the following: "welfare recipients are lazy," "gays and lesbians should be discreet," "women earn less than men because they work less hard than men and lack ambition." In trying to effect change, we need to realize that overplaying "the guilt card" can cause the oppressor to lash out even more. A good strategy is to appeal to the opponents' sense of fair play and goodwill, to offer them the means to expiate themselves from guilt, for example, by hearing success stories about poor immigrants who did not speak a word of English and who did well after receiving initial help from the government. This strategy draws on positive rather than negative emotions.

The more we can distance ourselves from the suffering of others, in short, the greater will be our sense of complacency and the more effective our denial systems. In her analysis of the dynamics of oppression, Bishop (1994) describes one of the processes by which the favored group solidifies its political and economic base—namely, through *ideological* power, the power of belief. If people can be made to believe that the injustice and inequality are right or at least inevitable, they will not try to change their society. On the other hand, involvement in social reform can expose the source of exploitation and release people from their docility into action.

Displaced Aggression

A more psychologically complicated strategy to enhance the power of the oppressor class is the strategy of *displaced aggression*. An individual might tend to displace aggression from a powerful source (for example, the boss) onto a less powerful source (one's wife or child). At the macro level, the nation's rulers or a political party, through skillful use of propaganda, can redirect the people's righteous anger against the people or politics responsible for their pain onto a vulnerable group such as criminals or immigrants or terrorists. In his insightful article, "Instigators of genocide: Examining Hitler from a social psychological perspective" social psychologist Mandel (2002) explains how collective violence against a designated group of people can be generated through media manipulation and constant repetition of lies and insinuations. Nationalistic slogans can be used to create an egotistic sense of in-group cohesion through emphasizing the shared greatness of the dominant group. Stigmatizing their victims, such as having them wear the Star of David, can increase hostilities by causing people to distance themselves from the designated others; Mandel calls this strategy "state organized moral exclusion" (p. 262).

Clearly, the master of displaced aggression of all time was Hitler (Mandel, 2002). How could Hitler happen? Certainly part of the answer is the severe economic crisis facing Germany following the horrendous defeat of World War I (Allport, 1988). And part of it is likely familial (related to the rigid norms of obedience to authority, militarism, and denial of feelings characteristic of the German family during that period). The evils of Nazism thus were perpetuated across all levels of the social structure. Jews, homosexuals, Roma (Gypsies), and conscientious objectors, among others, accordingly met a cruel fate now known to the world as the Holocaust. In a visit with her 17-year-old son to the U.S. Holocaust Memorial Museum in Washington, DC, an MSW student (T. Pearson, personal communication, July 2001) describes part of what she learned from this exhibit:

> The exhibit of the "burning of the books" in Berlin on May 10, 1933, welded me to that spot. There is a picture of a mountain of books, engulfed in tall flames while a crowd of jeering onlookers cheered wildly. Next to the picture of the burning books is a quote from Jewish poet, Heinrich Heine written a hundred years earlier that reads, "Where one burns books, one will, in the end, burn people." A sad prophecy was unfolding...

> The mobile killing squads single-handedly killed about one fourth of all Jews in the Holocaust. We saw pictures of mass graves, one containing over 7,000 people. It was a hastily dug trench on the outskirts of an Eastern European town where an *Einsatzgruppen* unit of soldiers shot their victims while they stood, kneeled, or laid face down. So many bodies, piled in layers, it was unnatural and your mind could hardly make out the human images. Past the life-sized photos and captions, we arrived at a real freight car. This was an

authentic, 15-ton *Deutsches Reichbahn* freight car. It is positioned in the path of the exhibition route, as a bridge to the next segment exhibits. My son and I stood together in there for a long while. We talked softly of Elie Wiesel's ordeal that he described in his book, *Night*. The reality gave me chills. Again everything, the people and their suffering, had to be multiplied as each train car would carry as many as 80 to 100 people and each train could carry one to two thousand people.[1]

The kind of anti-ethnic violence or hate crimes unleashed in connection with the hysteria of pre-World War II Germany occurs today as well in places such as Kosovo and Congo. *Hate crimes* are criminal acts stemming from prejudice based on race, religion, sexual orientation, disability, or ethnicity. Directed against persons, families, groups, or organizations, these crimes include arson of homes and businesses, harassment, destruction of religious property, cross burnings, personal assaults, and homicides (Barnes & Ephross, 1994). Often associated with a sense of powerlessness, or *anomie,* among young males reacting to a new visibility in society among vulnerable populations, hate crimes are seemingly on the rise throughout the world.

In one of the horror stories of the past decade, *Eight Bullets: One Woman's Story of Surviving Anti-Gay Violence,* Brenner (1995) argues that hate violence is bred when intolerance is socially endorsed. Brenner's survival of anti-lesbian gunfire in which her partner was killed, described in her book, is of a piece with the savage torture and murder of gay college student Matthew Shepard; killings at abortion clinics; the rape, impregnation, and torture of Muslim women in Bosnia; the persecution of women by the former Taliban regime in Afghanistan, and bride burnings in India. All these are examples of the rhetoric of prejudice and hatred gaining expression in individual acts of terrorism.

In times of uncertainty, many people are attracted to a leader with a simple message, a demagogue, over an emotionally mature leader who does not seem to have all the answers. While the mature leader may appear to equivocate on the issues, the demagogue is self-assured, simplistic, and zeroes in on the problem—taxes, national deficits, lazy poor people—and offers magical solutions—return to family values, end welfare, toughen laws (Goodwin, 1994). Today, as competition for well-paying and secure jobs in a global economy heats up, dangerous right-wing extremist movements are winning followers throughout the world. In the United States, the pro-life or anti-abortion movement has threatened the lives of people involved with abortions while hate groups, descendants of the Ku Klux Klan and the Nazis, form armed militias to prepare for violent insurrection. In Canada, a White supremacist movement is attracting a strong following among angry unemployed White youth; Asians, gays, and Jews are targeted. Popular political parties in Austria, France, and Italy fight to preserve their nation's cultural "pu-

---

1. For details of the U.S. Holocaust Memorial Museum, including haunting photographic displays, see the web site at http://www.ushmm.org.

rity." These developments, along with the suicide bombings of Palestinians and al Qaeda, in all probability, are linked to the disparity between the haves and the have-nots, and to a sense of alienation by the dispossessed.

Internalized Oppression

The scars of oppression, notes Bishop (1994), linger in those reared in an abusive society. The historic oppression of African Americans by Whites, for example, has understandably left a residue of self-hatred and suspicion. The effect works its cancer in ways that crush the spirit of many young people. The phenomenon of *internalized oppression*, or aggression turned within, is common among all oppressed groups throughout the world. Repeated exposure to maltreatment, whether on the basis of race, class, gender, nationality, or sexual orientation may lead members of the oppressed group to internalize the negative self-images projected by the external oppressor (Shulman, 1999). Here Shulman discusses the power of "oppression without":

> The external oppressor may be an individual (e.g., the sexual abuser of a child) or societal (e.g., the racial stereotypes perpetuated against people of color). Internalization of this image and repression of the rage associated with oppression may lead to destructive behaviors toward self and others as oppressed people become "auto-oppressors," participating in their own oppression. Thus, the oppressor without becomes the oppressor within. Evidence of this process can be found in the maladaptive use of addictive substances and the growing internal violence in communities of oppressed people, such as city ghettos populated by persons of color. (p. 36)

A fictional account from *Fried Green Tomatoes at the Whistle Stop Café* (Flagg, 1987) aptly captures the inner turmoil of a young woman scorned:

> What was this power, this insidious threat, this invisible gun to her head that controlled her life... *this terror of being called names?*

> She had stayed a virgin so she wouldn't be called a tramp or a slut; had married so she wouldn't be called an old maid; faked orgasms so she wouldn't be called frigid; had children so she wouldn't be called barren; had not been a feminist because she didn't want to be called queer and a man hater; never nagged or raised her voice so she wouldn't be called a bitch...

> She had done all that and yet, still, this stranger had dragged her into the gutter with the names that men call women when they are angry. (pp. 236–237)

Studies of battered women and also of prison inmates reveal how the negative label given by a partner or by society can set into motion a progression in the direction of a sense of helplessness and dependency. All six situations of oppression isolated by Bulhan (1985) and further developed by Shulman (1999) are the violations of an individual's space, time, energy, mobility, bonding, and identity. The violation to the injured person's identity, arguably, is the most harmful violation of all because it relates to his or her self-concept. The tragedy of internalized homophobia is reflected in an inordinately high suicide and alcohol abuse rate among youths with gender identity crises (see van Wormer, Wells, & Boes, 2000).

Sociological Theories

Although psychological processes, as seen above, are not directly addressed by sociological or macro-level theories about the nature of oppression, the impact of ideology and inequality on the human mind and human behavior are at the heart of these sociological formulations (Robbins, Chatterjee, & Canda, 1998). Central to these theories are notions of power alliances and imbalances in the social structure. Although all sociologists and other social scientists are concerned with both conflict in society and the impact of culture on behavior, we will look at two schools of thought that are complimentary in some of their representations and incompatible in others. How do proponents of each of the schools of thought explain oppression? Conflict theorists seek their explanation in terms of divisions in the social structure, for example, stratification on the basis of class, race, and gender. Cultural theorists, in contrast, seek explanations in terms of the social characteristics of oppressed classes. Whereas conflict theory, as the name would indicate, focuses on conflict and coercion, cultural theory explains harmony and maintenance of the present social system and the tendency toward equilibrium as opposed to systemic change (Mullaly, 1997). Where the conflict theorist sees alienation (as of the workers from their work), the cultural theorist is more likely to perceive group deviance from the social norms. Both schools of thought, as I am defining them, would accept the reality of cultural clash and of discrimination on the basis of race, gender, class, etc.

Keep in mind that there is much overlap between these schools of thought, and that elements from both approaches are crucial to our understanding of the social factors that sustain oppression in the society. We begin with these theoretical frameworks commonly associated with radical social theory.

Conflict Theory

Conflict theory, sometimes called radical/critical theory, is a polyglot group of theories, and proponents do not necessarily regard others as kin (Saleebey, 2002). Saleebey highlights three key themes uniting the theoretical orientations in this group: a rejection of positivism in social science research; a focus on a radical analysis of history; and an understanding that oppression is structural and issues from overbearing institutions and ideologies. Indeed the notion of oppression is central to the theory that falls under this rubric.

To explain the causes of oppression in society, sociologists of this radical school look to differential access to power and status (DuBois & Miley, 2002). Such an imbalance is an injustice in itself. The struggle to maintain such power and status perpetuates oppression in its many forms. The perception of society as torn by conflict rather than united in consensus had its origins in the writing of Karl Marx. The sociologist, C. Wright Mills, followed in this tradition. In his widely read *The Power Elite*, Mills (1956) revealed how the military-industrial complex joined industry, politics, and military planners in a common cause promoted by a common ideology. Because of the corporate control of the media, an image of "the just society" can be portrayed with great effectiveness and reduce the critical consciousness of the masses necessary to eliminate structures of injustice and oppression (see Gil, 1998).

In *Regulating the Poor*, Piven and Cloward (1993) present their theory concerning relief policies for the poor. The elites in society, according to this perspective, provide only enough aid, stigmatized at that, to prevent mass disorder and regulate labor. As enunciated by the authors in the updated appendix, "We gave primacy to conflict and social control rather than to the consensus and social altruism which figure so largely in traditional social welfare histories" (p. 457). *Regulating the Poor*, revised numerous times, has been one of the most influential books in the field of social work.

More recent representatives of this school of thought are Gil's (1998) writings on confronting injustice and oppression and Mullaly's (1997) work on structural social work. Both writers focus attention on the eradication of societal oppression. Change efforts, as Gil suggests, must be directed at entire policy systems rather than at more marginal adjustments. Mullaly agrees: "A truly just order can come about only through radical reorganization of society, not through extension of social control" (p. 125). A collective, participatory ideology is essential to the achievement of a just social order.

Both Gil and Mullaly are critical of mainstream social work. Gil (1998) urges social work to shift its focus from the symptoms of oppression and injustice to the actual causes. The challenge, as Gil convincingly argues, must be to the "systemic sources in capitalist dynamics" (p. 85). Such a paradigm shift, notes Gil, would be entirely consistent with the mandate of the profession's Code of Ethics to pursue social justice and resist oppression. Conventional policy analysis in social work, as Gil further argues, is erroneous in its treatment of single problems, single solutions. Elimination of supposedly unrelated social problems when viewed in isolation is unlikely because they all derive from a common cause. Each problem can be regarded as symptomatic of a weakness in the social structure. Homelessness and poverty, accordingly, may simply be a given in a competitive capitalist society.

Writing from a structural perspective, Mullaly articulates a major limitation of welfare capitalism and conventional social work as the narrow focus on economic inequality while often ignoring "the decision-making structures that determine economic relations in society" (p. 141). To truly understand the dynamics of oppression, as Mullaly asserts, we need to consider the role of exploitation in maintaining an unequal distribution of goods and services. At the practice level, social workers should avoid the role of expert and engage in a mutual learning process with clients.

Common to all the theories discussed under the rubric of conflict theory is a criticism of the existing social order. Solutions are geared toward major change, a transformation of the social structure. In a nutshell, inequality is inherent in our free market and highly competitive economy, and change efforts must be directed accordingly. Critics of conflict theory point to the limitations of a strictly structural approach in providing expert help to persons in serious personal difficulty. Criticism is also directed toward the neglect of the possibility of the empowerment of oppressed persons within the present social order (Payne, 1997).

Culturally Based Theory

Under conditions of oppression, norms and values arise congruent with survival in the system. Powerlessness breeds contempt; it also breeds deceit and manipulation as a way to "outsmart the system" and its representatives. As people come to feel themselves to be rejects and outcasts, the hope of becoming a part of the affluent society that surrounds them ceases to be a reality; it becomes a taunt. So said Harrington (1962) in his classical work on poverty, *The Other American*. People who no longer believe they have a stake in the system, such as the unemployed, can be destructive to the system.

Culturally based theory is not described in the social work literature as a specific model or theory, not even in textbooks on human behavior and the social environment (Robbins, Chatterjee, & Canda, 1998). Yet knowledge of culture and cultural history provide important perspectives for understanding human behavior (Saleebey, 2001). *Culturally based theory* is a term I am using for theoretical perspectives that explain many of the problems that oppressed people have in abiding by the norms of society, especially regarding achievement and independence. Such theory locates the source of oppression within the values, norms, and attitudes of the oppressed group but only as a legacy from earlier mistreatment, for example, slavery. History is important here. People who have been socially excluded and whose ancestors have been subjected to social exclusion over long periods of time develop survival mechanisms that may no longer be functional.

Illustrative of this approach, is Cattell-Gordon's (1990) analysis of the traumatic effects of the loss and absence of work over generations in Southern Appalachia. Introducing the concept of culturally transmitted traumatic stress syndrome to describe the character of the Southern Appalachian people, Cattell-Gordon records the history of those who have been alternatively exploited and abandoned throughout the 20th century. The distinct but not unique history of Appalachia reveals how external exploitation can leave a land and its people broken and bruised, and how the normative adaptations to the crises of unemployment and grinding poverty have become ingrained in the culture today. According to Cattell-Gordon (1990),

"These particular cultural traits then—an enduring sense of resignation, deep depression, disrupted relationships and hurtful forms of dependency—appear, again and again, in the culture as each new generation faces unemployment" (p. 43).

Blue and Blue (2001), similarly, speak of the legacy of cultural oppression of Canadian First Nations people related to the European invasion. The existence of these traumas must be taken into account when evaluating First Nations people within the Canadian penitentiary system, these authors suggest. Although oppressed populations, such as mountain people, Native populations, and inner-city residents, manifest similar patterns of cultural transmission that are often at odds, we might say, with the work ethic of the wider society, Cattell-Gordon argues vehemently against a culture of poverty premise. Perceiving a virtually autonomous subculture extant among the poor, culture of poverty theorists overlook the fact that the individual or group cannot easily break out of this vicious circle of social isolation. Cemlyn and Briskman (2002) echo these sentiments in their sociological study of Australian Aborigines and British "Gypsies" (Roma). Both groups' history of oppression includes persecution, assimilation, and genocide. Their relationship with land which diverges from the capitalist/colonialist norm, as Cemlyn and Briskman indicate, is treated as a threat by the majority. Cultural genocide has taken the form of child removal, leading these minority groups to fear state social services to the present time.

Naturally people at the bottom of the social heap lack faith in a system that appears to have very little to offer. In any case, we must agree that the social costs attended to the demoralization of generation after generation are immeasurable. Gradually the norm of "working the system" comes to replace the norm of working; rage, crime, and fatalism prevail. Then commentators such as Herrnstein and Murray (1994) blame these attitudes (and the welfare) for poverty. The interactive nature of external realities and belief systems may not be recognized; cause is confused with effect (van Wormer, 1997).

A closely related theory as discussed by Payne (1997) is "learned helplessness theory." If people find that the efforts they make to change their situations are in vain, they will cease to try. They may be seen as lacking motivation, depressed, and fatalistic. The response logically should not be blame but rather enrichment through providing situations of empowerment, as Payne thoughtfully suggests. A cautionary note about these cultural explanations of oppression is that they sometimes come across as deficiency formulations that are imposed on minority cultures (Robbins et al., 1998). Now we consider cultural values in relation to societal oppression.

Cultural Values Associated with Economic Oppression

The North American stress on independence and individualism militates against the provision of "cradle to grave" social services. Moralism, like independence and individualism, is a core American value singled out by Tropman

(1989) in his book on American values and social welfare. *Moralism* refers to the tendency to see human behavior in strictly ethical terms. Related to religious beliefs, the American brand of moralism derives from the 16th and 17th century Puritan creed. Moralism dictates that persons dependent on welfare suffer certain discomforts. When discrimination (on the basis of ascription) against minorities, women, aged, and disabled persons becomes played out as discrimination against the poor or non-achievers in society, it is hard for the social welfare system to get the public support to expand substantially. In the United States, as Tropman (1989) indicates, there is no mass political movement of the poor, and no labor political party with a strong working class allegiance.

As the tides of political change come and go, and as the public mood shifts, so do the social policies. Once ingrained, they tend to reinforce the social values. The cycle is complete with values shaping policies and policies, values. For example, religious belief in hard work and frugality can promote economic investment and growth; economic growth can reinforce the Protestant work ethic. Simultaneously, the religious value of compassion can influence a willingness to pay more taxes (economic consequences) in order to introduce programs to provide shelters for the homeless. Charity and philanthropy, which are institutionalized in tax write-offs and deductions, probably help assuage a sense of guilt on the part of the rich in a capitalist society.

Not only do values play into policies, but policies play into values. For instance, American means-tested programs associated with the poor and minorities generate more opposition than support. As Piven and Cloward (1993) wisely note, the effects of segregating programs for the poor are far reaching—dampening support for other welfare state programs. Citizens resent paying taxes for services from which they themselves receive no benefits. The value of providing social welfare is diminished when fragmented programs reach only narrowly defined groups. Some affirmative action programs, limited as they are in magnitude, have created resentment and hostility.

The United States prides itself on being one of the most generous nations. Yet social work educator and former labor organizer, Wagner (2001) in his book aptly titled *What's Love Got to Do With It?* makes a convincing case for the fact that philanthropy actually provides a cover for the dark side of the free-market economy. Organized charity has done more to benefit the rich (and make them feel better) than the poor, as Wagner observes. Most other industrialized societies place social rights obtained through welfare (tax) adjustments on an equal footing with political rights as an essential feature of social justice. This right of economic security is included as a basic right in the United Nations Universal Declaration of Human Rights (see Appendix).

The Anglo-American charity tradition is culturally related to calls for privatization and faith-based treatment. Such aid is given sporadically and is not considered an entitlement. Instead of constructing theories to explain "the culture of poverty," we can make a case for cultural beliefs that are characteristic of North

American capitalism. Perhaps we should define a "culture of affluence" as one that is strong on opportunity but weak on equality.

From my perspective, transformation of unjust and oppressive practices would require a shift in the priorities—away from values of independence and individual competition and in the direction of egalitarianism, cooperation, and faith in the system for ensuring a balance in the distribution of resources. (For a summary of Scandinavian and other European value orientations, see Gould, 2001, and van Wormer, 1997.) The popular assumption accepted by most Americans that just, non oppressive, egalitarian, and nonviolent societies cannot and do not exist is an assumption in need of re-examination according to Gil (2002). In *Confronting Injustice and Oppression*, Gil chides the profession of social work for buying into the system and system's values in "its dependence on powerful social elites" and failure to confront "the realities of injustice and oppression" (p. 77). As social workers increasingly gravitated toward practice as therapists, as Gil further suggests, sociology has come to have far less influence on social work practice and theory than psychology and medical models of disease and cure. With the exception of majority-minority relations and culturally sensitive practice, cultural content in general has received little attention in the social work literature (Robbins, Chatterjee, & Canda, 1998).

The Impact of Economic Globalization

The backdrop for any discussion of oppression must include, to quote Bishop (1994), "the amazingly powerful and well coordinated web of control of the multinational corporations and financial institutions have woven around the world" (p. 35). Political, military, and ideological power all come together in the service of global economic integration. The communications revolution enhances the political, military, and ideological power of globalization. Admittedly, life in the global age is not without its advantages. A search of the Internet and a hook-up to satellite TV links us instantly to a recent issue of Canada's *Globe and Mail*, Norway's *Aftenposten*, or a session of the British Parliament. Transfer of knowledge, perspectives, and direct communication through urgent e-mail announcements to persons thousands of miles apart can help popular social movements gain momentum.

Relevant to oppression, global communication helps inform people everywhere about conditions of oppression and bring pressure to bear on foreign governments to curb at least the appearances of mistreatment as of women and minorities. Also relevant to oppression is of course the impact of the global economy on the social welfare of the world's people. The link between globalization and inequality and the escalation of violent conflicts within and between countries is readily apparent (Torczyner, 2000). Disparities in wealth, whether within nations or between nations, are associated with greed, resentment, and war. Refugees created by bombings and warfare migrate from the poor countries into the wealthier ones, joining the already large number of immigrants who cross borders for economic reasons. This is only one way in which wars in one part of the world invariably involve nations from another part.

War and violence, in turn, are associated with ecological destruction as witnessed in the anti-capitalist attacks on the World Trade Center but also in the retaliatory bombings by the United States on Afghanistan and later, Iraq. War and violence, moreover, are associated with the erosion of the rights of dissenters, minority groups, and women. In a national military crisis, military spending takes precedence over all other spending.

Economic oppression of nations also results from conservative (or "neoliberal") global economic policies unrelated to military spending. *Laissez-faire* policy enforced by the world banks argues that market forces—the profit motive—will drive the economy to efficient outcomes (Stiglitz, 2003). Fiscal austerity, privatization, and market liberalization are the three pillars of the global market as Stiglitz, writing in the national bestseller, *Globalization and Its Discontents,* indicates. Such trends are enforced by the International Monetary Fund and the World Bank in connection with their money-lending policies requiring poor nations to reduce spending on social welfare in order to pay off the loans.

Structural adjustment programs generally involve cuts in government spending, strong promotion of exports, free trade agreements that favor the industrialized nations, and flexible wages to deal with international competition (Wilson & Whitmore, 2000). With the end of the Cold War, as Parenti (2002) suggests, there is no longer the incentive to enhance the social development of people to keep them from going communist. In Parenti's words, "Capitalism with a human face has become capitalism in your face."

Emphasis has been placed on economic growth at the expense of sustainable development and the well-being of human communities. In *Economics for Social Workers*, Prigoff (2000) spells out the social consequences, the increasing social problems stemming from the new economic realities. The rapidly growing gap between the rich and the poor (within and among countries) continues to widen while the degradation of the environment advances to threaten the life and livelihood of many of the earth's inhabitants. Because of regulations under Chapter 11 of the free trade agreement, corporations can sue governments to recoup their losses if environmental restrictions impinge on their profits (Moyers, 2002, February 2). The impact on individuals, families, and communities is profound. Accordingly, as Prigoff indicates, it is important for social workers to understand the theories and methods of the field of economics as they pertain to our clients and ourselves. Knowledge of such economic truths enables us to tune in to the experience of oppression and to help raise the consciousness of our clients and of the general public.

In the current context of serious economic constraints and welfare cutbacks, social workers should support and join with the growing coalitions of labor, religious, and non-government organizational groups that are working toward global social justice and human rights. In Seattle, Washington, social worker involvement in the anti-World Trade Organization project was palpable (British Columbia Teachers Federation, 1999). Until public consciousness is raised, notes Lee (2001), the real welfare culprits—corporations that receive very costly tax breaks and subsidies—will continue to exploit the American economy and poor workers while unemployed mothers will continue to be blamed for the public debt.

In 1996, the National Association of Social Workers' (NASW) Code of Ethics was revised to include a global mandate. Social workers are now enjoined to "promote the general welfare of society, from local to global levels" (Standard 6.01). In light of the current globalization of the economy, social workers inevitably will be working with persons who are unemployed because of outsourcing or downsizing or technological advances or who are exploited due to free trade competition from abroad.

Personal Narratives

In this final section of the chapter, we turn from the causes of oppression at the bio-psycho-social and global levels to its manifestations at the receiving end. The targets of victim blaming, displaced aggression, and economic exploitation are people who are differentiated from others on some visible or otherwise detectable basis by race, class, disability, sex, etc. Principles to keep in mind are that keynoted differences can derive from a physical or behavioral characteristic (such as drug use) and furthermore that it is not the difference itself that discredits an individual but the value assigned to that label. In the next chapter we will be concerned with whole populations that experience oppression. Here we will be concerned with the individual dynamics.

Individual vulnerabilities and the direct obstacles posed by discriminatory practices block opportunity structures, limit life choices, and pose threats to the development of "know-how" and self esteem (Lee, 2001). Through the use of personal narrative, we will see how oppression is played out in relations of dominance and subordination that are often humiliating to those believed to be less deserving and inferior. Persons victimized by word or deed rarely forget it; the slights, insults, and denial of equitable treatment may stay with the recipient forever.

The first step in challenging oppression and understanding what Bishop calls "power-over" relationships is to confront one's own personal experiences related to difference and privilege within the dominant culture (Van Soest, Canon, & Grant, 2000). An empowerment exercise that is extremely helpful in developing self awareness, especially when shared in groups, is presented in Box 2.2. Examples from MSW students and recent graduates from northeast Iowa are reproduced under the various topic headings below. Participants in the consciousness-raising exercise invariably shared that the experience was powerful; several tapped into emotions far deeper than they realized they still felt or that we as a class were prepared to deal with. Re-experiencing the visceral feelings of the personal rejection—the hearing, visualizing, smelling, tasting—is probably what triggered the intense reactions to events many had not relived in years. The lesson that we all learned is how great is the pain in personal oppression. Some respondents had been empowered in overcoming the experience of oppression; others clearly had been disempowered, and in at least one case, traumatized by the painful encounter. Note how the member of the privileged class, the "ally," was often injured vicariously by the episode. For the sake of illustration and organization, I have separated out several categories, for example, gender, race, and economic hardship. Just as the relationship between personal and political oppression is interactive, so is the link among the various categories of distinction. Gender, race, and class, in other words, are rarely discrete categories but exist in combination. The effect is beyond additive—race plus class—but synergistic. Take the female offender as an example. As a woman of color who is uneducated and a prisoner or ex-convict she will be deemed undeserving, a poor job risk, a threat to society. Conversely, achievement of high status in one category (becoming a doctor, for example) can modify the risk of experiencing discrimination by virtue of ethnic or class characteristics. As we consider the extent of oppression accruing to one factor, therefore, we need to be cognizant of the reinforcing or modifying effect of dual and multiple memberships. In Box 2.2 we hear from a staff member, herself an African American, privileged by virtue of her staff position whose heart cries out on behalf of a mistreated child.

Box 2.2   Consciousness Raising Against Oppression

The following empowerment exercise was presented at the feminist social workers Fem School Gathering in Bowling Green, Kentucky, in 1994. The purpose of the exercise is to raise awareness of the existence of oppression in our society and of ways that a negative event can be a turning point toward a transformation or a new beginning. The results of the exercise, when shared, make participants aware of ways that oppressive processes can be stopped and of strengths in the community.

Participants pair off, each with a partner who will read back to the group the other's response. Each participant fills in the blanks of this exercise with regard to an instance of oppression as follows:

I heard:

I saw:

I smelled:

I tasted:

continues...

I felt:

This to me was:

One participant provided the following compelling response which was recorded and read out to her partner. It demonstrates the spiraling effect of saying no.

Consciousness Raising Exercise: Saying No to Racism

I *heard* a group of people talking. I heard shuffling of chains. A man's voice. A psychiatrist's voice—white psychiatrist, saying everyone should close the doors. Everyone should lock this child out if she leaves my session. I *saw* two adult men carrying an overweight thirteen-year-old African American girl who was screaming out of her room. I saw frightened children. I saw panicked faces, angry faces. I *smelled* heat, sweat, grass. I *tasted* my saliva, salty saliva. I *felt* tension in my hands. Pressure in my ears, my head. Probably fear. Anger.

This to me was racism, sexism…oppression. And it was social work.

I said *no*. I will never close the door. This is not the social work I will do. I resisted. I took a risk. I sought support from my supervisor and co-workers. My supervisor was scared but took a stand. We both went on to be life-long activists working to transform the world—and social work along the way. To me this was resistance, taking risks and building alliances. It was *solidarity*.

Gender-Based Oppression

Because gender roles are assigned within the family and because the norms of patriarchy are so often learned at the mother's knee, oppression on the basis of gender can be considered the most enduring of all oppressions. To be liberated from such constraints often comes at the price of family ridicule and distress. In contrast to members of other oppressed groups, liberated women and lesbians (and feminist men) may have to seek out their own communities of support. Males as well as females can experience sex discrimination. Sometimes this occurs when passed over for a job because of affirmative action requirements or because of the employer's preference for a female. Because the male generally is in the position of privilege, however, our focus is on male-on-female sexism.

Power in any patriarchal society is typically exercised through the use of exploitation and force, manipulation and competition (Lee, 2001). And competition over scarce resources such as pay raises and salaries is often at the heart of discrimination. "We have to look at economics not only as the root cause of sexism but also as the underlying driving force that keeps all oppression in place," as Pharr (2001) notes. That unequal power relations exist between men and women in U.S. society is revealed in gender-based employment discrimination. Women generally earn less than men, even when performing the same job (CreditCareCenter.com, 2003). Yet many more women than men have child care responsibilities, especially among single parents.

The women's movement, the second wave of which began in the early 1970s, raised the consciousness of men and women, opened doors to professional advancement, and even changed the language. Never again would the masculine pronoun suffice; no longer would mature women be happy to be called girls, and a new word, "Ms.," entered the vocabulary. Non-discriminating laws and affirmative action initiatives have paved the way for women's entry into previously male-dominated fields.

Although women are still a long way from achieving full equality, the changes that have taken place—notably in the areas of control of reproduction, fairness in employment, and legal protection from harassment and other victimization—were resented by many men, especially those facing employment insecurity. Despite male resentment, the clock cannot be turned back on women's bid for equality, at least not in countries where women have entered the power structure. Women continue to enter the professions, such as law and medicine, in record numbers, and legislation has tightened up to protect female victims of domestic assault, while a new awareness of date rape and its connection with substance abuse has led to prevention measures and awareness campaigns on the college campus. Globally, women are beginning to organize to bring media attention to the needs of girls and women sold into sexual slavery and ravaged by genital mutilation.

Among the steps backward: attempts to stymie women's reproductive freedom, new coercive and highly punitive social welfare policies, the use of anti-conspiracy laws to punish the wives and partners of drug dealers for their role in perpetrating or covering up crime, a resurgence in the previously discounted myth of the "new female criminal," and finally, extensive press coverage of domestic violence statistics, which purport to show that women initiate violence against their partners as often as men do (van Wormer, 2001).

The backlash, the counter-assault that Faludi (1991) convincingly identified from events of the late 1980s, is now even more striking at the start of the 21st century. While the word "feminist" has come to be equated with male bashing and lesbianism among the younger generation of educated women (Pharr, 2001), other women at the bottom end of the social structure are falling victim to merciless "welfare reform" laws and harsh sentencing practices for drug violations. In the name of equality, gender-neutral sentences have been inflicted upon women who are now confined in record numbers in prisons built and run according to the male model (see Chesney-Lind & Pasko, 2003; van Wormer, 2001). A flawed notion lurks beneath the current policies: the assumption that women have achieved full equality and that men are suffering the consequences. The backlash related to women's advances at the upper echelons, ironically, is carried out against women who are the least able to take advantage of the new employment opportunities and the least feminist-identified. The media demonization of the "new violent female," a myth generated in the popular press, further aggravates the female offender's plight (van Wormer, 2001).

As Pharr (2001) reminds us, "we have to look at economics not only as the root cause of sexism but also as the underlying driving force that keeps all the oppressions in place." Women's (and minorities') gains are clearly a threat to the status quo, to White male privilege.

The consciousness raising statement I have chosen to end this section comes from a then MSW student who broke through professional barriers in an earlier career.

Consciousness Raising Exercise: Sexist Oppression

While serving in the US Navy I was one of the first women assigned to a ship on the West Coast. Upon meeting my department officer for the first time I experienced the following:

I *heard*: "You are a woman. Women don't belong in *my* Navy. Women belong in the kitchen, and the home. Not here."

I *saw*: "Old Navy," an institutional dinosaur, holding on with teeth and claws, fat, white and bloated.

I *smelled*: Fear—fear of change, fear of the future. I smelled power, anger, and hatred in his cigar smoke.

I *felt*: Diminished, unwanted, unwelcome. Resentful of the future struggles that were inevitable. Unfeminine in the extreme.

This to me was: My future as a woman in a man's world.

Printed with permission of Margaret Nichol, MSW.

Personal Victimization

This type of oppression occurs less from the category someone is in than as a result of power imbalance. Children are often victimized due to their inability to fight back. Child and partner victims of domestic violence pay a high psychological toll for their suffering. Fear, insecurity, and possessiveness are personality characteristics found in battering men who so often see themselves as the victims.

Due to such insecurity, perhaps because of a history of child abuse, jealousy and possessiveness of their wives and girlfriends are characteristic. Abusive men, as Marano (1993) suggests, may go into a rage when their wives go out with friends. Immigrant wives may even be discouraged from learning the language of their adopted country or from learning to drive as a way to keep them down, especially in a country in which women are relatively unrepressed. Power abuse by a man of a woman is thus as much about male insecurity (overcompensation through a show of bravado is typical) as it is about cultural attitudes. The interplay between power and control is visually represented by the widely used Power and Control Wheel developed by the women's shelter in Duluth, Minnesota. Represented in this Wheel is the system of privilege that perpetuates violence and the dynamics of maintaining that power (van Wormer, 2001). Economic abuse, use of children, isolation, and emotional control are represented in segments divided by the spokes of the wheel.

Clinicians who work with battering men will be especially cognizant of the psychology of male abuse. Intrapsychic attributes, for example, a hypersensitivity to abandonment, a seeming inability to control negative emotions and poor impulse control, combined with a biological predisposition such as low serotonin levels and brain injury, have been found to be linked in the backgrounds of women-abusing men (Marano, 1993).

When the mother in the family is beaten, the children are subject to victimization as well. An MSW student who wishes to remain anonymous records her memories in the following contribution.

Consciousness Raising Exercise: Child Mistreatment

I heard: The words "You bitch, I don't care, you make me do this."

I saw: My father's face above me, eyes bulging, saliva projecting from his mouth as he yelled, his whole body shaking.

I smelled: Cigarettes from his hands, sweat.

I felt: Panic, his hands around my neck, my body being crushed under his weight, my body slipping away into unconsciousness.

This was to me: A realization that I needed to survive.

Explanation: I grew up in a very abusive home. I was the brunt of all my father's hatred. In my family there was my mother and my brother. Before I was born my father beat my mom and once I was born it was my turn. I was worried that if I wasn't there that he would hurt my younger brother next. This is why I felt as though I had to survive, I couldn't leave this house, I couldn't tell anyone for fear that they would take me away and my brother would be alone enduring the wrath of my father.

Economic Oppression

Economics, as we have seen, is at the root of most oppression, both in terms of cause and consequence. The concentration of economic and political power in the hands of corporate elites brings its effects to bear in declining social and economic conditions for the vast majority of the world's population (Wilson & Whitmore, 2000). The more powerful the major corporations become (witness the growth of the private prison corporations) the greater their political clout and ability to shape social and economic policies. Punishment of the poor for petty theft is often harsher than that of grand corporate crime. One is reminded of the Biblical observation, "Whosoever hath, to him shall be given…but whosoever hath not, from him shall be taken away even that he hath" (Matthew 13:12).

The trend toward declining investment in human development carries immense social costs. The documentation is found in statistics showing that in the United States just under one in six children live below the poverty level (Cooper, 2001). Although this was a decline from earlier years, a decline attributed to the labor shortage in the late 1990s, the economic recession of 2001 will see a reversal in these numbers. Meanwhile, as Ehrenreich's (2001) revealing documentary *Nickel and Dimed* proves, surviving on a minimum wage job is not easy. At such an income level, there is no margin for car trouble, new clothes, medical expenses, or any other unexpected crises.

In her widely reported participant-observation study, Ehrenreich tried to survive on jobs that paid $6 or $7 an hour. She worked as a waitress, motel maid, and Wal-Mart sales clerk but needed to hold two jobs to make ends meet. And that was without children. Such economic struggles are characteristic of working class Americans. The jobs that Ehrenreich describes are typical of those jobs often taken by refugees and other immigrants.

Women on welfare hardly fare better. Punitive social policies reappeared in the 1980s under the guise of welfare reform (Abramovitz, 1999). The new wave of Puritanism, combined with an intensified thrust to discipline poor and minority women who seemed to challenge traditional gender roles, culminated in the Personal Responsibility Act of 1996. Poor single mothers, according to Jimenez (1999), were demonized in this legislation, legislation which marked the climax of a 20-year campaign of stigmatizing and stereotyping welfare mothers for their perceived laziness. The values ingrained in this act, as Jimenez argues, paradoxically were given new life by the modern feminist movement and the sexual revolution. Congressional hearings that preceded the passage of the act, bolstered by uncharitable media accounts, linked welfare mothers with crimes ranging from child abuse to raising juvenile delinquents, to a lack of the ability to delay gratification. Behind the media attacks condemning bad mothers, behind the assaults on women accused of having babies to get state aid, another message flashes: "You have won equality; now you will be self-sufficient." The cult of traditional womanhood, as Jimenez suggests, was overturned by the modern feminist movement. In any case, the day of entitlements for poor women was now over. Men who depended on state general welfare assistance were thrown off the rolls as well. Many of them were unemployable for one reason or another.

As the major portion of the county budgets in the United States go to the building and running of new jails, public funding for prenatal health care and early child care and mental health treatment is greatly diminished. Poverty not only causes pain and suffering, as Prigoff (2000) indicates, it also kills. Low-income children are several times as likely as other children to die from all causes—disease, birth defects, and fires. Child poverty increases the risk of school failure and in turn adult poverty.

In a society with a weak safety net, however, a major life crisis can throw even the highly educated among us into dire circumstances. Many of us, it is often said, are just one paycheck away from such misery. Witness the struggle of the following undergraduate student:

Consciousness Raising Exercise: Woman on Welfare

I *heard* only one end of the conversation. The landlord, it seemed, didn't quite know how to ask the question that was foremost in his mind. Talking with the social worker from the housing department on the phone, I could sense the information given out about the rental assistance program was really the least of his concerns.

I *saw* her tactfully try to steer the conversation away from that single question: "What kind of people *were* these, if they were on assistance?" He was worried about his property being damaged.

I could *smell* the prejudice in the air, fought the *taste* of bile rising in my throat as anger swelled inside, and tears threatened to spill.

"I am college-educated," I wanted to shout. "My kids are clean! Both are in advanced academics at school and are well liked! We are moral, decent people! The divorce wasn't my fault! I've published! I'm very well liked and respected in the community!"

I *felt* all of these things but could not say a word. The worker assured the prospective landlord that we would make excellent tenants. Yet he remained skeptical. He'd never rented to a divorced person before, let alone a divorced *female* on *public assistance*, with *children*...

This to me was stereotyping. Stereotypes abound surrounding persons on public assistance programs. Despite the presentation of facts and figures, accurately depicting exactly who is (and who *isn't*) on "welfare," these misguided impressions exist. For my part, in my corner of the world, I will do all I can to educate. It is my firm belief that this is the most devastating form of oppression: *ignorance*. Fighting this particular form of oppression is instrumental to social work.

Printed with permission of Sandy Hartstack.

Political Oppression

Rarely mentioned in the literature is the form of oppression thought to be more characteristic of a totalitarian society than a democracy, oppression based on one's belief system—political oppression. Yet the "don't talk, don't tell" policy for gays and lesbians in the military is an example of what I have in mind. This policy provides punishment on the basis of speaking one's mind. Not to be able to state who you are or to advocate for civil rights for people of your kind is the greatest silencing. On the tombstone of a former sergeant, Leonard Matlovich, are the following words: "When I was in the military, they gave me a medal for killing two men, and a discharge for loving one" (cited in van Wormer, Wells, & Boes, 2000).

The first casualty of war, as the saying goes, is the truth. It is also freedom of speech. There have been a number of reports in the newspapers of journalists and academics losing their jobs for expressing skepticism over the "war on terrorism." In a totally military-run society, of course, there is no freedom of speech because speaking out against the government can be equated with treason. To learn of the suppression of free speech of social workers in Nazi Germany and in the United States during the McCarthy era, see Reisch and Andrews' (2001) *The Road Not Taken: A History of Radical Social Work in the United States.*

Awareness of the extent to which conformity rules our lives or of how unwelcome dissension is in the workplace is rare. Until they step out of line, whether from moral convictions or for other motives, dissenters often find out the hard way that their "differentness" is unappreciated. Academics and social workers who are right wing and "politically incorrect" are probably as likely to be made to suffer for this outspokenness as are left wing individuals. Within the addictions field, the agency often has followed a "party line" of sorts (see van Wormer & Davis, 2003).

To provide a relevant contribution for this section and because I have lost more than one job due to unpopular affiliations or expressions of opinion, I am providing my own submission to exemplify political oppression.

Consciousness Raising Exercise: Tenure Denial by All-Male Faculty, Kent, Ohio, 1984

I *heard*: You do not understand the mission of the criminal justice department. You are too pro-black and pro-women in your minorities class. How about the other students? There have been complaints...Students mock you behind your back: "She's the woman in pants," they say.

I *saw*: The formal denial of tenure statement: "She has a strong feminist bias; this is evidenced by her writings. This bias is a disservice to students who need to appreciate freedom of thought."

continues...

I *tasted* nothing, *smelled* nothing but maybe a burning from within.

I *felt* stunned, depressed, defeated—anger turned within, a stabbing pain in my stomach, pounding heart.

This to me was the ultimate defeat, a career destroyed, unanimous rejection from my peers and my boss.

I said nothing. I will share this with the press, I vowed. I will not go quietly; I will stay and fight until the bitter end. Then when I lose I will find a niche for myself, take the kids south and move back in with my Mother, go to graduate school for an MSW. And someday I will write books about injustice. This to me was a turning point.

Oppression Based on a Disability

Charlton (1998), a longtime disability-rights activist, studied the plight of people with disabilities across the world. Compared to many nations, the U.S. disability rights movement has achieved some success. Nevertheless, people with disability in the United States have little economic power and are surplus people. Charlton contrasts "disability oppression" with empowerment. Empowerment arises when disabled persons come to reject "the shame program" to which society subjects them.

Barriers in architecture, transportation, communications, economics, and legal rights, as Dubois and Miley suggest, impose serious limitations in the environment. Above all, prejudicial attitudes keep persons with disabilities from full participation in the environment. Malicious parodies of people with disabilities provide evidence of what Dubois and Miley (2002) term *handicapism*.

There are many kinds of disability; most of these delimiting conditions are stigmatized especially when they appear to be self-inflicted in some way. Thus persons who are disabled as a consequence of poor health practices or addictions are especially disregarded and in the case of obesity, often ridiculed. Recently reported research presented at the North America Association for the Study of Obesity revealed the depth of obesity stigma. In a study from England, female student reactions to two prom photos were measured. Ratings of an average size man embracing a very large woman were far more negative than the same person seen with a slim woman. Even students who were overweight themselves rated the man harshly in the first instance. As was also reported at the conference, overweight people are often discriminated against by doctors who ascribe all their problems to their weight (Associated Press, 2003, October 14). Enter the world of an overweight 13-year-old:

Consciousness Raising Against Fat Oppression

I *heard*... the grind of the engine as the bus pulled away from the curb, the excited voices of the different kids, the snickering, name-calling, "hey fat ass!," the following laughter, the whispering amongst themselves, the unmistakable gross sound the boys would make when preparing to spit...I heard my heart beating faster, beating inside my ears, my ears ringing, making other sounds seem distant and muffled...

I *saw*... the boys, a year older than me, laughing and pointing, their faces distorting as they prepared to spit and their faces contorting in laughter...I saw the mucus running down the sleeve on my new blue winter coat, and the other kids turning and looking away, even the driver appearing oblivious to what was happening...I stared down at my glove-covered hands holding on to the back of the seat in front of me, staring at the floor, willing myself to sit and stare ahead and not turn around...

I *tasted*... the salt from my tears...

I *felt*... the bouncing and jolting from the bus ride to the high school, my face turning red, like it was on fire...I felt like I wanted to shrink inside myself and disappear from this moment, from this world...I felt my stomach muscles contracting and my feet going numb...I felt fear, anger, despair, shame and guilt...

This to me was... Just part of my life, a daily occurrence of cruelty, an example of humiliation, an embarrassment in front of my family as I walked through my kitchen door, spit dripping down and soaking into the back of my brand new coat, panting and crying after having run home the five blocks from the bus drop-off at the high school... *this to me was* the evening of my 13th birthday party.

Printed with permission of Suzanne Schwartz.

Racial Oppression

Race discrimination manifests itself on two different levels: individually and structurally. Individuals discriminate through expressions of prejudicial attitudes and behavior such as in denial of housing, employment, etc. Personal oppression of people on the basis of race derives in part from personality traits in the racist. The tendency to be authoritarian and rigid regarding diversity is correlated with a strict childhood upbringing in which no tolerance of misbehavior or difference was allowed (Allport, 1988; van Wormer, 1997). The hostility generated by the harsh discipline cannot be expressed toward the authoritarian parents so it may be displaced toward powerless groups in society. In contrast, children brought up in democratic households are more likely to tolerate and appreciate differences.

At the structural level, discriminatory practices in one social institution limit opportunities in others (DuBois & Miley, 2002). Competition over scarce resources is also related to discrimination due to people's own insecurities or a situation of intense competition, as over well-paying jobs, for example. The influx of immigrants into a community, accordingly, is apt to be associated with resentment by members of the community for "taking jobs away" or "holding wages down." One working-class group thus is often pitted against another working-class group. The employers such as factory owners and the business class they represent stand to benefit economically and politically by such ethnic rivalry within the working class. Conservative politicians tend to benefit from such a split in the working class as well.

Oppression, exploitation, and injustice by social class usually intersects and overlaps with the dynamics of racism because of joint inequalities in the social system (Gil, 1998). Then when people in poverty are forced to apply for welfare aid, say because of the limited educational and job opportunities in the inner city, that aid and the entire welfare system become associated with minorities.

In a thought-provoking book titled *The Color of Welfare: How Racism Undermined the War on Poverty*, Roberts (1996) argues that racial politics has dominated "welfare reform" efforts, that Americans falsely imagine that the mythical Black "welfare queen" has babies for the sake of a monthly welfare check. People generally do not want to be accused of racism so they express disapproval of people on welfare. The word welfare, in this sense, has become a code word for race. Black single mothers are the targets of measures designed to force them into the workforce.

Whites' perceptions of people of color reflect ambivalence and contradiction (Appleby, Colon, & Hamilton, 2001). Simultaneously there may be guilt over the mistreatment of Blacks in the society and resentment over affirmative action measures, and admiration for Black heroes existing side by side with denigration for poor and uneducated Black people. Pretending to be color-blind, Whites usually maintain that they treat African Americans and Latinos just the same as anybody else. Discussion of race is avoided as such discussion can be uncomfortable for Whites. In mixed company and where there is evidence of discrimination, discussion of race can be uncomfortable for African Americans as well. In the following illustration, an African American social worker regrets her own reticence in joining a White ally and speaking up for her race.

Consciousness Raising Against Racial Oppression

I *heard*: open air, silence, one voice begging for acceptance, one voice seeking affirmation.

continues...

I *saw*: the pleading face of a person rebuked, a wrinkled face, small frail hands then I saw blank faces, heads turning, no speaking, heads down, legs crossed, eyes glaring into space, eyes rotating back and forth.

I *smelled*: stale air.

I *tasted*: sticky saliva.

I *felt*: tension, my heart pounding, my body heating up in expectation, a flood of emotions, nervous, scared, out of control, the need to escape.

This to me was racism, racism disguised as professionalism, unacceptable, especially for a group of well-educated professionals, especially for a profession that embraces differences. But in the midst of this intolerance, there was courage. One woman who looked like these others; she had straight hair like them, and she was privileged like them. What was the difference, what made her not like them?

She thought like us; she related to us; she identified with our struggle, she tried to empower us, and on that day I should have taken a risk, to stand up for what I believed in, to challenge the authority, to risk my cloak of protection that my silence was affording me. Never again will I remain silent. I will stand for my beliefs, I will stand for my race, I will stand for all humanity and if all else fails, I will simply stand.

Printed with permission of Charletta Suddeth, MSW.

Summary and Conclusion

In a society that stresses opportunity over equality, individualism over collective thought, and competition over cooperation there will inevitably be oppression and exploitation as people who do well come to dominate others. Under the highly competitive capitalist order, the values reverberate throughout the system and are reflected in the socialization practices, cultural belief systems, the mass media, and economic and political institutions.

In order to understand the dynamics of oppression and how it can be so institutionalized within the social system as to go unnoticed, we have explored psychological factors in oppression—how the oppressor rationalizes and the oppressed internalize, social factors—the ideological control of the power elites, and even biological factors that come into play relevant to aggression and male dominance. We have, in short, viewed oppression and injustice from a multidimensional, biopsychosocial perspective.

To me the most intriguing part of this chapter is the psychology of oppression and the individual consciousness-raising experiences shared by a group of budding social workers. Why do we blame the victim and often ignore the perpetrator of crimes or injustice? How is victim blaming related to the Protestant ethic? What do we learn from excerpts from concentration camp studies about human behavior? These are among the baffling questions pertaining to psychology.

We are all at various times oppressors (at least in terms of group membership if not deliberate behavior), and among the ranks of the oppressed. To furnish first-hand accounts of circumstances of oppression I solicited testimonials from a group of graduate social work students. The results were powerful. Examples of oppression by virtue of gender, politics, disability, and race show how the political forces can have disturbingly personal consequences.

Because much of oppression is rooted in economic competition and has economic consequences, economics kept cropping up in the writing of this chapter. When you think of the women and today's backlash (played out in "welfare reform" and tough sentencing practices), race discrimination, exclusion of disabled persons, you are thinking of economics. Hence the attention in this chapter to pressures from the global market, pressures associated with heightened competition among nations and among residents within nations.

Oppression by race, gender, and class can each be illustrated by separate examples as was done here to show the impact of oppression on people of diverse backgrounds and orientations. The feelings generated by each manifestation are personal to each individual. And yet, as Gil (1998) informs us, the dynamics of injustice and oppression are universal; the solutions are not separate but call for macro-level social change, systemic reorganization. But before we come to the chapter on innovations and social change, we will explore more deeply in Chapter 3 the collective impact of oppression, this time on marginalized populations in today's world.

Three
Confronting Social Exclusion and Oppression Worldwide

> I have a dream that my four children will one day live in a
> nation where they will not be judged by the color of their skin
> but by the content of their character.
>
> Martin Luther King, Jr.

Social work is unique among the professions in its commitment to the welfare of the most vulnerable members of society, to populations at risk. Poverty, structural unemployment, environmental destruction, mass migration, human rights violations, disease, national debt—these basic social problems cannot be critically analyzed outside the context of global concerns. And although our accrediting bodies have been slow to require international content in the social work curriculum, this is an area in the process of development (Healy, 2001). In fact, the accrediting body, CSWE (2003), now evaluates course content for the inclusion of international issues in social welfare policy.

If anyone thought America was an "isle entire of itself," September 11 should have dispelled even the most confirmed isolationist of that notion. Such hate violence as was unleashed in the horror of that day can only be understood within the broader social and economic context. Key features of this context include the shift in public spending from investment in human needs on the home front to militarization and a world view based on "us versus them," on the construction and labeling of designated "enemies" as evil.

Whether our nation seeks corrective action through spreading goodwill or in mobilizing a permanent warfare economy, one thing is clear: as the world around us continues to jolt our consciousness, connections are revealed between troubling issues in distant lands and those closer to home.

To acquaint ourselves with "the global interconnections of oppression" (CSWE, 2001, p. 11) and an understanding of the form that oppression takes, we turn our attention in this chapter to forces that promote the social exclusion and marginalization of people. *Marginalization*, or the process by which a people (or category of people) are held down in terms of their socio-economic position, race, or other status in society, is often rationalized through ideologies such as sexism, racism, and heterosexism. Societal *isms*, as DuBois and Miley (2002) indicate, are the prejudicial attitudes directed against groups that society identifies as "lesser" —less capable, less productive, and less normal then others such as themselves. The isms, as DuBois and Miley further suggest, provide rationalization for stratified social structures that provide fewer prospects and fewer resources for those who are marginalized. Generally, as we saw in our analysis of the dynamics of oppression in the previous chapter, those reaping the benefits of power differentials—the cheap labor, access to resources—will fight very hard to maintain their advantaged, superior position.

We are going to deal here in this chapter with the global dimensions of power abuse, not the causes but the *consequences*, the way the oppression is played out. Ethical issues will be addressed where relevant, for example, in situations involving cultural values (e.g., machismo) or government policies (e.g., cutbacks in benefits) that are in clear conflict with the mission of social work to strive "to end discrimination, oppression, poverty, and other forms of social injustice" (NASW, 1996, p. 1).

Sexism

The topic of gender oppression was visited in Chapter 2; the focus of that discussion was power relations and a backlash against women's (middle- and upper-class women's) earlier accomplishments. The backlash in America has been played out against poor women on welfare and the girlfriends of male drug dealers. Now we will take the same theme, the backlash against women, and view this phenomenon globally, what we might call "the world's war on women." Worldwide, as competition for well-paying and secure jobs in a global economy heats up, dangerous right-wing extremist movements are seizing political power. Even in the United States, the pro-life, anti-choice movement has threatened the lives of individuals working at abortion clinics. More profoundly, the withdrawal of much needed funding for international family planning where abortions are sometimes performed has resulted in the deaths of large numbers of women. Such deaths are related to unsafe abortion in the absence of other forms of birth control through the loss of family planning money to organizations unwilling to comply with the abortion gag rule (Otis, 2001).

The mistreatment of women globally tends to be expressed in the guise of an attack on modernization, including the threatened liberation of women. Perhaps we should start with the Taliban. The persecution of women in Afghanistan went far beyond traditionalism into the realm of torture and genocide. There were many professional women in Afghanistan—teachers, nurses, and doctors—who were educated under the Russian-dominated communist regime. When the fundamentalist Islamic extremists seized power in 1996, a backlash ensued. Afghan women were beaten and stoned to death for teaching girls to read or failing to conceal their bodies beneath the shroud-like burqa. Many were captured and forced to wed Taliban soldiers and then discarded or sold to brothels in Pakistan (McGirk & Plain, 2002). The burqa and the laws imposed by the Taliban rule represented the most extreme form of repression against women in modern memory. They also served as reminders of other ways, obvious and subtle, in which clothing and other practices have shackled the female gender form and imprisoned women's spirits (Gardner,

2001). Even following the overthrow of the Taliban government, the progress of women and female education is compromised by the behavior of ultra-conservative local leaders and many women still dress in the burqa (Coursen-Neff & Sifton, 2003).

"Human rights are women's rights." This saying has become a motto of the international movement for human rights. Today, attention increasingly is drawn to the 1948 United Nations Universal Declaration of Human Rights (see Appendix), which included women as an at-risk population whose rights need to be protected. Feminist groups today are networking globally around issues of injustice, violence, structural inequality, and women's right to resist fundamentalist religious movements that deprive them of human rights (Corrin, 1996).

Half of humanity is systematically excluded from institutions of power and governance. Women perform two thirds of the world's work but earn only one tenth of all income and own less than one tenth of the world's property (Human Rights Watch World Report, 2001). Violence against women is commonplace. In the United States, one woman is raped every seven minutes, and one woman is battered every 18 seconds (Human Rights Watch World Report, 2001).

According to a conference document of the United Nations Fourth World Conference on Women (Mason, 1995), the cultural origins of this violence are in the historically unequal power relations between men and women. Indeed, the low social and economic status of women can be both a cause and a consequence of violence against women. The dowry bride burnings in India (an illegal custom in which a bride is set on fire by her in-laws if the demands for dowry payment from the bride's family are unmet), which number over five a day, illustrate crass materialism at its extreme. A report by the United Nations Children's Fund (UNICEF, 2000) calls for international solidarity against anti-female homicides such as the honor killings in Pakistan (to "restore honor" to a family when an unmarried woman lost her virginity whether she had been raped or not), the acid attacks on women in Bangladesh who had displeased men, and the bride deaths in India. Stone and James (1995) studied the phenomenon in India in terms of recent changes in women's roles and sources of female power. Bride burnings not only reflect women's relative lack of economic power in India but also, given the diminished emphasis on fertility today, a reduced function in producing the next generation. Bride burnings occur most often in cases of arranged marriages and among the urban middle class. As India has shifted to a market cash economy, the new consumerism puts more value on the size of the dowry itself than on the woman. Forever vulnerable to being beaten and killed by disgruntled in-laws, many women in India are rendered powerless to challenge what is happening to them. Thus economic discrimination against women and their vulnerability to violence are intertwined (van Wormer, 1997).

See Box 3.1 for a global digest of facts pertaining to gender oppression across the world.

Box 3.1   International Women's Day

Press Release from Worldwatch Institute
by Danielle Nierenberg

Despite the widespread belief that women have "come a long way," International Women's Day will still see millions of women from all parts of the world trapped in lives where they are not allowed to attend schools, own property, vote, earn wages, or control their bodies and where violence is a constant threat.

Unfortunately, statistics point to a much bleaker world where on too many fronts, women are still struggling to gain equal rights.

- Over half a million women die each year from preventable complications during pregnancy and childbirth; another 18 million are left disabled or chronically ill. In other words, more than 1,300 women will die while giving birth on International Women's Day alone.

- Worldwide, AIDS infection rates are now higher for women than men. In sub-Saharan Africa, where AIDS is spreading faster than anywhere else on the planet, women account for 55% of all new cases of HIV. Sadly, most of these women lack the sexual autonomy to refuse sex or demand that their "partner" use a condom.

- Twenty to 50% of all women have experienced violence from a so-called "loved one." Gender-based violence takes many forms and plagues girls and women throughout their lives. An estimated 60,000 girls are considered "missing" in China and India because of sex-selective abortions, female infanticide, and neglect. In 2000, their parents or other family members murdered more than 5,000 girls because they spoke to boys on the street or "dishonored" the family by becoming a rape victim. More than 2 million women undergo female genital mutilation each year, which leads to a lifetime of suffering.

- Two-thirds of the world's 876 million illiterate people are female. In 22 African and 9 Asian nations, school enrollment for girls is less than 80% that for boys, and only about half of girls in the least developed nations stay in school after grade 4. In sub-Saharan Africa and South Asia, only between two and seven women per 1,000 attend high school or college.

- In most parts of the world, women-headed households are much more vulnerable to poverty than those headed by males. In the United States,

continues...

single-mother households are raising one-third of the children living in poverty.

- Throughout most of the world women earn on average two thirds to three fourths as much as men for the same work. In addition, women perform most of the invisible work that keeps families going day to day. However, house-keeping, child care, water fetching, collection of firewood, and other activities mainly performed by women-are rarely included in economic accounting, although their value is about one-third of the world's economic production.

- Women are still vastly under-represented in all levels of government and in international institutions despite high profile leaders like Gloria Maca-pagal-Arroyoomen, the President of the Philippines, and former First Lady and now Senator Hillary Clinton. At the United Nations, women only made up 21% of senior management in 1999. In only 9 countries is the pro-portion of women in national parliament at 30% or above. And as of mid-2001, at least seven nations (Djibouti, Jordan, Kuwait, Palau, Tonga, Tuvalu, and Vanuatu) did not have a single woman sitting on their legislatures.

"There is ample evidence that when women take political power, issues im-portant to women and their families—such as maternal care, nutrition, and family planning—rise in priority and are acted upon by those in power," says Worldwatch Staff Researcher, Danielle Nierenberg.

And providing the resources to keep girls in schools can be more effective than improved sanitation, employment, or higher income in boosting child survival rates. U.N. sources show that the nations with the highest levels of schooling in sub-Saharan Africa—Botswana, Kenya and Zimbabwe—are also the nations with the lowest levels of child mortality, despite higher lev-els of poverty than many of their neighbors.

"Ultimately what is good for women is good for the world. The full partici-pation and full empowerment of the world's women is a keystone for any meaningful sustainable development strategy. But we still have a long way to go before women have the same rights as men."

Source: Worldwatch Institute, 2003. Reprinted with permission of World-watch Institute.

The United Nations adopted the Convention on the Elimination of All Forms of Discrimination against Women in 1979. President Jimmy Carter signed the docu-ment but the U.S. Senate has never ratified it. The only other nations that have re-fused to sign are Afghanistan, Iran, Sudan, and Somalia. We will discuss human rights documents in greater detail in Chapter 7.

The battle for women's rights will have to be fought on the international arena. Influential international organizations such as the World Bank and the United Nations will need to do their part to ensure progress toward a transformation in attitude and behavior toward women's equality, and to provide external funding of grass-roots organizations for educating women about their legal and social rights. According to UNICEF (UNICEF, 2001), the best assurance that women will limit the size of their families and protect themselves from AIDS is in the education of a nation's girls. Women of the world are beginning to recognize the extent to which the global market exploits women economically, thereby reducing their power on the domestic front. At the 1995 United Nations Fourth World Conferences at Beijing, 30,000 women (by some estimates) organized globally to tackle problems from sex slavery to genital mutilation to employment discrimination. In demanding that women's rights should supercede national traditions, the Beijing accord marked a historic breakthrough (Chesler & Dunlop, 1995). The age-old dilemma is whether to err on the side of cultural insensitivity to a nation's traditions or to err on the side of neglecting a minority group's (for example, women or children) ability to have their needs met.

Practitioners today work with families that subscribe to cultural norms that are often quite alien from their own. The feminist slogan, "the political is personal" is an apt description of the situation practically all social workers will see in their work as sexual politics restricts a woman's options. Sometimes there is no easy resolution, as the following ethical dilemma will show.

Case: Ethical Dilemma Related to Sex Roles

Both feminism and social work seek to bridge the gap between the personal and political through the process of empowerment. In situations of marital disputes, the empowerment task may be complicated by the fact of conflicting interests between the parties. When clashing cultural values enter the picture, the complications are intensified.

I mention these contingencies because, in the case I have chosen for analysis, there is both a cultural crisis and a serious conflict of interest between the two parties—three parties, in fact, including the child. First we will look at the situation facing the social worker or workers, then at social worker values, then see how the social workers drew on their powers of critical thinking to resolve the issue.

The case: McMahon (1994) provides this extremely volatile situation in her textbook, *Advanced Generalist Practice with an International Perspective*. The case took place at the Social Office in Norway; social worker involvement pertained to concern for the welfare of the child. Initially, the parents, Iranian refugees, had appeared at the agency for financial help due to employment problems when Mrs. A. was laid off from her job. Mr. A. could not find employment and wanted to return with his 11-year-old son to Iran. Mrs. A., however, had become acculturated to the Norwegian way of life and wished to stay in Norway and have custody of her son. She did not want to share her husband with other wives, which it was his plan to obtain. The son was happy in Norway and wished to stay. The dilemma is double-edged, involving conflicting interests of husband and wife. It was clearly not a win-win situation. There was no solution that would empower each member of the family given that the father was determined to return home.

From my knowledge of Norway, having practiced social work there for two years, I concur with McMahon that gender equality is a major cultural value in Norway. Norway, in fact, along with Sweden, leads the world among the 94 countries on the "Mothers' Index" computed by Save the Children (Associated Press, 2001, May 8). Top on the Norwegian list of values is the welfare of children. For example, physical punishment of children is of course against the law; new parents receive instruction in childcare, extensive work leaves, and family allowances from the state. Iran, too, has produced many well-educated and determined women. The recent surge in religious fundamentalism, however, has been a major setback for women's rights.

McMahon guides us through a systematic assessment, intervention, and evaluation of the ethical dilemma according to the process that she developed to engender a standardized treatment of problems of this sort. Her concern is reminiscent of that enunciated by Gambrill (1997) and oriented toward process rather than outcome. The process, as Gambrill describes it, consists of "critically evaluating our view no matter how cherished, and considering alternative views" (p. 126). And always we must be forever open to our own biases or prejudices.

Social Work Values

The preamble to the NASW (1996) Code of Ethics lays out the mission of the social work profession as rooted in a set of core values. "These are values," states NASW, "enhanced by social workers throughout the profession's history, are the foundation of social work's unique purpose and perspective." They include the following:

- service
- social justice
- dignity and worth of the person
- importance of human relationships
- integrity
- competence

These core values, as NASW cautions, must be balanced within the context and complexity of the human experience. We need to attend to the spirit as well as the "letter of the law" in using the Code. Their own and their clients' religious and cultural values need to be weighed carefully in following the code.

Within the Code of Ethics itself, the key items most relevant to our case illustration of the divided Iranian family are in the following standards: 1.05, Cultural Competence and Social Diversity, which urges that we recognize the strengths that exist in all cultures, and 4.02, Discrimination, which states that social workers not practice any form of discrimination on the basis of race, ethnicity, sex, or religion, among others. (The Norwegian Code of Ethics is similar on these points.)

The social work conflict is apparent in the situation of Mr. and Mrs. A. between the need to respect a foreign culture although that culture subordinates women in many ways and the need to uphold the principle of non-discrimination on grounds of sex. Standard 1.02, Self-determination, also enters the picture as social workers are instructed to respect client wishes. Here the wishes of the mother are in conflict with the wishes of the father.

Resolution

Making a list of options is the first step in the process of critical assessment, according to McMahon's scheme. The social worker gives consideration to each option, weighing the probable outcomes on a scale from negative to positive. The impact of the outcome on the values/norms of the participant are assessed along with the impact on their quality of life. A key question is how each option fits with the worker's professional ethics.

In the case example of the Iranian family, Mr. A. argued that his son would have a better future with him in Iran where he would not be a foreigner. Mrs. A. was enjoying the freedom for women she had experienced in Norway and planned to stay and begin a career. In Iran there was no equality for women and fathers had all rights to child custody.

At the assessment stage, the parents explored the options. In the end, the social workers placed a strong weight on the culture of origin of the family members and helped the family accept that the child return home with his father. Eventually, Mrs. A. accepted the decision and remained in Norway to pursue a new life. In follow-up sessions, Mrs. A. was helped to deal with her sense of loss. In follow-up interviews, the social workers conceded that the values that were instrumental in the decision were contrary to workers' personal and professional ethics.

Given the same set of facts, I would have tried to craft a solution that was consistent with my orientation toward egalitarianism and sense of justice. Children of all ethnicities thrive in Norway; Mrs. A.'s liberation was understandable and admirable. Mr. A. was returning to a situation of much promise, occupational success, and multiple wives and children. His decision to return home, under the circumstances, was understandable but his sense of loneliness without his son would have been brief. Mrs. A.'s options of starting a new family were more limited.

The significance of this case history lies not in the decision that was reached but in the process of resolving a dilemma through a thoughtful analysis of values and outcomes. The discrepancy between the decision that the Norwegian social workers made, and that theoretically I would have made, says a lot about our value prioritizing. Whereas the social workers were prepared to set aside their own belief systems presumably not to err on the side of ethnocentrism, I would be more willing to err on the side of ethnocentrism in the interest of sexual equality and the seeming best option for the child. My personal aversion to cultural oppression and patriarchy comes to the fore. The fact that professionals, although using the tools of critical thinking, might arrive at different recommendations for a family in conflict attests to the difficulty of weighing one value against the other. In the final analysis, who can say which solution for the family is the better (more empowering) one?

Heterosexism

Related to sexism and to the rigid codes of gender conformity is the societal oppression of gays, lesbians, and bisexuals. Cultural attitudes play a significant role in all matters related to sex and sexuality. Discrimination against persons perceived as sexually deviant can be horrendous.

The term *heterosexism*, as discussed in Chapter 1, is for gays and lesbians the counterpart of sexism to women. Prejudice is involved but here, because homosexuality is so often hidden, there is the presumption that the world is heterosexual. For this reason, gays, lesbians, and transgender people (although they are approximately 5% of the population) get left out of the equation ("Gays Comprise 5 percent of Electorate in 2002, New Poll Finds," 2002). Sex education in school, for example, tends to be strictly heterosexual education. Homophobia in a sense is the opposite of heterosexism; it entails a heightened attention to the doings of gays and lesbians and often a scapegoat of persons of different sexual orientation. Homophobia derives from anxiety concerning the perceived threat of homosexuality (van Wormer, Wells, & Boes, 2000).

Hate crimes against gay males and lesbians have become particularly pronounced in both military and civilian life in recent years. The torture and murder of Matthew Shepard in Wyoming in 1998 represented gay bashing in the extreme (see van Wormer, Wells, & Boes, 2000). The New York Gay and Lesbian Anti-Violence project recorded more than 2,100 anti-gay hate crimes in 2000, and 1,887 incidents in 2001. Crime against transgender persons made up 13% of the total (Douglas-Brown, 2002).

More commonplace is the razzing and innuendo directed toward youths by others seeking to prove their own heterosexuality and to separate themselves from non-normative behavior.

In May 2001, Human Rights Watch issued its comprehensive report aptly titled "Hatred in the Hallways" (Human Rights Watch, 2001b). This report offers the first comprehensive look at the human rights abuses suffered by lesbian, gay, bisexual, and transgender students at the hands of their peers. (Transgender persons are those who identify with the gender different from their biology; they often dress as the opposite sex, and may or may not take hormones or have surgery). When taunting remarks were uttered, teachers and administrators looked the other way. Interviews with 140 youth and 130 teachers nationwide combined with data from state surveys revealed that:

- Youths identifying as sexual minorities reported a rate of alcohol/drug use over three times that of their peers; the rate for use of injected drugs was nine times as high.
- Around a third of the students reported recent participation in unsafe sex.
- Although the exact numbers are unknown, a substantial percentage of homeless youths are gays and lesbian who have been forced out of their homes because of "lifestyle" issues.
- Gay, lesbian, and bisexual youth are over three times as likely as other youth to report that they attempted suicide; being perceived as gay or lesbian and harassed on that basis appeared to be the key factor.

Kids who survive the cruelties and injustices preserved for those who are "different" rarely forget. Consider the following poignant description contained in the writing of social work educator Bricker-Jenkins (2001):

> Kids know when their teachers are talking about them. If they are feeling shame, confusion, or have "secrets," they *really* know. They see their teachers' averted eyes, the glances at other teachers, counselors, and even other kids; they hear the sudden silence when they walk by school administrators or the coach. Fear and self-degradation are likely consequences. Or bravado, risk-taking, and defiance. Or all of these and more, but seldom anything positive.
>
> I am speaking from experience here. I was one of those kids who "knew they knew" and did everything I could to please them. But nothing worked, because they *knew*. When I was denied admission into the "gold leaf" club despite my stellar academic performance, when I did not make the team despite my athleticism, when I was not invited to return to the boarding school I loved, I knew exactly why. The hurt was magnified to suffering and despair when there was nobody to talk with about what was really going on in my life. Sometimes, when nobody was around to see which stacks I was exploring, I skulked around the library looking for a name for my "condition." I didn't find anything good. I was "circling the drain," sometimes contemplating suicide, when a teacher took me aside and showed me some kindness. She talked to me about the life of the mind, about the theater and music and poetry, about my friendships, about my wild ideas about a just world. She made me her assistant director for the annual school play. She saved my life. (pp. 93–94)

Of all the forms of oppression, the oppression of gender non-conformity is perhaps the most virulent. Unlike other victims of acts of prejudice and discrimination, sexual minorities are taunted on the basis of behavioral characteristics and inclinations that are thought to be freely chosen. There is an element of teaching persons so disposed to non-conformity a lesson, often a very public lesson. Unlike members of other minority groups, moreover, the very groups they might use for support—their families, their church—may be the first to turn against them. The psychological toll of being attacked on all fronts can be enormous.

Sometimes society's hatred is turned within. In their research on the relationship between suicide risk and sexual orientation, Remafedi et al. (1998) found evidence of a strong association between suicide risk and bisexuality or homosexuality in young males. A Canadian study conducted through the University of Calgary's center for the study of suicide interviewed young adult men who answered questions on portable computers (King, 1996). Results were startling, in that gay and bisexual subjects were found to have 14 times the rate of attempted suicide as heterosexuals. The sample size for celibate males, however, was extremely small. The Canadian study is unique in that it is based on a cross section of young males, not on a sample of persons already known to be gay.

Religious fundamentalism was found to be associated with a risk of suicide in gay males, presumably because of their unresolved feelings of guilt and rejection by their church. Since the 1980s, fundamentalist Christian extremists have come to wield political power in North America. Operating as a moral crusade to defend the traditional family, the Christian Coalition is a well-financed campaign against the rights of women, gays, and lesbians (Berzon, 1996). The ex-gay movement, Exodus, has received media attention in its "conversions" of homosexuals to heterosexuality.

Lesbians suffer a double whammy from homophobia because of its link with sexism. A woman who steps outside the rules of patriarchy and threatens its authority expects to be hated and feared by men and heterosexual women who seek social change but fear the lesbian label (Pharr, 2001). The effect on the women's movement—as women are divided from women by the male power structure—has been devastating. The passage of the equal rights amendment was defeated in several states because of its linkage by opponents with homosexuality and the right of same-sex marriage.

Living at the margins without a clear-cut identity as either gay or straight, bisexuals have been the pariahs in whichever circles they choose to move. "To a social order based on monogamy," writes Leland (1995, p. 47), "bisexuality looms as a potent threat...as a rupture in the social structure, conjuring up fears of promiscuity, secret lives, and instability." With the threat of AIDS today, many are horrified when a person identifies himself or herself as "bi." In reality, bisexuals need not be involved with members of both sexes simultaneously; they simply have a flexibility that is an anomaly in a world that thinks in terms of polarities and clear-cut labels.

Legal Oppression

Homosexuality is outlawed in many parts of the world including Zimbabwe, Nigeria, Ghana, India, and Nicaragua. Having such laws on the books makes gays and lesbians particularly susceptible to violence. Incidents of robbery and violence cannot be reported to the police under the circumstances, and the attackers know this (Jost, 1993).

Within the United States, anti-sodomy laws were still on the books in several states; those states could use the laws to separate gay parents from their children

(Reasons & Hughson, 1999). Happily, in June 2003, the U.S. Supreme Court overturned Texas' sodomy law, while Canada became the first non-European nation to legalize gay marriage ("Burst of Milestones for Gays Is Really a Long-Term Trend," 2003).

Employment discrimination against gays and lesbians is commonplace; except in some cities that have passed anti-discrimination ordinances, such discrimination is perfectly legal. In Iowa, for example, an employee can be fired on the grounds of being homosexual. Dismissal in the U.S. military occurs under the "Don't ask, don't tell" policy when gays and lesbians let their sexual orientation be known. Today some branches of the military seem bent on engaging in a witch hunt to weed out gays and lesbians (Reasons & Hughson, 1999). In contrast to U.S. policy, the United Kingdom, Australia, and Canada integrated their military forces with little fanfare.

Despite the large numbers of hate crimes inflicted upon gays and lesbians (assaults resulted in injury or death to 867 victims in 1996), hate crime legislation only includes sexual orientation as a protected class in 21 states (Reasons & Hughson, 1999).

The denial of marital rights to same sex partners is one of the deprivations of gays and lesbians with the gravest social and economic consequences. These consequences range from denial of income tax deductions, family health benefits (with most companies), the right to have a say in medical emergencies, and child custody or visitation rights of the partner's biological child.

Gays and lesbians and their allies are currently organizing at the grassroots level to end discrimination in the law. The AIDS pandemic, in particular, galvanized sexual minorities in many communities to establish case management services and direct aid for people living with HIV (Robbins, Chatterjee, & Canda, 1998). This movement connected with AIDS has effectively united gays, lesbians, and bisexuals in a common cause.

A major success in the appeal for legal rights came when Vermont passed the Civil Union Law in 2000. This law grants the same legal benefits, protections, and responsibilities to partners in a civil union as are accorded spouses in a marriage. Germany and the Canadian province of Quebec passed similar laws ("Montreal Civil Union is Canada's First", 2002). Meanwhile, in other parts of the world such as the Netherlands, Denmark, and Sweden, and now Canada, partner unions now provide to same sex partners *all* the benefits of marriage including the right to adopt children and for lesbians the right to qualify for artificial insemination. German law allows for certain partner benefits as well.

Case: An Ethical Dilemma

"I don't agree with it; it is against my religion." This phrase is commonly heard in the social work classroom, especially among highly religious African American and White students. As these students move into the practice arena there may be a conflict between their personal values—sex out of heterosexual marriage is immoral—and the NASW Code of Ethics standard against discrimination on grounds of sexual orientation.

In her comparative survey of social work students, Sun (2002) confirmed that female social work students are significantly more homophobic than female non-majors on the issue of whether homosexuality is a sin and whether it is disgusting. On other issues, however, the social work majors are less discriminatory than non-majors. The male non-majors were the most homophobic of the groups. Significantly, the large majority of all students in the sample (of 130) supported the statement that gays and lesbians should have full civil rights.

Sun explains the female social work agreement to the statement "homosexuality is a sin" (about 37% of them agreed with this while over 19% were undecided) in terms of the strong emphasis on Judeo-Christian values in their backgrounds and their awareness of Old Testament admonitions against homosexual practices.

In today's world new family forms have emerged and are likely to continue to emerge. Social workers will encounter these forms wherever they work—in health care settings, private practice, and in child welfare. In working with gay and lesbian families, as Laird (2000) suggests, the practitioner's own narratives, shaped in a homophobic and heterosexist society, need to be examined critically for unwitting biases or faulty assumptions.

For our case example, let's take not the usual client-worker situation but rather the professor who faces the challenge of preparing students in a social work practice class for practice with family groupings of various living and parenting arrangements. Remembering that approximately one third of the female social work students are apt to see homosexuality as a sin, the professor might approach this topic with a generalized discussion of heterosexual privilege and the roles that religion, law, and school systems have played in reinforcing society's gender ideology.

Three key aspects of critical thinking from which the professor can draw are a critical analysis of the facts; empathy for the population at risk; and self-awareness. Because religious beliefs are seemingly so closely correlated with the stigmatizing of gay, lesbian, and bisexual alliances, an effective exercise is for students to consult their Bibles and to read the host of forbidden behaviors included in Leviticus along with the proscription against homosexuality. Consideration can be given to the fact that passages allowing for slavery and the subjugation of women are also found in the Bible (Appleby, Colon, & Hamilton, 2001). The point of the discussion is to encourage healthy skepticism concerning beliefs against the evidence. Thinking critically about beliefs, as Gambrill (1997) notes, requires raising questions about our views, even "politically correct" ones.

For working with multicultural and other non-mainstream populations it is immensely helpful to know members of that population personally. Research has shown that homophobia is far less prevalent among individuals who know gays and lesbians personally than among people who think they do not know any such people (Cramer, Oles, & Black, 1997; van Wormer, Wells & Boes, 2000). On numerous occasions I have invited gay/lesbian panels to speak. Results confirmed the importance of personal contact, especially with an oppressed group surrounding which there is so much comment; many students who previously had expressed reluctance to work with gay and lesbian youth changed their minds following the personal encounter. Others whose beliefs were more entrenched were helped to see the correct professional response was referral of clients who had the competence to counsel gay or lesbian clients and their families.

There are many excellent self-awareness exercises in which students may engage to explore their own sexuality. They may want to contemplate the continuum of sexual orientation to see where they rank between 100% heterosexual and 100% homosexual. The famous Heterosexual Questionnaire devised by Rochlin (2000) that begins "What do you think caused your heterosexuality?" is very effective in getting heterosexuals to discover how it feels to be put on the defensive about one's sexual orientation.

The rejection of gays and lesbians by the major social institutions deprives a sizeable segment of the population of the help and support they need. Alienation from the traditional church's teachings, lack of awareness of counseling services, the living of a lifestyle that is taboo in most circles, and abuse inflicted by peers and family members all combine to close the avenues to much-needed social support. The results are a loss not only to gays and lesbians but also to the society, which deprives itself of the gay and lesbian contribution.

Racism

Racism is the subordination of any person or group because of skin color or other distinctive physical features characteristic of a certain group of people such as a certain shape of nose or hair texture. Racial, like sexual, oppression is reflected in both individual and institutional acts, decisions, and policies that neglect, overlook, or subjugate the individual or the group (Appleby, Colon, & Hamilton, 2001).

That racism is a worldwide phenomenon was evidenced in the United Nations Conference Against Racial Discrimination, Xenophobia and Related Intolerance held in 2001 in Durban, South Africa. This conference addressed issues of race hatred against minority groups ranging from the Roma (Gypsies) of Europe, to the slaves in Sudan, to the "untouchables" (Dalits) of India, to the indigenous peoples of Australia. When the Palestinians threatened to hijack the discussions, however, the United States and Israel pulled out. There was much criticism at the time of the American refusal to participate (Hanson, 2001).

Included under the rubric of U.S. racial minorities, or people of color, are African Americans (at 12.7% of the population), Latinos and Latino Americans (now the largest group at 13%), Asian Americans (about 4%), and American Indians (0.9%) ("Hispanics Now Largest U.S. Minority," 2003). The term Black is reserved for people of African descent. Throughout other parts of the world such as Britain, however, the term "Black" is used for all racial minorities. In the Bosnian context, for example, as law professor Wing (2000) points out, the Roma, most of whom would be considered White from the American perspective, are literally considered "Black" and treated in all the derogatory ways of a stigmatized minority group.

Is globalization racialized? Wing (2000) points to the racialized massive redistribution of wealth, power, and resource from the "developing" world to the "developed" and the exploitation women of color for cheap labor. Davis (2000) observes how the globalization of the U.S. war on drugs with its attendant demonizing of people of color has moved across natural borders into Australia, for example, where the brunt of the new laws are borne by young aboriginal women.

In most Latin American countries, class divisions dominate over racial ones. Race, as Wing indicates, is socially rather then biologically constructed. Speaking of herself, she says:

> In South Africa, because of my light skin tone, shape of nose, and wavy hair texture, I am regarded as a colored or mixed-race person. I am far too light to be considered Black...In Brazil, I discovered I am considered white...Within the Black American group, my coloring has historically led to a privileged position, because I am something known as "high yellow." (p. 8)

Due to the rapidly changing racial and cultural composition of the U.S. population, the exclusive White/Black model of racism is no longer applicable. In the 2000 census, for the first time, mixed racial categories were included to more realistically reflect the ethnic identity of citizens: 7 million Americans listed themselves as of mixed race (Cohn & Fears, 2001; see also Table 3.1). A conceptualization of a unified, people-of-color category would have the advantage of uniting minorities on the basis of common interests. For doesn't the present state of affairs, as Martinez (1994) suggests, encourage the isolation of African Americas from potential allies? What is needed, as Martinez further argues, is a new race paradigm to encompass experiences common to Black and brown, such as police brutality, including Border Patrol brutality along the Mexican border.

Table 3.1 Telling Statistics

Compared to non-Hispanic Whites, African Americans have:

- A life expectancy of six years less on average for women and men.

- An annual income that is about half as much as Whites ($21,659 vs. $31,213).

- A significantly lower marriage rate (32% vs. 57%).

- A college completion rate about 7% lower than that of Whites (11% vs. 18.6%).

continues...

- Death rates among children 5–14 that are 30–50% higher.

- Teenage pregnancy rates that are twice as high compared to Whites (20.7% vs. 10.9%).

- An infant mortality rate that is over twice as high (15.1 vs. 6.3 per thousand) (HHS).

- A homicide rate for men that is 8.2 times that of Whites (HHS).

- A child poverty rate for children under age 18 that is over three times the White rate (36.7% compared to 10.6%) (HHS).

- Imprisonment rates that are disproportionately high: 12% of young Black males compared to 1.8% of White males were in prison or jail; approximately 40% of all death row inmates are Black (BJS).

Statistics compiled from U.S. Census Bureau, 2000. Those marked CDC are from the U.S. Centers for Disease Control and Prevention (2002) and those marked BJS are from the Bureau of Justice Statistics (2003a) and (2003b).

Racism Directed Against African Americans

When people are judged not by the content of their character, but by the color of their skin, as Martin Luther King so eloquently said, that is racism. In a multiracial society with an uneven balance of power among the various racial groups, racism is probably inevitable. Guilt feelings on behalf of the dominant group lead to racist rationalizations while resentment by injured parties will lead to race hatred as well.

Such grim statistics both reflect the institutionalization of racism in the society and the reaction of an oppressed group to the existence of such hostility. A rare survey conducted by *The Washington Post* and Harvard University measured the impact of race discrimination in America (Morin & Cottman, 2001). A nationwide telephone sample of almost 2,000 persons revealed that from restaurants to the workplace to police traffic stops, Blacks experience more discrimination than any other group. In answer to a question concerning discrimination over the last 10 years, 46.7% of Blacks, 40% of Hispanics, 39% of Asians, and 18% of Whites responded in the affirmative. Black men said they had experienced such discrimination more than Black women.

In response to the survey, Nelson (2001) calls for the creation of a national Black history museum, dedicated in part to promoting an understanding of slavery and its consequences, to help the nation acknowledge "the lingering effects of several hundred years of systematically being broken, beaten, and chained, of being denied economic opportunity, prevented from raising a family freely or simply realizing God-given potential" (p. 22).

Looking for the roots of racism in the United States, we can begin with the genocide against American Indians which made possible the American land base crucial to Euro-American settlement and early capitalist growth (Martinez, 1994).

Racism is perhaps the "original sin" in U.S. history, the curse upon the land,
which could never be expunged. Chao (1995) briefly summarizes racist practices
starting with the Constitution and the Bill of Rights, which did not include African Americans or the Native people. The passage of the Chinese Exclusion Act
and the herding of 100,000 innocent Japanese Americans into internment camps
are often overlooked examples of racism involving Asian American and Asian
people. Such measures were adopted both in the United States and Canada.

Davis, an African American political scientist and activist once accused of a
conspiracy to aid convicts in an escape attempt, recounted an autobiographical experience in a jail cell: The woman next door is in the throes of some type of mental
collapse. Hearing her pour forth a tirade of racist obscenities, Davis reflects on the
pitiful inadequacy of psychiatrists to treat her (Davis, 1974).

How could she be cured, Davis asks, without an awareness "of the way in which
racism, like an ancient plague, infects every joint, muscle and tissue of social life
in this country?" (p. 37). For it was from the society that such a woman had so
perfectly learned to hate Black people.

Whites are rarely aware of the extent to which racism permeates American life.
Even individual social workers, on the whole, often have taken a color-blind attitude toward the issue of race (Christodoulou, 1991). (The social work profession,
however, has strongly endorsed firm commitment to protect the gains realized
by policies of affirmative action (National Association of Social Workers New
York City Chapter, 1996). Stokely Carmichael coined the term *institutional racism*
to describe this indirect and often unwitting mistreatment of minority groups in
modern America. The tendency to overlook the Black contribution to American
history and to history in general is an example of something that is more than
oversight. Institutional racism expands the parameters of racist behavior beyond
the person-to-person realm of deliberate individual acts to a relatively constant
pattern of prejudice and discrimination between one party who is favored and
another who is not (Greene, 1995).

One form of institutional racism that surfaces from time to time in the news and
then is quickly forgotten is the form called *environmental racism*. In his collection
on environmental racism, *Unequal Protection*, sociologist Bullard (1994) documents
the glaring disparities in who pays the price of the nation's extravagant use of
energy. Contained in his book is the story of Louisiana's "Cancer Alley." There
in the lower Mississippi River Valley where more than a quarter of the nation's
chemicals are produced, incredibly high cancer rates are found. Thanks to grassroots organizing and legal help, Louisiana passed its first air quality act (van
Wormer, 1997). More recently in Anniston, Alabama, poor Black residents whose
water supply had been contaminated by the chemical division of the Monsanto
Company, exposing them to a high cancer risk, won money in a legal settlement

as compensation for the heath problems (Associated Press, 2001, April 25). In California, Latino/Latina politicians and voters have united with environmentalists to push for clean water and open space bond measures (Rogers, 2002).

At the macro level, environmental racism takes the form of degradation of biodiversity, depletion of natural resources, and the dumping of hazardous wastes. The persons most affected by such practice are those living in non-industrialized countries at the mercy of the global corporation and indigenous peoples, and other minority groups within countries. The issue of global environmental racism was on the agenda of the non-governmental organization at the World Conference Against Racism in Durban, South Africa (Environmental Justice Resource Center, 2001). Such environmental justice advocates agree with Bullard (2001): "The poisoning of African Americans in Louisiana's 'Cancer Alley,' of Native Americans on reservations, and of Mexicans in the border towns all have their roots in economic exploitation, racial oppression, devaluation of human life and the natural environment, and corporate greed." (p. 3) Phenomena associated with racism range from what Angelou (1989) terms "the little murders and petty humiliations" to "the grand executions," which are life-threatening. The constant barrage of negative remarks, looks, and threats take their toll in terms of generalized stress and internalized racism.

Internalized racism involves picking up the prejudices of the dominant culture and turning them within, onto the self. Feelings related to low self-esteem, powerlessness, and rejection of Blackness may play an indirect role in high-school dropout rates, drug use, high homicide and suicide rates, and teenage pregnancy. The reduced availability of young African American males compared to African American females is associated directly and indirectly with racism. The death rate (often through shootings) and incarceration rate of young Black males is high enough to create a severe sex ratio imbalance in the population (Davis, 1993; Morales & Sheafor, 1995). Due both to perceived danger and racism, police beatings and homicides perpetrated against young Black males are disproportionately high.

Violence leads to violence and racism leads to racism. The already overfamiliar and numbing picture of White police officers standing idly by while two of their number savagely beat a helpless Black man, Rodney King, has now entered the annals of history. The shocking aftermath of hordes of rioting people—young, male, and Black or Latino—beating innocent bystanders, trashing Korean stores, and setting a section of Los Angeles aflame demonstrates the racial tension present in the United States. More recently, Cincinnati has exploded into anti-police riots, as has Los Angeles after a videotaped beating of a 16-year-old. The teen, Donovan Jackson, was handcuffed and could be seen on the tape having his head slammed on the hood of the car.

Racism Against American Indians

In considering hate crimes against minority groups, again one thinks of White on Black, to a lesser extent Anglo on Latino, and rarely of anti-Indian attacks.

Given that most violent crimes are intraracial rather than interracial, some recent statistical findings concerning American Indian victimization are chilling. Data collected by the South Dakota Advisory Committee in a report to the U.S. Commission on Civil Rights revealed that of the violent victimization of American Indians, 70% of the assailants are White. For Indian rape victims, 82% of the perpetrators similarly are White (Williams, 2001).

Within the criminal justice system, there are reports in South Dakota of Whites who attack Indians being given lenient sentences while Indians serve long sentences for theft and other property crimes (Steinberger, 2000). In South Dakota, Native Americans comprise 10% of the population but are 21% of male prisoners and 34% of incarcerated women.

About one third of the American Indians live permanently on the reservations, one third in urban areas, and one third moving back and forth. The statistics for income, education, mental health, and crime present a bleak picture. Almost 31% of all Native Americans have incomes below the poverty level. The major health problem facing the American Indians (like the Australian aborigines whose history parallels the Natives of this continent) is alcoholism. The death toll due to alcohol abuse is mind-boggling. The present day social conditions, the poverty, drinking, and so on are a cruel legacy from the past.

Keep in mind that upon "discovering" America, Europeans practiced ethnic cleansing with regard to the native population with whom they were in fierce competition over land and resources. Much of the worst devastation occurred in the earliest years of contact, when previously unexposed populations lacked acquired immunities to European diseases and were especially vulnerable (Wood, 1992).

As a result of deliberate policies of exclusion and extermination, not to mention the illnesses, firearms, and alcohol, the Indian population went from an estimated three to seven million to 240,000 by 1920 (Green, 1995). Today, in part because of renewed interest in genealogy, the number of American Indians has soared to more than 2.4 million. According to an article in the *Chicago Tribune* (Glanton, 2001), the surge is greatest in the Deep South. Members of federal tribes who have stringent requirements for membership see the many new pale-skinned claimants who get their membership through state tribes as "wannabes" seeking a share in government programs and the lucrative gambling industry. Still, these Southern descendants of Cherokee, Creeks, and Choctaws, who identified themselves as Indian in the new census often did not learn their true heritage until recently because of family secrecy related to past discrimination and even genocide.

Native Americans, like many Mexican Americans, did not choose to become part of the United States; they are a conquered people, in fact, defeated after several battles with the U.S. Army. American Indians and many of the Mexican Americans are different from other minority groups in that they did not arrive here from other lands. Lewis (1995), a member of the Cherokee Nation and a professor of social work, turns to the socioeconomic theories of colonialism to describe the relationship between conqueror and the conquered.

Lewis defines *colonialism* as a situation in which the destiny of a nation or an identifiable group within a state is controlled by external authorities and their agencies. Under the colonial relationship, the dominant partner extracts benefits from the subordinate partner. Two types of colonialism singled out by Lewis are structural and cultural.

With regard to American Indians, *structural* colonialism is illustrated by the political controls that resulted in the seizure of lands through battle, treaties, and the passage of federal acts calling for the placement of Indians onto barren lands in the West.

The tribes of Indians who inhabited the regions further west experienced the pattern of cultural colonialism in the form of forced assimilation. The settlers' sense of religious superiority over persons considered barbarians and heathens fed into these efforts. Tribal religious traditions and ceremonies were outlawed; by 1930 the majority of Native Americans professed a Christian affiliation (Longres, 1995). Children were removed from reservations to attend boarding schools hundreds of miles away where they could become acculturated. The speaking of Indian languages was strictly forbidden.

A member of the Cheyenne/Lakota tribe mourns the death of his culture through his grief for a fallen man:

I *heard* the Eagles cry. I *smelled* the sweet grass and sage. I *saw* a once proud native man, lying in his vomit, dying. A broken whiskey bottle on a bare wooden floor. I *tasted* the bitterness and pain within my spirit. I *felt* a great sadness, and the shame, at not having done more. I held him gently, and sang a death chant. *To me this* was the continuation of one of our worst oppressions. *This to me* was the continuation of extinction. (Printed with permission of David Thunderhawk.)

War on Drugs as a War on Minorities

The ultimate social control of the oppressed is carried out in the criminal justice system. And it is on the basis of gender, race, and class in combination that an individual is either deemed deserving of protection and respect, or as a threat and/or burden to society. Black and Latina women have been herded into prison since the passage of the 1986 and 1988 Anti-Drug Abuse Acts established harsh mandatory minimum sentencing guidelines targeting crack cocaine. This is the drug associated in the public mind with inner-city crime. The 100-to-1 ratio in punishment for crack cocaine compared to powder cocaine has been considered racist and classist by most observers. One of the results of this federal law, which was modeled at the state level, was that the number of Black women incarcerated for drug offenses increased 828% between 1986 and 1991 (Bush-Baskette, 1998). This increase was more than three times that of White women.

A glance at the Bureau of Justice Statistics (1999b) report on women offenders provides further evidence of racism engrained in the system. While nearly two thirds of women under probation supervision are White, nearly two thirds of those confined in local jails and prisons are minority. Hispanics account for about 1 in 7 women confined in state prisons and nearly 1 in 3 female prisoners in federal custody. Relevant to occupational status, about 60% of women, in contrast to 40% of men, were unemployed at the time of arrest; 30% of the women were receiving welfare assistance. These poor and minority women are the major casualties of America's war on drugs. Many of those incarcerated in the federal sector, besides, are immigrant women who were transporters of drugs or "mules" (van Wormer, 2001).

Because the majority of female prison inmates are women of color, the stridency of the attacks on the "new violent criminal females" can be perceived as a thinly veiled instance of institutionalized racism. In her justifiably scathing book review of Pearson's (1997) inflammatory *When She Was Bad: Violent Women and the Myth of Innocence,* Chesney-Lind (1999) reminds us of the racism engendered in the zealous prosecution of offending women.

The war on drugs is considered one of the most serious obstacles to achieving racial justice in the United States and internationally. This fact was argued in a petition signed by more than 100 U.S. civil rights and religious leaders and presented to the U.N. World Conference against Racism. The group cited statistics showing that Black men are sent to prison for drug offense at 13 times the rate of White men and that half of those arrested for using marijuana are Latinos. Blacks constitute 57% of the drug offenders in U.S. prisons and Latinos account for 22% ("Petition Asks U.N. Racism Conference to Take Up U.S. War on Drugs," 2001).

Case: Ethical Dilemma Unresolved

Often ethical dilemmas are resolved in ways that benefit no one. My involvement in the following situation was as a board member of the substance abuse agency in Waterloo, Iowa. So impressed was I with the agency's branch in the poor section of East Waterloo that provided specialized services to African American and Latino residents that I highlighted this programming in a book:

> The second program attempt involved a merging of the original program with a large, financially secure provider of treatment for low-income persons. The merger allowed for the existence of the innovative culture-centered model within the sound fiscal structure of the parent organization. Because of the degree that it has been integrated into the black community's natural support system, the program has been effective and well received. For continuing success, the emphasis is on working with extended families and other neighborhood caregivers, such as church and youth leaders. A strong minority representation on the board of directors of the parent organization is essential to continuing progress.

> The Northeast Council on Substance Abuse (NECSA) serving Northeast Iowa has successfully adopted an exemplary community-focused approach. The

culturally specific outreach office was described by program director Jo Ann Qualls-Carr in a classroom presentation as "very different from traditional treatment programs." The traditional setup emphasizes red tape and billing procedures. Clients may become suspicious, angry, and resentful. The minorities-oriented counselor, in contrast, must be prepared to be an advocate, for instance, to help a client get money to get a tooth filled, to cut through the paperwork and build up trust. Traditional treatment centers on an agency in the community and is focused on the individual and immediate family. Cultural-specific treatment reaches out to the community, and the family includes extended family and close friends.

My interview with a recovering crack user from NECSA reveals culture-centered content of a treatment group. The group consisted of fifteen men and five women, all African American. The group leader, himself a recovering drug user from the community, drew a parallel between addiction and slavery. Under both conditions there is a total lack of control over one's body and mind. "Do we want to go back into a slave frame of mind or do we want the control our forefathers fought for?" the leader asks. (van Wormer, 1995a, pp. 182–183)

The dilemma that came about was related to managed care constraints, the enforcement of which was the death knell of innovative culturally specific treatment. Accountability, the requirement for assessments, financial statements, and the like, meant that treatment services took priority over outreach and prevention, workers from within the community left in frustration, resigned, or were fired (one counselor for complaining on office stationery to a judge that the laws concerning crack cocaine were racist; he had also failed to get the proper release forms signed). Today the so-called outreach center is only a former shell of itself; clients are referred to the integrated main office several miles away.

Although today the treatment center, under new and progressive management, continues to meet the needs of poor, mostly court-ordered clients, the fiscal constraints and endless paperwork requirements continue to define the treatment milieu. And for African Americans and Latinas, treatment is no longer provided within their community. This, as Daly, Jennings, Beckett, and Leashore (1996) indicate, runs counter to African American styles. Other ways that the treatment is no longer Africentric are the reduced emphasis on extended family ties (third-party payers do not cover the family members) and the focus on productivity and cost effectiveness rather than relationship (Daly et al., 1996).

As the case example of the Northeast Iowa treatment center (now called Pathways) shows, creating culture-specific community treatment centers alone, even exemplary ones, is not enough in the face of state-level pressures for standardized, one-size-fits all services. The size is invariably that of the dominant culture. As the NASW (1996) policy statement on affirmative action informs us, "colorblind" policies cannot survive racist biases still prevalent in U.S society. Colorblind policies, in ignoring the structured barriers that keep the majority of poor people of color from accessing services, fail the very people who the services were set up to help in the first place. Because policy and practice are intertwined, economic forces at the highest levels can kill the most innovative and successful of programs. Managed care, as Tice and Perkins (2002) suggest, is an example of how social policy dictates practice. "Not only did the practitioners have to adopt their service delivery to align with managed care," they write, "social work educators had to educate students for a changing health care environment as well as new market realities" (pp. 304–305). Change efforts will have to be directed, therefore, at the policy level.

Classism

In American society no force is so entrenched nor so denied as class. Class is implicated in our educational options, speech patterns, attitudes, and as we saw in the discussion of environmental racism, in the very air we breathe.

Classism is defined in *The Dictionary of Social Work* (Barker, 2003) as "stereotyping and generalizing about people, usually negatively, because of the socioeconomic class to which they are thought to belong" (p. 75). To shape the meaning to directly parallel racism and sexism, I am broadening my definition to signify a system of inequities based on the distribution and control of wealth and opportunity. Class is relative by country; of course, persons in the United States living below the poverty level (the level below which people cannot get their needs met) are far better off than some persons in other lands and considered by them to be relatively prosperous. The poorest 10% of Americans are still better off than two thirds of the world population (Elliott & Denny, 2002).

Just as we cannot talk about class without talking about race and ethnicity, so we cannot talk about race apart from class. As bell hooks (2000) reminds us:

> Class matters. Race and gender can be used as screens to deflect attention away from the harsh realities class politics exposes. Clearly, just when we should all be paying attention to class, using race and gender to understand and explain its new dimensions, society, even our government, says let's talk about race and racial injustice. It is impossible to talk meaningfully about ending racism without talking about class. (p. 7)

Class and race/ethnicity are closely linked as prejudice and discrimination lock disproportionate numbers of minority groups into the lower classes of society. This is accomplished in ways subtle (arguing for color-blind policies, end to affirmative action) and not so subtle (having poor, overcrowded schools in poor neighborhoods). And because the lower class is composed of minority groups who are differentiated on the basis of race, ethnic background, and/or disabilities, other members of society are apt to judge its members harshly. Class privilege is thus maintained ideologically as well as practically through abandonment of government responsibility. Although it is now not fashionable in most circles to be prejudiced, it is now fashionable to crack the whip on welfare recipients (and also on prisoners). Illegitimacy, laziness, freeloading, irresponsibility—labels such as these are bandied about in a society built on a creed of independence, individualism, and equality. Because the social work profession is associated with advocacy and programming for persons at the bottom tiers of society, the stigma accorded this population has generalized onto the helpers.

So stigmatized are the poor in America that all politicians have to do is make a program means-tested (there was talk about doing this to Social Security a few years ago) and the program becomes stigmatized and even resented. The myth prevails in America that hard-working people suffer much loss in income in taxes that go to poor people on welfare.

In her book aptly titled, *So You Think I Drive a Cadillac?*, Seccombe (1999) assembled data from personal interviews with 47 women welfare recipients to counter the negative images perpetuated in the media and by politicians of mothers in need of financial assistance. That these women were well aware of their status is revealed in comments like the following:

> And I've went in the grocery store and when you get ready to buy your groceries, people have made nasty little remarks about the groceries you are buying (p. 56).

> They say you lazy. They say your lazy and don't want to work (p. 51).

> I heard one girl was going to quit working because all the taxes come to us... They say we look like slobs, we keep our houses this way and that way (p. 51).

The effects of class stratification are seen in a walk down inner-city streets or Kentucky rural roads, a look within a nation's sentencing laws and prisons, a tour of a city's schools (suburban and urban), a study of the income tax structure, consideration of health care provisions, and a comparison of wage/salary pay scales. The gap in income between skilled and unskilled workers, and in the possession of wealth between the highest and lowest echelons is key to the level of social equality in a given society. Whereas some countries, namely those in Scandinavia, put a premium on equality, others like the United States value opportunity in a free market economy over policies to equalize social benefits.

The growing gap between rich and poor within nations is recapitulated on a macro scale in the power imbalance between rich and poor nations. Just as persons with political clout within a nation shape the laws to their benefit, so nations with international clout set up the rules for international loans through the International Monetary Fund (IMF). The concept of social exclusion applies to the countries that lose out in global competition and to classes of people within nations in the grips of poverty.

Countries of the Global South whose economies are not based on modern technologies cannot compete on the same terms and therefore become excluded from the development process, amassing huge debts through loan interest payments to nations of the Global North (Elliott & Mayadas, 1999). According to the dictate of the "new world order," financial development has become antithetical to social development. Central to an understanding of the forces operating to the disregard of a nation's most vulnerable people is an awareness of the significance of the current debt crisis. Most of the international debt accumulated by the poor countries has come from the purchase of sophisticated weapons systems and other technologies by the state. Under pressure from the IMF to improve the balance of payments and reduce the national debt before receiving more loans, the industrializing countries have been forced to reduce government welfare spending and to encourage exploitation of economic resources. A legacy of destruction is seen in ecologically damaging projects such as the construction of roads through rain forests and clearing land for pasture. Overdependence on the growth of cash crops for export to other nations in exchange for hard currencies has been associated with unrestricted use of pesticides and the displacement of indigenous peoples who have gotten in the way of "progress." The sharp decline in the marketability of local products, in turn, has resulted in severe loss of income, unemployment, and mass migration.

The trickle-down approach, according to Wilson and Whitmore (2000), is seriously flawed. It has not been effective in raising living standards of the world's women or for their families. The richest 1% of the world, in fact, has income equivalent to the poorest 57%. This figure, recently calculated by a concerned senior World Bank economist, represents a staggering increase in global inequality (Elliott & Denny, 2002). The significance of the global market is that external economic forces dictate internal policies to the detriment of those on the periphery of the power structure. The free market economy approach considers direct attention to the preservation of the physical environment and to people's needs as a wasteful and unnecessary diversion of resources. A focus on sustainable development, in contrast, is concerned when balancing energy needs, agriculture, and food security with ecological considerations to ensure a habitable earth (Healy, 2001). A focus on sustainable and localized agricultural (as opposed to cash crop) production is the best way to eradicate hunger and poverty worldwide.

A focus on sustainable and prevention-focused health care is crucial as well. Today the greatest scourge that human kind has ever faced, in terms of quality of life, is the AIDS pandemic. AIDS is infecting as many as 39% of adults in some countries in sub-Saharan Africa, yet development assistance from the prosperous nations, especially from the United States, is at the lowest level in decades (Lite, 2002).

Of all the global problems, poverty is the most pervasive and intractable (Healy, 2001). Perhaps one of the reasons that, as the Bible says, "the poor always ye have with you," (John 26:8) is because having what was in the mid-90s pejoratively called an *underclass* serves many functions, latent if not manifest, for the society. In a now classic article, sociologist Gans (1976) explained the persistence of poverty in terms of 15 functions that poverty and the poor perform for the rest of U.S. society. Among these were assuring that society's "dirty work" is done; subsidizing through low wages many activities of the affluent; the creation of jobs for a number of occupations including correctional officers; and maintaining the legitimacy of dominant norms by identifying the poor as deviants.

But what is functional for the elite in society is not likely to be functional for the society as a whole. The dysfunctions are seen in festering poverty, poor health, crime, substance abuse, and homelessness.

Wilson and Whitmore (2000) deride the structural adjustment programs required by the global agenda, which allow for the global concentration of wealth. Such adjustments generally involve cuts in government spending on welfare, promotion of exports, privatization of public enterprises, and free movement of trade and labor. They cleverly quote Dr. Seuss's (1971) jingle:

Business is business!

And businesses must grow

Regardless of crummies in the tummies you know.

The point of this discussion is not to dwell on the misery of living in poverty or of the plight of the working poor in America, about 25% of whom earn below a living wage (Sharpe, 2001), or of welfare efforts that force single mothers to work in the absence of affordable child care arrangements, or that one in six children lives in poverty and fewer families are getting food stamps than before (Oliphant, 2001). No, the point is the classism itself, a classism bolstered by the ideology of freedom over security, an ideology continuously reinforced by the corporate-controlled media. Unlike in countries of the European Union, as Link (2002) tells us, recognizing that the roots of poverty are structural has never taken hold in the United States. The American focus on opportunity has a darker side; the opportunity to be rich is the opportunity to be poor as well, as Link further suggests.

The military budget, in large part to feed the military industrial complex, is now 15% more than the Cold War average (in figures adjusted for inflation). Compared to other countries, the U.S. military budget is six times greater than Russia's, nine times greater than China's. According to the War Resisters League, which calculates the budget based on government figures for each year, the $396 billion expenditure for the 2003 budget request represents a commitment to international relations based on economic competition rather than cooperation. See Figure 3.1 to study the pie chart of government expenditures presented by the War Resisters League and compare to that provided by the government.

**Figure 3.1   Where Your Income Tax Money Really Goes:
The Government Deception**

According to the War Resisters League, the government's presentation of the budget distorts how income tax dollars are spent, because the information includes trust funds (e.g., Social Security) and past military spending is not distinguished from past nonmilitary spending. The first pie chart shows the government's breakdown, while the second comes from the War Resisters League.

The U.S. Federal Budget for Fiscal Year 2004
Total Federal Funds: $1.731 Billion

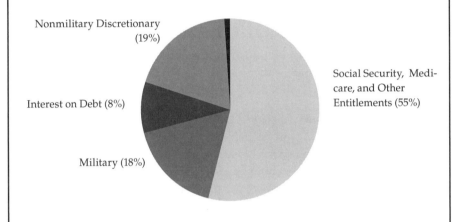

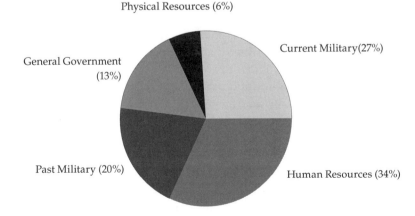

Adapted with permission from War Resisters League (2002), Where Your Income Tax Money Really Goes, http://www.warresisters.org/piechart.htm.

As long as the United States lacks a true labor party, there is little chance to counter the conservative ideology and therefore to end the sharp disparity between workers' benefits in Europe (where work weeks are short and wages are high) and in the United States where the opposite situation applies.

One positive development related to the very forces of globalization is the spreading wave of protests against the multinational economic institutions. Mobilization for these protests depends on the rapid exchange of information that is possible, in large part because of advances in information technology. Principal demonstration targets are the World Trade Organization, World Bank, and IMF; major rallies are held wherever the leaders of these economic conglomerates meet. Protests are directed against low wages, minimal health benefits offered by multinational companies, depletion of rainforests, and use of pesticides. Seattle, Genoa, Washington DC, and Calgary are among the cities that have been the scenes of such gatherings.

Concurrent with this phenomenon of anti-globalism is the growing skepticism concerning the role of big business in American politics. By more than two to one, a poll's respondents said the administration was more interested in protecting the interests of large companies than those of ordinary Americans (Stevenson & Elder, 2002).

Case: Ethical Dilemma

What is the role of social workers in a society/world in which fewer and fewer people benefit directly from economic transformation, where budget cuts at the state and local levels are threatening social service provisions and client well-being? We remember from the NASW *Code of Ethics* (1996, Standard 1.01): "The social worker's primary responsibility is to promote the well-being of clients." And, according to Standard 6.04, "Social workers...should advocate for changes in policy and legislation to improve social conditions in order to meet basic human needs and promote social justice."

In the following chapter we will read of the direct action projects of the Kensington Welfare Rights Union, which has so empowered women on welfare and their social workers in joint efforts to arouse the social consciousness of others. And we will learn how policy and practice can merge according to the principles set forth in Gutiérrez and Lewis's (1999a) framework for empowering women of color.

The moral dilemma we are dealing with here concerns social workers at a wide variety of agencies at a time when social services are weakening and needy clients are being forced off the welfare rolls while those hindered by mental health problems are finding it harder to obtain psychotherapy and family therapy due to cutbacks. At the practice level, one can adopt a "we're all in this together" approach and help clients seek alternative services such as kinship care or a self-help group so as to maintain whatever level of progress was being made.

Gambrill's (1997) advice in such circumstances is well taken:

You may have to lobby, persuade, bargain, teach, inform, advise, and analyze formal and informal power structures. Mobilizing voters, forming coalitions, and gaining access to the media to educate or expose problems may be required. (p. 607)

As Manning (1997), writing about ethical dilemmas in an earlier fiscal crisis, notes, social workers who have the courage to engage in the public debate about contemporary social transformation integrate social work values into the public dialogue and ultimately shape culture.

Ethnocentrism

Because of the interconnectedness between oppression on the grounds of race and oppression due to ethnicity, this section can be regarded as a logical extension of our discussion on racism. Here our focus will largely be on anti-immigrant sentiments in the United States, especially pertaining to newly arrived Mexicans and other Latin Americans. We will discuss the anti-Arab fervor in the next section on sectarianism.

Ethnocentrism is defined as the tendency to view another culture through the lens of one's own culture; the inherent belief in one's own cultural superiority is ingrained in this outlook and perhaps inevitable. In the study of other cultures, ethnocentrism is treated as a bias that impedes objectivity. The implication is that within higher learning, one can rid oneself of such a bias. True, we can shed some of our biases through going "native," but we would always be outsiders. There is no way around it: Ethnocentrism is a part of the human condition in the sense that we will invariably see the world through the eyes of our culture. Culture is imbedded in the very language that we speak and in our tastes for food and music and beauty. Ethnocentrism becomes an evil, however, when we disregard the humanity of others in their differentness; when we are unaware of our tendency to see our way of doing things as the only correct way, we may try to impose these ways on others. Self-awareness of the uniqueness of our cultural beliefs, such as in the importance of the work ethic and the prioritization of the nuclear family, is a pre-requisite to critical thinking; it is the gift of perspective.

Carried to extremes, ethnocentrism can lead into ethnic hatred, warfare, and even to attempts to exterminate a people. The world today has been reintroduced to the notion of ethnic cleansing. During the wars of secession in the former Yugoslavia, Croats, Bosnians, and Serbs have tried to create ethnic enclaves free of the other ethnic groups. In an earlier war, World War II, many Croats and Bosnians collaborated with the Nazis in persecuting and exterminating Serbs, Roma, and Jews. The generally dark-complected Roma (who do not like to be called Gypsies), originally migrated from India around the 14th century. Today the Roma are socially excluded throughout Europe. Recent examples of ethnic cleansing have taken place in Afghanistan and Israel/Palestine.

In Europe, from Norway in the North to Italy in the South, far-right extremist groups have scored one electoral victory after another (Daalder, 2002). In the United States, right-wing politicians, representing the interests of big business, historically have welcomed the inflow of immigrants as cheap labor. The scapegoating of undocumented workers, accordingly, is related to the low-wage, low-skill economy. Europeans express their anti-immigrant prejudices in terms of the need to preserve the homogeneity of the society (Lorenz, 1994; Daalder, 2002). Americans and Canadians clearly have no homogeneity to preserve. In the United States and Canada, restricting the unrestricted tide of immigration is a major concern; yet, ironically both nations are known as "nations of immigrants." U.S. history books refer to this country as "the great melting pot" or crucible, a blending of old world nationalities into a new American alloy. The comparable Canadian concept is of "a mosaic of people," a concept that stresses the retention of unique cultural identity.

Population migration is perceived as a problem in most industrialized nations and in many non-industrialized nations as well. The United States, Canada, Australia, and Israel are the only countries that willingly accept large numbers of immigrants. Although these countries like to regard themselves as lands of freedom and opportunity, a backlash against foreigners has been occurring here and elsewhere. Competition over scarce jobs, resentment over costs to taxpayers, and racism seem to be behind the populist cry to close the borders. Immigrants are in a double bind. If they do not work hard they are considered lazy. When they do work, as most of them do, they are "stealing American jobs." Resentment is built into the system due to capitalism's incentive to keep the unions from organizing by having a steady pool of cheap labor from south of the border. Thus the interests of one group are played off against the interests of another. Both groups are effectively excluded from access to material resources or economic decision-making. The profession of social work has a unique opportunity, as Prigoff (2000) indicates, to help local communities respond effectively to the challenge of economic globalization. Social workers need to have a grasp of the big economic picture, to be prepared to work with the victims of the global economy (and of warfare) who migrate into the community, as well as with those local workers who are displaced from their work due to downsizing and technological advances.

Attacks on Latinos/Latinas

The U.S. economy has long depended on the labor of millions of Mexican workers. Southwestern industries such as construction, agriculture, and mining were built on the backs of Mexican immigrants and their migration has been actively encouraged. Yet, as with every wave of immigration, the newcomers have faced fear and hostility, especially during times of economic hardship or foreign wars.

All across the North American continent today, the influx of Mexican and other Latin American workers who have been recruited to work in meatpacking, the building trades, forestry services, and the hotel industry have brought an element of diversity to the continent previously known only in the Southwest and large eastern cities. The controversy over language in the last few years seems to have been resolved in favor of English over bilingual offerings. In reference to the issue of whether to teach Latino/Latina children in Spanish or immerse them in English, my belief is that we are going about this all wrong. It is the non-Hispanic children who should be taught Spanish from kindergarten on up. Those who speak Spanish at home need fluency in English for later occupational success in the United States. To prepare for life in a bilingual society, we all need to be able to speak both English and Spanish. Even the presidential candidates and other politicians now use their Spanish proficiency for political gain. Social work job ads across the United States seek bilingual, bicultural applicants; Spanish-speaking persons will be given the hiring preference. Because language is best learned in early childhood when the brain is the most malleable, the present practice of introducing foreign language in high school makes little sense.

In the 1990s, fanned by anti-immigrant extremists and based largely on myths about immigration's effects on the nation's economy, a virulent anti-immigrant movement has sought to curtail the rights of many Latin Americans living in the United States (American Civil Liberties Union [ACLU], 1997). In California, with the largest Latino/Latina population in the nation, the voters approved a controversial ballot initiative in 1994, Proposition 187 that sought to deny education and other services to undocumented immigrants. Although it was later declared unconstitutional and never enforced, its popularity shows the build-up of resentment toward the influx of Mexican workers and their families. Today about one in three Californians is Latino/Latina. Compared to other ethnic groups in California, they have the lowest levels of educational attainment. One in four Latino/Latina voters are foreign born (Public Policy Institute of California, 2001).

Hate crimes against Latinos/Latinas are on the rise (Knickerbocker, 1999). Official estimates indicate that hate crimes against Hispanics (as against Asians) were roughly 5% of reported offenses (Political Research Associates, 1999). Because many of the Mexican victims no doubt lacked the proper documents, these estimates are extremely low. The inhumane treatment of Mexicans—the beatings, sexual assaults and even fatal shootings by U.S. Border Patrol agents—has been widely documented by human rights groups (ACLU, 1997). A number of states have passed "English-only" laws as a symbolic statement against persons who have not yet mastered the English language.

Mass media studies of the racial breakdown of lead characters on television, such as a recent article from *Time* magazine, reveal that Latinos/Latinas are highly underrepresented in this form of American culture (Pohiewozik, 2001). Only 2% of the characters on television are from this minority group.

Post September 11, curiously, attacks and animosity directed toward Mexicans have mounted. According to a report by Leyva (2001), the federal government has instituted stricter border-crossing procedures for entering the United States. Partly due to layoffs related to the economy, but partly due to fears that the border might be closed, more than 300,000 Mexicans have returned home since September 11. George (2002) cites still another reason for migration: Hispanics say they can feel employers and immigration officers scrutinizing them more after the terrorist attacks. In this climate of uncertainty, social workers have been working with Latinos/Latinas in Colorado to advise them of their constitutional rights. At the office of the federal Equal Employment Opportunity Commission, 166 complaints were received nationwide of workplace discrimination specifically related to the September 11 attacks. Most of these complaints presumably were from workers from the Middle East. Ethnocentrism meets sectarianism, the topic of the next section, in these acts of discrimination.

Case: Ethical Dilemmas

The example provided above under the section on sexism (the Iranian family torn by the decision of whether the son should stay in Norway or return with his father) is a dilemma with equal relevance to the phenomenon of ethnocentrism. The conflict was between cultural norms promoting Western values of sexual equality versus Iranian beliefs that children, especially sons, belong with their father. The choice facing social workers was to err on the side of cultural relativism (which they did) at the expense of sexual equality or to err on the side of universalism and human rights at the expense of cultural acceptance (which would have been my choice).

In working with clients from foreign countries, ethical dilemmas are a constant. Consider the situation facing social workers in California when Proposition 187 was passed. The measures that would have been put into law would have required the reporting of persons suspected of lacking proper documentation and a refusal of services to undocumented residents. For social workers who were committed to nondiscrimination, provision of access to services, client confidentiality, and welfare, but for whom lawbreaking was wrong, the dilemma was real. Many of the social workers, true to their values, signed a pledge of noncompliance with the dictates of Proposition 187. Fortunately, these discriminatory measures were never enacted into law.

Pinto (2002) presents an interesting situation of value conflict between a client's family system and the social worker. Even the U.S. government was involved. The situation is an outgrowth of new welfare reform requirements, which have forced immigrants to become American citizens to receive full benefits. In the case presented, the father wished to maintain his Mexican citizenship while the wife wanted him to become a citizen so they could qualify. Keep in mind that social workers are expected to uphold the value of self-determination and to provide for their clients and the clients' children's welfare. The only reasonable course of action for the social workers, in Pinto's analysis, was to help guide the father to find a way to maintain his cultural identity while also protecting his wife and children by becoming a naturalized citizen. This was painful for the father, however, as it might be for us to give up American citizenship. Meanwhile, the social work profession will continue to work through political channels for the eradication of laws that create difficulty for people in forcing them to renounce their own citizenship in order to enjoy financial protections from the government.

In training American social workers for the challenge of multiethnic settings, Nakanishi and Rittner's (1992) Inclusionary Cultural Model is helpful. Developed in Southeast Florida for work with a large variety of diverse immigrant groups from various class backgrounds, this model engages the worker in critical analysis from an international perspective. Under the circumstances, learning one foreign language or the social norms of one ethnic group will not suffice. Unlike the cultural competence model that teaches facts about one particular culture, Nakanishi and Rittner's model is relevant to working with diversity across the board. The starting point is a thorough and searching analysis of one's own culture and an awareness of how even aspects of their personality is culture- (and class-) based. The following questions exemplify the instrument: What childhood lessons were taught through catchy maxims (for example, "the early bird catches the worm")? Which lessons were family-idiosyncratic and which ones were seemingly universal? Such a process of discovery encourages openness to diverse ways of living, a reduction, in other words, in cultural insensitivity and above all "to see ourselves as others see us" (Burns, 1786).

Sectarianism

The pervasive racism and ethnocentrism that festers under the American skin boil to the surface at times of national crisis (Petchesky, 2002). So it is with sectarianism. *Sectarianism* can be defined as political oppression in the name of religion. When I lived in Northern Ireland, for example, I was told the differences between Protestant and Catholic were not about religion but about politics. As in most situations, it was not a case of either/or but of both/and: Politics and religion were combined. So it is with Islamism, the fundamentalist branch of Islam (not to be confused with Islam proper), the revival of which has marked a tremendous setback for Muslim women throughout the world. Muhammed, the prophet and founder of the religion, preached for kindness toward women and showed great tenderness for his wife. So when women are forced to cover their bodies in the suffocating garment, the burqa, is the driving force religion or is it sexism? And in its expression of terrorism, is Islamism an attack on the infidel, a "holy war" or *Jihad* against Jews and capitalism, or is it an expression of macho brotherhood?

Suffice it to say, religious fundamentalism is behind much of the extremist politics today. And religious hatred is as virulent as any other kind; fanaticism of any sort is dangerous. From mass bloodshed in the Bible and the slaughter of the Crusades to today's terrorist attacks in the United States and suicide bombings and Zionist retaliatory strikes in the Middle East, violence in the name of religion has a long history.

Religious oppression at its most extreme took place in Afghanistan, which fell under the control of Taliban zealots. The Taliban, allies of the United States in its earlier war with the Soviets, used their CIA training and weaponry to set up a fiercely violent regime in which educated women were persecuted. The teaching of Christianity became a capital offense; Hindus were ordered to wear an identifying label; and the largest Buddha statues in the world were ceremoniously blown up.

Theologian Armstrong (2001) puts this kind of religious fanaticism in context. "During the 20th century," she explains, "the militant form of piety often known as fundamentalism erupted in every major religion as a rebellion against modernity… Fighting, as they imagine, a battle for survival, fundamentalists often feel justified in ignoring the more compassionate principles of their faith" (p. 48).

The World Trade Center, of course, was the prime symbol of capitalism, of the global economy. Anti-Semitism figured in as well in that in the terrorist's eyes, American capitalism is conceived of as Jewish finance capitalism (Petchesky, 2002).

Although the American response to the mass destruction on New York City was far more nationalistic than sectarian in character, the anti-Arab backlash by the American people took on a character that was sectarian. The government's "war on terrorism" similarly took on a character that was decidedly moralistic.

In the immediate aftermath of the September 11 attack, the targeting of Arabs, Sikhs and others from India, Latinos, and even Jews mistaken for Arabs occurred in the United States and in parts of Europe as well. The Council on American-Islamic Relations recorded just fewer than 1,500 anti-Muslim incidents in the two months following the hijacked airplane attacks. Some examples provided by Wipf and Wipf (2001):

- In Illinois, 300 protesters yelled "USA!" as they tried to storm a mosque.
- A Molotov cocktail in Chicago destroyed an Arab-American community center.
- Australians stoned a school bus carrying Muslim youngsters; a Lebanese church was also set afire.

Out of the fear that gripped America following the unprecedented hijackings and anthrax scare, the U.S. government was able to pass repressive legislation that would have been unthinkable pre-September 11. In conjunction with a major reorganization of federal law enforcement priorities, more than 1,000 detainees were rounded up due to immigration violations. Some 40 militant groups were designated as terrorist organizations in a crackdown to identify possible terrorist sympathizers (Johnson & Locy, 2001). With close to unanimous support from Congress, the President signed into law the USA Patriot Act, providing for expanded government powers of surveillance, intelligence sharing, and detention. Civil liberties affected are the right to freedom from discrimination based on religion and the right to *habeas corpus* and to a fair and speedy trial.

Case: Ethical Dilemmas

Social workers cannot provide counseling to clients and their families, cannot assess the strengths and resources available to their clients without attending to their religious beliefs and affiliations. In its guidelines, CSWE (2001) now recommends that courses on human behavior address spirituality along with biological, sociological, and psychological development across the lifespan. Religion is included along with other kinds of diversity that need to be recognized as possible sources of discrimination. For practitioners, an understanding of the key role that religion plays in the lives of clients and their families is crucial in knowing how they respond to their world and to others (Mindell, 2001).

Ethical dilemmas relevant to religion arise in a disjunction between the social worker's beliefs, such as when one is pro-choice and the other is pro-life; in helping a family from a minority religion negotiate the system; and when confronting religious oppression within a fundamentalist family. The example we will look at is conflict within the religiously divided country of Ireland.

Jonathan Swift's (1905) memorable words, "We have just enough religion to make us hate, and not enough to love one another" still apply today. Even today, only 5% of Catholics go to non-Catholic schools, and virtually no Protestants attend Catholic schools in Ireland. "Mixed" marriage is a strong taboo. Unemployment is very high; for Catholics the rate is twice that of Protestants.

Between 1969 and 2002 more than 4,000 people have died and 30,000 have been injured due to political violence. Political murders, car bombings, police killings (of and by police officers), and internal Irish Republican Army disciplinary shootings have given Northern Ireland the highest levels of internal political violence of any member-state of the European Union.

One's religious identity in Northern Ireland goes beyond mere church membership to determine a person's residence, employment opportunities, and experience of political violence.

Houston and Campbell (2001) forthrightly probe the relationship between sectarianism and social work in Northern Ireland during the time of "The Troubles." Because the issues have been so volatile, so divisive, and fear of the "other" so strong, social workers in the North of Ireland have retreated into cold bureaucracy and their educators into a focus on individualistic casework skills. As Houston and Campbell describe it:

> The understandable response by practitioners to the social conflict has been to avoid engagement in community-based politics and action, and to accept, sometimes too easily, a "value-free," technocratic approach to problem-solving. It is almost as if these functional attributes were "bought," by the "system," at the expense of more radical, empowering forms of practice that might have challenged the status quo of the "system." (p. 70)

Kapur and Campbell (2002) present a case study of a client (presumably Protestant) so torn by political strife from the terrorism in the wider society, subscribing to the notion of "attack before being attacked," and a paranoid Catholic client out to get "those bloody Protestants." In this climate, clinicians have been reluctant to speak about the Troubles or reveal their religious identity for fear of retaliation. And therein lies the dilemma—whether to keep the silence or to break it. Houston and Campbell applaud the resurgence of a community focus, open dialogue, and the development of more progressive interventions such as working with political factions newly released from prison in community service. Such strategies, as the authors suggest, encourage social inclusion.

Other Forms of Social Exclusion

Oppression on the basis of old age (ageism), physical or mental disability (ableism), and youth (adultism) all relate to vulnerability based on physical or mental characteristics. Regarding social services under the American residual form of social service provision—treatment after the fact is favored over preventive measures—the needs of one group, such as children, is often played off against another, such as the elderly.

Ageism

Gil (1998) traces the roots of age discrimination to a partial counter-reaction to the power wielded by elders in earlier societies. This gradual reversal in the respect accorded to the elderly is also related, as Gil suggests, to the decline of their knowledge power due to the new technologies, which favor the young, and the relative decline in the size of the needed work force. Other factors are the migration to cities of the younger generation and the breakup of the extended family.

Thanks to the Social Security Act of 1935 and other government programs such as Medicare providing for health care, only about 10% of the elderly live below the poverty line. Among elderly African Americans, however, the majority live below the poverty line. Two factors may push many of the elderly into poverty—the much publicized expenses for medication that easily reaches several hundred dollars per month and nursing home care at the end of life. Over the years, moreover, inflation reduces the value of one's retirement pension. There is a higher rate of poverty in the over-85 age group compared to the 65–85 age group.

As federal Medicare and Medicaid reimbursements for nursing home care fail to meet the expenses to the state, there increasingly are many reports of inadequate and health-threatening conditions in nursing homes and even elder abuse in such institutions. Treatment of the advanced elderly in society and in nursing homes is often, as Beechem (2002) reports, condescending; the tone of voice used by staff is that usually reserved for use with small children, for example.

The major official dilemma concerning the elderly concerns the need of the frail elderly to maintain control of their own lives, to maintain their living arrangements and finances. Typically, social workers must weigh the value of self-determination for clients against available options when home health services are weak. The younger generation may feel sandwiched in between their obligations to their children and their parents, and public transportation in smaller communities is often inadequate for non-drivers to maintain independence. Given their not inconsiderable voting power, senior citizens can expect to see more in the way of adequate home health care in the future. Senior citizens are organizing in various ways. The AARP (American Association of Retired Persons) is one of the largest U.S. lobbying associations; the availability of affordable health care is a major concern. Self-help organizations of older persons to help other elders and families meet their caretaking responsibilities is a strengths-based activity consistent with those advocated by Brownell and Moch (2001). "The young of today are the old of tomorrow," as these authors remind us (p. 66), and strengthening the social contract across generations is vital for the health of all.

Adultism

When I look back on my childhood I wonder how I survived at all. It was, of course, a miserable childhood: the happy childhood is hardly worth your while. Worse than the ordinary miserable childhood is the miserable Irish childhood, and worse yet is the miserable Irish Catholic childhood. (McCourt, p. 11)

A strange-sounding word used by Bishop (1994), *adultism* refers to "a social/political/economic/ideological system that allows adults to exploit children" (p. 126). I am using the term here to refer to such systemic neglect and mistreatment of children. Sometimes the neglect (or abuse) by the mother is related to poor living conditions such as the lack of affordable child care or a situation of wife battering. In her book, *The Price of Motherhood: Why the Most Important Job in the World Is Still the Least Valued,* Crittenden (2001) shows how the U.S. tax code, workplace policies, immigration laws, and welfare system all devalue the job of raising children. Perhaps it is not surprising that on the United Nations Children's Fund (UNICEF, 2001) *State of the World's Children,* the United States was 32nd in the rankings for the mortality of children under five years of age. Cuba and the United States were tied. UNICEF's slogan puts it very well: "Caring for children = caring for women" (p. 23). There is a vast difference in the nutritional and other health/mental health standards affecting children throughout the world as the UNICEF report documents. Among the most appalling facts highlighted in this report:

- Worldwide, 1.3 million children under age 15 live with HIV/AIDS.
- In some African countries, 10% of the children are orphans
- Almost half the children in the developing world live in extreme poverty.
- Over the last decade, 2 million children were slaughtered and 6 million seriously injured.

Conditions have improved, according to UNICEF, since the widespread adoption of the UN Convention on the Rights of the Child in 1989. We will discuss the implications of this document still not ratified by the two countries—United States and Somalia—in Chapter 7.

A comprehensive report compiled by the Federal Interagency Forum on Child and Family Statistics on the state of child welfare in the United States shows a decline in the numbers of teenage pregnancies, firearm deaths of children, and of the number of children living in poverty (Cooper, 2001). On the negative side, childhood asthma rates are increasing, and 10 million children still have no health insurance. Parents are in the workforce but need high-paying jobs to lift them out of poverty and pay for health insurance. White mothers and children are faring much better than are families of color (Link, 2002).

In the United States, cost-cutting efforts related to family welfare benefits are matched by cost cutting of child welfare services. The situation that exists is that now that the primary responsibility for the welfare of children is passed down to each state (devolution), budget cuts by the state are necessary (Perez-Koenig, 2001). Typically these reductions are being drawn from higher education funding (making it harder for single mothers to escape from poverty) and the U.S. Department of Health and Human Services (DHS). Child protective services are now desperately underfunded during a time that reports of child abuse and child neglect are holding steady.

Witness what has taken place in Iowa following drastic staff reductions in human services. This editorial, built on the resignation statement that a social worker provided on her last day of work at the Iowa DHS, was printed in *The Des Moines Register* ("Editorial: The Reluctant Quitters," 2002):

A heartfelt resignation letter offers a look at the strains on overburdened social workers. Today is Melissa Ellis's last day at the Department of Human Services. Her position as a front-line social worker has simply become overwhelming.

Responsibilities of these workers include serving children and adults who need assistance. Their clients are kids who are abused, neglected and in foster care and adults with mental illness. Workers do everything from testifying in court to checking on kids in foster homes. Extensive record keeping and report-writing is required. With an average of 120 cases per worker in Polk County in January, the job has simply become unmanageable.

Social workers are quitting. Ellis is one of them. Her resignation letter shared with the Register explains why. After thanking her for working so hard to support her, Ellis writes about what social workers at DHS are experiencing. "I came to the department for a reason. I am here because I have a passion to help and serve at-risk children and their families, but after only a few months it was clear that I would struggle. I had approximately 55 cases and more were coming. I began to experience lack of sleep and a different type of anxiety. Not just a nervous, jittery anxiety, but anxiety that caused me to doubt myself and the work I was doing.

"There are so many dedicated staff that could do wonderful work, but morale is down, workers spend time trying to return phone calls, addressing envelopes, making copies, writing reports, attending court hearings, filing paper-work, making payments and trying to keep things manageable. Meanwhile clients are not being seen or even talked to via the phone."

Ellis's resignation letter explains the plight of other social workers who vomit before coming to work in the morning and are visiting mental-health profes-sionals due to the constant anxiety. If these workers make the wrong deci-sions, kids can end up hurt or worse. The stress of being responsible for the lives of children is a unique pressure. And it's gotten to be too much. Good professionals leave the department.

And they're leaving in droves. During this fiscal year, there has been a 39% turnover of front-line workers in Polk County. According to Dale Schmitz, an administrator at DHS, 27 of 69 workers have left.

"Young energetic, talented workers come in and find the caseload isn't man-ageable," he said.

Iowa's decision to underfund and reduce staff in human services is resulting in the exodus of the most dedicated and qualified people. After years of previ-ous experience working with children in private agencies, Melissa Ellis spent only seven months in the job of a state social worker. Her time there is done. And she's just following her co-workers out the door. (p. 10A; reprinted with permission of *The Des Moines Register*)

Childhood is oppressive for many children in the society, especially for those in homes where there is heavy drinking or other drug use, partner violence, homelessness, or other forms of poverty. Unrelieved childhood pain, as Bishop suggests, seems to be a key mechanism for learning how to behave as oppressors or oppressed. The psychological dynamics are complicated but adults who have endured but not survived oppression may project their hatred (of themselves or of others) onto their weak, dependent children. The social psychological dynam-ics are that when reared under conditions in which the family suffers oppression on grounds, say, of race, ethnicity, or poverty, children may lose their faith in the social system and become fatalistic about working to improve their condition. Conversely, of course, they may develop empathy for the underdogs and pursue education as a way to help persons who had it hard like themselves. (Such is the story told in the narratives of many social work majors, some of whom received help in childhood from a friendly social worker.)

Ethical Issues in Child Welfare

Ethical dilemmas abound in the field of child welfare. There are so many is-sues, the more so in the absence of family-friendly social policies. Some of the child welfare policies that do exist are ill-conceived or unworkable because of underfunding. For example, disproportionately high numbers of poor, minority children are placed in out-of-home care, often for living in neglectful situations related to family poverty. For Black children there is a short supply of African American foster and adoptive families. Among the reasons provided by McRoy (1995) are barriers within the agencies themselves. These barriers include institutional racism, adoption-agency fees, negative perceptions of agencies, inflexible standards, lack of minority staff, and poor recruitment techniques. The challenge to social workers within such a system is to work proactively through community outreach to reduce the barriers to African American families and, as McRoy emphasizes, develop culturally specific approaches to service delivery.

This example involves working within the system. The ethical problems that social workers face in achieving justice for their clients may seem insurmountable in a system in which the mounting poverty is blamed on the poor people themselves rather than seen in the demands of the global market economy. The dilemma then becomes should social workers continue to enforce society's norms with regard to their clients or work with the clients to change the system? These issues are the topic of the following chapter.

We cannot leave ethical issues pertaining to children without mention of the issue of physical punishment. Some countries, of course, outlaw corporal punishment or spanking of children both at school and in the home. They are Austria, Denmark, Norway, Finland, Sweden, New Zealand, Cyprus, Croatia, Latelevisionia, Italy, and Israel. In the United States, most parents spank their children and in 23 (mainly Southern) states, corporal punishment is allowed at school (Boser, 2001). Research, such as the meta-analysis of the major studies of corporal punishment by psychologist Elizabeth Gershoff, however, reveals serious long-term effects in children who were spanked ("Study: Spanking is a No-No," 2002). These include aggression, anti-social behavior, and mental health problems. The United States is unlikely to endorse a legal ban on parental physical punishment, she concedes. NASW has taken a stand against this form of discipline.

The controversy comes into play as social workers work with families who "whip" or spank their children. Some are in treatment following complaints of drug abuse; many are engaging in family counseling for other reasons. The social work literature encourages non-violent methods of discipline; at women's shelters, for example, no hitting of the children is allowed. Many shelters have programs to help teach more effective forms of discipline.

Cultural and racial differences concerning child discipline practices are pronounced. Because African Americans more than European Americans tend to use physical forms of discipline, the question then becomes, should there be a double standard in considerations of abuse to make allowances for cultural differences? Or are standards universal? While pondering this issue, consider these words uttered by Femi (1997):

I grew up with these views of child rearing, which are partly a residue of slavery. During the time of slavery, African American parents figured out that they could save their children some suffering by teaching them to show no willfulness in their encounters with white people. The process was brutal. That parenting style represented a kind of survival strategy, but it has had far-reaching effects, many of which we're still living with today. (p. 19)

Ableism

From the point of view of able-bodied people, disability involves a limitation, a deficiency in some area. People with disabilities are thus seen as unhealthy (medical model), non-productive (economic model), or not capable (functional limitation model) (Roth, 1987). A newer definition consistent with the strengths perspective views disability as a socially defined category; the problem of disability is located in the interaction between the disabled person and the social environment (Karger & Stoesz, 2002). Oppression is revealed in the labels used for people: retard, idiot, lunatic, nutcase, drunk, cripple, and fat slob.

The stigma attached to the possession of disabilities is universal; as an extreme case, consider persons with leprosy in the Bible. There is a pronounced risk of social exclusion in our society for members of diverse groups such as persons who are mentally ill, mentally retarded, obese, and prone to epileptic seizures. Persons with physical disabilities—deafness, paralysis, survivors of stroke, arthritis—usually feel themselves to be undesirable company in many ways. Here we will consider two examples of oppressive conditions that are disabling: mental illness and obesity.

A great advance in the history of treatment of disabilities occurred in 1990 when then-President George Bush signed into law the Americans with Disabilities Act (ADA). This act was a partial victory in changing society's perception of disability by the passage of major legislation that extended to persons with disabilities civil rights protections similar to those on the basis of race, sex, color, and religion. Today, accordingly, public accommodations and services have to be handicap accessible. The ADA resulted in large part from the advocacy efforts of people with disabilities joined by allies. Another powerful force for disability rights was the independent living movement that started in the early 1970s. In their focus on discrimination of an oppressed minority group and on the roots of problems of disabled persons, they helped set the stage for a civil rights effort that continues today.

Social work and the other counseling professions are attractive areas of employment for individuals with personal experience with disability. As social work professor Mackelprang (2003) comments, "While we will serve as a profession a disproportionate number of people with disabilities, we should not only look at folks with disabilities as our clients, but as our colleagues" (p. 4). We should welcome them to the field as role models. Until recently, social workers regarded disability in the realm of the problematic, but today the focus is increasingly on diversity (Mackelprang, 2003). Nevertheless, as Karger and Stoesz indicate, discrimination against persons with disability is still widespread. A psychiatric diagnosis is a particularly negative valuation which gets to the heart of a person's social identity, to the extent, as Rapp (1998) contends, that the person becomes the illness.

The award-winning 2001 movie, *A Beautiful Mind*, brought moviegoers into the world of mental illness in a way that all the scientific studies cannot. Because the view was from the inside out, empathy rather than blame was elicited for the leading character, John Nash. As the drama unfolds we become delusional along with Nash.

In the real world, sadly, neglect and blame are the usual responses to the abnormal mindset of mentally ill men and women. While mental institutions have largely closed, the local jail has become the dumping ground for persons whose behavior violates the norms of polite society. Behind jail and prison walls, other inmates prey upon mentally ill and retarded inmates. The correctional officers resent dealing with them because they often do not obey or act out in disturbing ways. Chemical sprays, shackles, handcuffs, rough treatment and solitary confinement are routine, according to a shocking 1999 NBC News special, "Back to Bedlam." One consequence of the deinstitutionalization movement of the 1970s which freed mentally ill patients from confinement in mental institutions, is that more than 150,000 mentally ill Americans are homeless today. About one million mentally ill people are arrested each year, often for minor crimes related to their untreated disease. Jails and prisons have thus become the new mental institutions. A promising development that is both cost-saving and humane is the mental health court. Such courts are non-adversarial and designed to get minor offenders with mental illness the help they need.

One group for whom the prejudice linked to their disability is probably most pronounced is the seriously (often called morbidly) obese. Fat oppression, as we learned in Chapter 2, is especially painful for the victims as even their friends and family members blame them for creating the condition for their own victimization.

Throughout the media, negative perceptions of overweight people are reinforced by images of emaciated fashion models and ever-dieting television and movie stars (Fiske, 2002). Prejudice against fat and obese people exists across the entire spectrum of society and affects every aspect of life including finding a marriage partner to getting hired for a job. The strong stigma attached to being overweight is associated with low self-esteem in both men and women and with eating disorders.

A clear ethical issue relevant to disability arises for practitioners torn between the value of self-determination and the welfare of the client and sometimes of society. Should hard-drinking pregnant women, for example, be involuntarily confined for the duration of their pregnancy? And to what extent should forced treatment of persons with severe mental illness (for example, paranoid schizophrenia) be sanctioned? Often the dilemma centers on whether the family's interests or the client's wishes should gain priority. The resolution of cases like these depends on individual circumstances and the availability of appropriate treatment facilities. Court-ordered medical treatment (the taking of anti-psychotic medication) is designed to help keep psychotic people from getting into trouble with the law or from harming themselves or others. Court-ordered care has gained in popularity because of highly publicized crimes committed by mental patients off their drugs (Associated Press, 1999). In the meantime, the lack of adequate affordable community health care services and halfway houses often leaves mentally ill persons left to their own devices.

The medicalization of mental disorders and, to a large extent, the psychological determinism of *The Diagnostic and Statistical Manual of Mental Disorders* (DSM) (American Psychiatric Association, 2000) are inconsistent with the strengths perspective and person-in-the-environment conceptualization of social work. Social workers provide most of the mental health services in the United States, yet their guiding diagnoses and treatment protocols must conform to the DSM for third-party payer reimbursement purposes.

The role of the pharmaceutical companies in treatment is problematic as well. Gambrill (2002) cautions us about the commercial factor in setting up drug treatment as the panacea for mental health problems. Indeed, on an almost hourly basis, advertisements for expensive mood-altering drugs fill our television screens. Astonishingly, the American Psychiatric Association makes money in sales of DSM-related products, as Gambrill notes, and from pharmaceutical companies eager to medicalize troublesome behaviors. Social work educators and practitioners need to be continually alert to the prospect of inflated claims of success of recently introduced psychotropic drugs. The profession can play a vital role in listening to their clients who often relate the unwanted side effects of drugs and helping clients express their concerns to physicians.

While criticizing the constraints that Medicaid managed care imposes upon vulnerable clients and their therapists in imposing unrealistic, seemingly cost-effective limits, Congress and Sealy (2001) urge social workers to document individual and community need and help clients advocate for themselves within the political arena.

Summary and Conclusion

"None of us is secure while some of us are hungry; none of us can truly experience well-being while some of us are excluded." So writes Link (2002, p. 23). The evil that society does to some of its citizens will eventually come back to haunt *all* the citizens. The effects will be felt in poverty, homelessness, and crime.

In contrast to Chapter 2, which focused on the *why* of oppression and injustice, this chapter focused on the *what*, the "isms" of oppression. We dealt not with ethnic groups but with ethnocentrism, not with race but with racism, not with gender and sexual orientation but with sexism and heterosexism, not with religion but with sectarianism, and not with poverty but with classism. Because the process of social exclusion is universal, the perspective of this chapter has been international.

Although each topic was presented as a separate form of oppression for the sake of organization, in reality the caregivers are rarely separate. For example, the boundaries between racism and classism are often hard to find, and much of sectarianism overlaps with ethnocentrism. Persons who are threatened by the liberation of women, similarly, are also inclined toward homophobia.

Except for discrimination against gays and lesbians, which is probably largely tied in with attitudes (and "hang-ups") related to sexuality and procreation, economic interests underlie much of the mistreatment of subjugated groups. Yet even in regard to heterosexism, as well as racism, sexism, and sectarianism, those who control the wealth in society can force people to behave in certain ways in order to survive. The power balance is skewed. The major tactic of the dominant class, according to Pharr (2001), is to arrange for inadequately compensated labor through limiting educational and training opportunities such as for women and people of color. This fact is borne out in the new standards for welfare reform reducing benefits for higher education. Nevertheless blaming the victim of economic forces for his or her lack of achievement is common. The phenomenon of victim blaming both lowers the victim's self-esteem and provides a rationale for perpetuating the system. The threat of violence against women and of other minority groups who oppose the status quo is a strategy used the world over by the oppressor group to maintain power and control of jobs and other resources. Another effective strategy that has long been practiced in countries ranging from Northern Ireland to the United States is the divide-and-conquer strategy to split the working class politically along religious and racial lines. So it is that oppressive power relations are associated with racism, gender, and sexism.

Given the vulnerability of people who are emotionally or mentally challenged, or who are disempowered on the basis of class, gender, sexual orientation, or race, or any combination thereof, social worker sensitivity to issues of human diversity and oppression is essential. An awareness of the origins of the conflict—whether structurally induced or culturally based—is essential as well so that social workers can anticipate ethical dilemmas that might arise. Because the same social problem can be resolved in different ways in different cultures and even by different social workers due to inherent value dilemmas, these situations are extremely complex. In reconciling a conflict between one ethical value (self-determination) and another (promoting the general public welfare), for instance, social workers will need to draw on all their powers of critical thinking. In the struggle against social exclusion and poverty at the societal level too, they will need to draw on their critical thinking skills and social work imaginations to be at the vanguard of policymaking and program development. But the road from policy analysis to policy change is a long and winding one. To this topic we now turn our attention.

Four
Anti-Oppressive Policy Analysis

If the people lead, the leaders will follow.

Popular bumper sticker slogan

Of all the helping professions, social work uniquely maintains a dual focus—to help people who are disadvantaged and to challenge aspects of their oppression as rooted in the socioeconomic environment. It is not, as is so often claimed, just about bandaging people's wounds. Social work, as Popple and Leighninger (2001) proudly proclaim in the title of their book, is "the policy-based profession."

The core values of challenging inequities and promoting democratic ideals have been formalized in the social worker's code of ethics (NASW, 1996). To this end, students of social work study policy analysis and policy practice. How to change the system by working within the system is a typical theme of instruction. Social workers are enjoined to be proactive, not reactive.

That policy and practice are inextricably linked is a major assumption of this book. *Policy*, as Bibus and Link (1999) indicate, is the "intent or goals and the procedures to accomplish them" (p. 106). The aim of social welfare policy, according to these authors, is to meet "particular human needs related to people's well-being" (p. 98). But sadly, many policies do just the opposite. Under a conservative regime, for example, many policies even institutionalize injustice and promote oppression. Thus, subsidies for the rich such as extensive tax deductions for purchases only remotely related to business and various other "welfare for the rich" schemes are enjoyed as a right. In contrast, consider the often demeaning and controlling programs available for the poor in need of food, clothing, and affordable shelter. Social policy, we must not forget, is crafted and sustained by the rulers of society, the "power elites," in accordance with however much the general public will tolerate. According to the sociological view, the ruling policymakers must offer relief only insofar as is necessary to quell mass discontent and rioting of the "have-nots," while maintaining credibility with the middle classes (Piven & Cloward, 1993).

Such policies as are enacted apply at both the macro or micro levels. Laws and legislative acts of Congress are *macro*-level policy. *Micro*-level policy is more at the level of the petty bureaucrat determining such matters as agency protocol, the stated goals of service, the characteristics of clientele served, and the eligibility criteria for service delivery. The science of policy decision making or *policy analysis* concerns the who, what, where, when, and why of policy development, implementation, and revision. According to *The Social Work Dictionary* (Barker, 2003), *policy analysis* is defined as:

Systematic evaluations of a *policy* and the process by which it was formulated. Those who conduct such analyses consider whether the process and result were rational, clear, explicit, equitable, legal, politically feasible, compatible with social values, cost-effective, and superior to all the alternatives in the short term and in the long term. Three approaches to policy analysis are (1) the study of process (socio-political variables in the dynamics of policy formulation), (2) the study of product (the values and assumptions that inform policy choices), and (3) the study of performance (cost-benefit outcomes of policy implementation). (p. 330)

This chapter is concerned with all three of these study areas—process, values, and cost effectiveness, which are integral to the science of policymaking and policy shaping. Learning how process works can be regarded as a stepping stone to policy practice. Barker (2003) defines *policy practice* as "efforts to influence the development, enactment, implementation, modification, or assessment of social policies, primarily to ensure social justice and equal access to basic social goods" (p. 330).

The skills required for policy practice are the same skills as those required for social work practice in general—people skills, and the possession of a probing, creative mind. If one door closes, use of one's social work imagination is essential to finding another passageway. In addition to the skills required, a second connection between direct practice and policy practice is that conflict at the higher, policy level inevitably spills over into agency directives affecting front-line work with clients. Even the definition of who may be a client is affected by higher-up decrees. Thus, in child protective services, the conflict over whether to prioritize child protection or family preservation permeates the whole child welfare system, a conflict often exacerbated by political pressures. For social workers within the child welfare setting, ethical dilemmas abound; the worker is prone to err on the side of the family or on the side of the child depending on policy directives that fluctuate over time. As another example, consider what state managed care requirements for extensive and immediate paperwork have done to regional initiatives such as gender- or culture-specific programming. Much of the spontaneity and uniqueness of focus may be lost to standardization requirements. (I saw this happen at a substance abuse outreach center at Waterloo, Iowa, a tremendous loss to the African American and Latino communities.)

The purpose of this chapter is spelled out in its title: "Anti-Oppressive Policy Analysis." The adjective *anti-oppressive* is chosen to denote the purposive and political nature of this endeavor, an endeavor designed to help students and practitioners ask the right questions and discover the right answers toward the end of influencing social welfare policy. Policy analysis can be conceived as an artificial device, an exercise through which to master techniques of persuasion that may inform a lifetime career. Policy analysis to the social worker is equivalent to learning scales for the pianist, the keyboard to the typist, or basic leg movements to the dancer, techniques that later become automatic. This prerequisite exercise is conceived as an overture to the change effort, not an end in itself as the subtitle of this book, *From Policy Analysis to Social Action*, makes clear. All graduate programs in social work and many undergraduate programs offer courses in policy analysis. Central to such courses is a critical examination of the political, historical, and cultural context in which a particular policy was formulated and is now applied. Usually policies are provided from the fields of child welfare, health care, corrections, or mental health counseling. Class debates may serve to stimulate research needed to bolster one's arguments and to anticipate strategies by the opposition. To pursue such activity, knowledge of the present political climate is necessary so that we can separate the doable from the unrealistic, but less obviously, knowledge of the political ethos (such as a fear of communism of the 1950s or social activism of the 1960s) that existed at the time a measure was introduced is essential in order to gauge the chances for change in a given policy that we might want to eliminate or defend.

Even when the time is ripe historically for change in a favorable direction, economic considerations may well be the key variable in preventing such change. Naysayers will readily attack a popular proposal with the words, "We can't afford it," or "The public will not stand for a tax increase." Or simply, "Not at this time."

For purposes of rebuttal, a grasp of the economics of the situation is crucial. Supportive politicians and other policymakers must have the convincing facts at their fingertips: How much will a given policy cost? How much will implementation cost or save the taxpayers? At this time of tight budgeting at the state and local levels, such key considerations often become the overriding component in making the case for new programming. Consider, for example, the following argument that is currently making the rounds in treatment circles: $1.00 of substance services saves $7.00 of loss to the state in terms of drug-associated crime, imprisonment, and hospitalization (see van Wormer & Davis, 2003). This compelling rationale for the introduction of county drug courts and other means of treatment can be presented in the form of simple charts and graphs to compare the effectiveness of drug treatment with the ineffectiveness of money spent on the war on drugs (see also Join Together Online, 2002).

Unique to this book is the inclusion of a category within our policy analysis for an international investigation. What is entailed here is a search for innovative models already in use elsewhere that are successfully dealing with the problem at hand. (As students of social work will remember, The Hull House of Chicago had it origins in Toynbee Hall of London, and women's shelters begun in Britain and the United States are now spreading across the globe.) The familiar saying, "think globally, act locally," can take on a new meaning as we look globally for common solutions to common problems or make the discovery that something that sounds good in theory, for example, privatized social security, may not work so well in fact. Finally, to bolster the case for policy change or innovation and our own credibility, an honest analysis of policy limitations, a summary of what it can or cannot do, needs to be carefully documented.

This chapter is not so much about effecting social policy in general as it is geared toward the shaping and refining of policies that relate specifically to oppressed populations or, better yet, the prevention of oppression in the first place. The writing of this chapter is guided by the beliefs that the best way for social workers to confront oppression and injustice is through providing input into the shaping of public policy. Consistent with other progressive approaches to social work, themes of power relations and empowerment inform this discussion.

How do values shape policy development? What are common barriers to progressive policy change within a conservative society? How can political support be mobilized for definitive action? These are among the issues addressed in the following pages. The capstone of this chapter is the Outline for Anti-Oppressive Policy Development. Presented as a series of questions, this framework concludes this discussion on policy analysis. It is a framework that, hopefully, will serve some purpose in classroom exercises or professional workshops. The outline encompasses the major aspects of policy development including problem description, historical, international, economic, and political analysis.

Models of Policy Analysis

Dobelstein (2003) presents three ideal types of arrangements for analyzing policy. The first is the *behavioral or rational approach*. The behavioral approach, which emphasizes value neutrality, describes alternative solutions relevant to the targeted social problem, with an emphasis on benefits per unit of cost. This is the model more for an accountant than a social worker. The second variety of policy model, the *incremental policy model*, carries out elements of change on an incremental basis. Practitioners develop small-scale changes experimentally and then measure the results. We can call this model the "trial and error" approach. In contrast to the previous design, the analysis of underlying values and evaluation of consistency of goals and values are crucial aspects. Third is the *criteria* or *value-based model*. This formulation, which seems more social work- than sociology-oriented, starts with a value orientation for the given criteria, then gathers data appropriate to the most politically acceptable solutions to the problem. Costs and benefits are weighed systematically against the desired goals. The anti-oppressive policy analysis introduced in this book is clearly oriented toward the value of countering oppression. It is therefore most compatible with the criteria-based model.

Anti-oppressive policy analysis we can define as a design for fact-gathering toward the end of advocacy—obtaining support and resources—on behalf of disadvantaged persons. Such an exercise can be considered the intellectual component of social action. Ideally, as mentioned earlier, such an undertaking will be the first step on the road toward community/political organizing. Lobbying for sentencing reform, the founding of a methadone clinic, the closing of mega-schools in favor of neighborhood schools, the offering of perinatal public health services—these are just a few of the examples of progressive programs that might have been inspired by social workers trained in techniques of policy analysis.

As introduced in this text, anti-oppressive policy analysis can serve as an empowering tool that helps social workers, even as seeming outsiders to the political system, have some influence on that system. The social work contribution to shaping policy is often through a legislator or other public official. That influence may be indirect and it is rarely acknowledged, but it is certainly not insignificant in the number of persons affected.

Policymaking begins with analysis of the facts relevant to a specific proposal. Before delineating the major steps in policy analysis, let us digress a moment to consider the sociology of decision making and explore the process by which a social condition comes to be defined as a social problem in the first place.

Theories of Policymaking

How are important decisions made in a community? What kinds of special interest groups are involved? Who do the political decisions, the instituted policies, really benefit? That is the question.

The two opposing views in sociological discourse are termed the pluralistic and the power elite positions. *Pluralism*, a major model of social scientists in the 1960s, strives to show that policymaking is a democratic process in a democratic society, that it involves agreements and trade-offs among diverse interest groups. According to this perspective, all voices are heard, at least to some extent, in the ultimate decision that is reached. The *power elite* position, in contrast, operates at the other end of the political spectrum. Proponents of this view consider how corporations, the major banks, and influential politicians shape policy in the interests of the moneyed class. Control of the media, whether deliberate or not, is a major component in politics inasmuch as the media rely on advertisements from large corporations. More direct is the corporate buying of the support of key players in the passage of legislation that is of benefit to their special interests. The "little people," according to this view, very much sit on the sidelines of the decision-making process.

The way researchers phrase their research question has a bearing on the findings. Note the difference in wording of these questions: When the question is, How do local policy decisions take into account the needs of diverse groups in the community?, the answer is apt to give credence to the *pluralistic* notion. When the question is, How do powerful interest groups shape social policy?, the answer is likely to support the *power elite* position.

There is some truth in both worldviews—the pluralistic and power elite, as Popple and Leighninger (2001) suggest. Some decisions such as funding for the defense industry over social welfare spending are clearly decisions taken by members of the "military-industrial complex." Other decisions, such as legislation for the rights of persons with disabilities, on the other hand, involve input from a number of different constituencies. Over the years, however, the political clout of major interest groups, from pharmaceutical companies to gun manufacturers to insurance companies, has grown increasingly pronounced. To what extent political campaign reform legislation, itself representing a compromise among opposing factions, will curb the "buying" of social policy legislation remains to be seen.

Defining the Social Problem as a Problem

The strategy of policy analysis can direct policymakers to the aspect of the policy or law that needs redressing, but only if the timing is right. A well-publicized crisis can stifle progressive initiatives or, conversely, precipitate an outcry for action. Take the death of a child who was known to the state Department of Human Services to have been a victim of abuse or neglect. The subsequent public outcry may lead to recommendations for the hiring of more social workers or to a policy change toward more immediate removal of a child from a family situation of abuse.

Theoretically, from the social work perspective, the primary purpose of shaping policy is to resolve social problems for the smooth functioning of society and to help people access the services they need. As social conditions such as homelessness or inadequate foster care come to be defined as problems, concerned social workers will want to consider how to get the word out on helpful strategies to significant parties. The problem/solution formulation from the social work point of view would not necessarily be the problem formulation from the government's point of view. Keep in mind that the strengths perspective is premised on the belief that many of the societal social problems tend to come from class, educational, and political exclusion, in other words, from demographic rather than individual characteristics (Chapin, 1995). The inclusion of the people most directly affected by proposed policies in problem definition and policymaking is an absolute necessity in the shaping of strength-based policies.

Due to the American tendency to look to individual/cultural pathology as the explanatory factor in the existence of social problems (the victim-blaming fallacy), the solutions sought tend to be curative and treatment-oriented, rather than preventive. For this reason, the United States is commonly referred to as "the reluctant welfare state" (Jansson, 2001), a *residually* based society as opposed to a universally-oriented social structure, such as that found in Scandinavia where social supports are built into the system rather than derived from an external, means-tested source.

The way a problem is defined usually determines how it will be resolved (Dobelstein, 2003). Examples of social problems as conceptualized by public officials and the corporate press are welfare fraud, Medicaid fraud, teen pregnancy, a high drop-out rate from high school, underage drinking, and drug dealing. Examples of social problems as conceptualized by social workers and their clients are more likely to be the non-living wage, industrial job loss due to global competition, absence of nationalized health care, unequal access to exemplary educational offerings, high infant mortality rates, marginalization of disabled persons, lack of affordable substance abuse treatment, punitive drug policies, lack of affordable housing, etc.

The challenge to injustice and oppression begins here, in short, with the definition of the problem. An integration of an empowerment perspective at this stage of the policymaking process helps ensure that the end product will be consistent with the social work value of preservation of the work and dignity of the client and whether, in fact, there will be any challenge to forces of injustice and oppression at all. In a society such as the United States, guided by the principle of individualism, the responsibility for social problems is often thought to rest with one or more segments of the population, usually the people who have the problem in question. Such a society will tend to ignore the need for change in social institutions (Chapin, 1995). Analysis of the definition of social problems must take into account the cultural ethos. Such a critical analysis may reveal that the major stumbling block in initiating change lies in this individualistic bias, the all-too-familiar tendency to locate the root of social problems in individual pathologies rather than in flaws in the social structure.

Barriers to Change

Imagine that a consensus develops for policy change due to a perceived inequity in the system or an expense to taxpayers beyond which they are willing to pay. The widespread dissatisfaction over health care provision is an example provided by Popple and Leighninger (2001) that transcends both categories—inequity and expense. The sense of inequity relates to the large numbers of uninsured workers and their families in a country that provides outstanding health care for the roughly one third with adequate coverage (Dinerman, 2002). The expense of U.S. health care has remained at a percentage of the Gross Domestic Product (around 14%) and is well beyond that of any other country, even those with universal coverage. (The United Kingdom spends around 6.7% and Germany, 10.6% [The Commonwealth Fund, 2003].) That we are not getting our money's worth from the health care system is quite obvious.

Consensus concerning the problem of health care provision has not been matched by consensus concerning what to do about it. Despite considerable political backing and the strong support of then President Bill Clinton and many members of Congress, extensive lobbying by groups representing private hospitals, pharmaceutical companies, and the insurance industry bombarded the nation with TV ads claiming if "big government" took over, patients could no longer choose their doctors.

NASW strongly lobbied on behalf of national health care as did the labor unions. But in the end, the scare tactics worked. Managed care stepped in with the promise to reduce health care costs. Costs have continued to rise, nevertheless, as has the paperwork, and the choice of physician has grown extremely limited (Kanenberg, 2003). Yet the barriers to change a system already intact remain prohibitive.

Analysis of such barriers is essential in countering the influence of powerful interest groups. We have been talking of barriers at the macro level. At the agency level, similarly, persons in the position of power have vested interests in maintaining the status quo. Innovators and social change agents are likely to meet resistance at both macro and micro levels, accordingly. Gambrill (2001) cites Sackett, Straus, Richardson, and Haynes (2000) in identifying common barriers to the implementation of effective services. Among the political barriers are disagreement over value of services, organizational policies that prohibit a service, traditionalism, authoritarianism, concerns about litigation, problems in applying the innovations, and/or client resistance. The policy analyst anticipates such barriers to innovation and must decide whether to proceed further preparatory to the change effort or to pull back pending the garnering of greater public or internal support for corrective action.

Historical Analysis

As social values change in the society, so do the meanings attached to certain kinds of human behavior. Sometimes the consciousness of a nation is raised through grassroots activities and media attention to the extent that the previously taken-for-granted (for example, segregation in the South, sex discrimination) becomes suddenly controversial and is recognized as a social problem. Healy (2001) presents the example of family violence against women. Thirty years ago, in almost every country, domestic violence was regarded as a private issue. As a result of the feminist movement and extensive consciousness raising and fund raising activities, today there are women's shelters in towns across the world and legislation criminalizing partner/spouse abuse.

The key question to consider in historical analysis is put forward by Chambers (2000, p. 38): "Who are the actors now defining this issue as a social problem and how are they different from past actors?" Each time a new formulation of the problem is put forward, new solutions will be sought (Chambers, 2000). We may alter the service-delivery system to accommodate the new demand (such as benefits for homeless veterans following war); we might create a whole new structure (such as home health care for isolated elderly persons); or we might ignore the situation altogether (for example, large numbers of homeless children in homeless families).

Taking a long-term view helps us to see the rhythms and patterns in things, to anticipate the tendency for oppressors to fight to maintain their position of preeminence, and to latch on to an ideology that justifies their position. Fundamentalist Christians, for example, rely upon carefully chosen Biblical passages. In the past, passages accepting of slavery and harsh punishment for children were actively applied. Today, we see the same pattern in the quoting of passages against homosexuality. With regard to capitalism, however, scripture provides a poor fit; storing up riches is actively condemned. So the same conservatives who quote the Bible on some issues draw on other sources instead. Thus capitalism is apt to be justified in slogans such as "a rising tide lifts all boats" (quote attributed to John Kennedy), or the more self-serving "trickle down theory." According to the "trickle down theory," the accumulation of vast wealth by big business will enrich the whole society. Interestingly this belief, which was popular in the 1920s, fell out of favor during the economic disaster known as the Great Depression. In reaction, an opposite ideology of ending poverty through government intervention carried the day (van Wormer, 1997). As long as the social welfare state seems to work fairly well, the predominant ideology, which we might call the "trickle down ideology" is not questioned. Through repetition and the role of the news media, the national ideology shapes public policy, and public policy, in turn, shapes ideology.

The tendency is for the same constituencies to have the same interests over time, for example, for big business interests to promote low wages and a high enough level of unemployment to keep wages low (Chambers, 2000). This tendency can be traced backward through the Middle Ages, at least. Chambers contemplates the reverse scenario in which the American Medical Association (AMA) successfully fought against nationalized health care in the 1930s and unsuccessfully against the Social Security Act. Today, however, the AMA is often at the forefront of the battle as doctors fight on behalf of their patients and their right to make decisions in accordance with good medical practice, over and against business considerations imposed by the dictates of managed health care.

In striving to initiate change we can learn much from strategies that were applied and were effective or ineffective in the past. Thus Martin Luther King studied the life and philosophy of Gandhi, successfully emulating his strategies as he moved from a position of weakness to one of strength. He began, like Gandhi, by using the mass economic boycott as a device for both creating harm to one sector and gaining in esteem in the eyes of important external observers. The Montgomery bus boycott galvanized the nation; social organizers in later years (e.g., peace protesters, women, elderly and disabled persons, gays and lesbians) borrowed the tactics of mass organization at the grassroots level with varying degrees of success.

The policy analyst's task is to identify key factors that inspire the adoption of new attitudes concerning old issues and to analyze mistakes that led to setbacks along the way. A further task for the policy analyst is to study the effectiveness of a government's official stated (manifest) goals but also with cognizance of the key role of unstated or latent goals that may be less palatable for public consumption. The difference between these two motivations, the manifest and the latent, can be discerned through reading the research literature and/or interviewing key players who are no longer in the system and therefore more apt to talk freely. Statements like, "We testified that...but we also recognized..." may reveal the underlying reason for the success of a campaign to sell the public on a certain course of action. Historians sometimes arrive at the truth about a practice through a perusal of documents from that period, sometimes of those that only recently were made public, as for example, once-private government communications. One suspects the stated goal actually may have been otherwise when seemingly rational and much less costly solutions to problems (such as the introduction of a mass transit system to solve pollution and transport problems) are dismissed out of hand. Popple and Leighninger (2001) provide the example of the school system's policy of forcing children to stay in school even when they are unwilling to try to learn, when they could work temporarily and perhaps return at a later date when their minds are more ready to absorb the material. The *manifest* goal is education but the *latent* goal may be to keep teens off the job market.

And why is schoolwork so often tedious, especially in the early years? The blame is often wrongly placed on schools of education. In her provocative, *The Overworked American*, Schor (1991) examines the schoolroom from a historical perspective: In the early days of the Industrial Revolution, Americans were too undisciplined for the monotony of factory work. So the school was given the responsibility of disciplining a new generation to meet the demands of labor. An understanding of the latent purpose of this historical tradition can thus explain how entrenched are certain educational practices and unyielding to change, even when the technologies that produced them are changed.

Policy Formulation

The policy formulation phase is the core phase of policy analysis; this is when policy intent and content are specified and agreement is secured (Healy, 2001). One effective strategy, often as part of a grant-funded project, is to evaluate several competing programs (for example, motivational and 12-step drug prevention initiatives), ideally conducting experimental and control groups. One can then compare the findings in terms of cost effectiveness and success in meeting policy goals. In addition to empirically based research data, we must, at each stage of development, not neglect to draw on the strengths and insights of people who" have been there." Policy formulation, as Chapin (1995) reminds us, will only be relevant and meaningful to the extent that it is inclusive. Who knows better the disincentive to working under the new "welfare reform" act, for instance, than the single mother who is trying to support her family? Sometimes, as a certain William Faulkner character once said, we are rendered "unable to listen, too busy with the facts." Read Box 4.1 (p. 114) for such first-hand material and to learn how a concerned parent became her son's advocate, and through this experience, ended up challenging bureaucratic oppression and empowering herself and others.

In doing the essential background research, social workers must take care that clients have input in the shaping of questions (Chapin, 1995). Once the agenda is set, policy planners will need to mobilize public opinion in favor of their plan. Again, the voices of persons who will be most directly affected by a policy change need to be heard, this time by the public and their political representatives. Mindful of historical attempts to get a certain measure enacted, policy analysts can anticipate likely barriers to change and prepare their arguments accordingly. When the research results are complete, their dissemination through press releases, publication in a professional journal, and sharing with key policymakers, as Healy notes, can be useful, especially if the authors have credibility.

The Social Work Imagination and Policy Input

Often out of the most dismal crisis or setback comes an opportunity that was unexpected. So it is with the crisis of *devolution*. Devolution is the word used for the turning over of many social work functions from the federal government to the states. State legislators have far fewer resources at their disposal than do members of the U.S. Congress, but they are placed in the position today of allocating scarce resources. Because they live in local communities, they are far more accessible than are federal legislators to local influence. Enter the social worker lobby to fill the void with friendly phone calls, letters, and well-prepared fact sheets. So it is, as Sherraden, Slosar, and Sherraden (2002) inform us, that the challenge of policy devolution opens the door for social workers, in collaboration with community leaders, to influence state policy. Social workers are the perfect liaisons between private troubles and political solutions, between the populations at risk and the decision makers who can "make or break them."

Sherraden, Slosar, and Sherraden look to Mills' (1959) classic concept of "the sociological imagination" as a source for guidance in shaping program proposals and carrying them through from start to finish. As spelled out by Mills, the success of a productive idea depends on the following: the ability to connect private troubles and public issues; a multidisciplinary perspective; possession of a scientific understanding of the issue; and the use of imagination and creativity. These qualities, which are the essence of social worker resourcefulness, I refer to as *our social work imagination*. The social work imagination entails a combination of "know-how" and a vision that competent social workers acquire in helping their clients "find a way of no way," in helping them tap into their inner resources at a time in their lives when their resources are severely limited. Social workers can take this same "know-how" that they rely on in their daily work to come up with solutions on the larger scale. The road from agency practitioner to spokesperson for policy change to policy shaper is a road that is increasingly traveled today as state economic crises call for imaginative and cost-effective solutions.

Box 4.1   Consciousness Raising Against Disability Oppression

by Jamie Paige, LMSW, Medical Social Worker

I remember thinking: there is something terribly wrong with my son. He had been struggling more and more in school with each passing year. He was very bright, was involved in many activities in school, including the talented and gifted program. Yet, my instincts were telling me, there simply was something wrong.

I asked the school to do some testing on him. In Iowa we are under the auspices of what are called Area Education Agencies (AEA). The AEA called together a team of professionals to discuss with me my concerns about my son. At the very first meeting, I anxiously and naively walked in, expecting a unified group of people all coming together to give us the help we needed.

As I sat by myself, surrounded with the "powers that be," I felt immediate intimidation. I tried to shirk off those feelings, as I did not know why I would be having them. These were school personnel—a social worker, guidance counselor, and school principal, and surely they shared my genuine concern for the well being of my son.

After introductions of the AEA social worker, the guidance counselor, and myself, the social worker asked me why I was there. I shared my concerns that I felt my son had a learning disability. I asked them to test him for that. The social worker (who I had hoped would give me some support), meeting me for the very first time at this meeting, leaned forward and stated, "You know, we have noticed that your son seems to feel a great pressure to succeed and we wonder what it is you are doing wrong at home to make him feel this way."

I was absolutely stunned. He proceeded to tell me that since my son was doing grade-level work, he could not be tested for a learning disability. He stated that according to law, my son had to be two grade levels behind the other students in order to qualify for testing. I did not know at the time this was in fact incorrect information. I left that meeting feeling defeated, unsupported, and indeed, victimized. How dare they insinuate that I was doing something wrong with my son? They did not even know me. Little did they realize, that on this day, they had planted a seed inside me. It was the seed of advocacy and self-determination. And this seed was about to grow into an amazing educational experience for us all, over the next few years.

continues…

Here is how it felt to me as a parent at this very first meeting. Let me share with you on a more personal level, what I remember feeling as they spoke to me in their unified circle of black suits and ties.

I heard: All problems are the parent's fault. The school is perfect. There is nothing in this atmosphere that causes problems except parents. If parents would just stay out of school affairs and let us do what we are professionally trained to do, everything would be all right. You are not welcome.

I saw: Uncaring faces, trained to show power, control, and intimidation. Arms crossed, mocking smiles. A show of force, like wagon wheels pulled into a circle to keep "them" on the inside protected, safe and unchanging. While I was left on the outside looking in feeling confused, alone, and violated.

I smelled: Expensive professional men's cologne. The staleness of the school. The remnants of the noon lunch. All mixed together in an airtight room. I smelled their patronizing air.

I tasted: Raw emotion. My mouth went dry. I actually could taste my anger and resentment.

I felt: Anger, intimidation. Indignation. Experienced words burning into my skin intended to hurt and scare me away. Yet at the same time I felt oddly energized, motivated to change this system which blamed victims and was so used to getting its way.

This to me was: Oppression, injustice, intolerance. The power and control of a school and its internal bureaucracy. An antiquated system set up years ago, in which single mothers stood no chance in discussions concerning their own children. This to me was a "system" begging for change, for help, for growth. This to me was my opportunity to help my son; my motivation to help others, a new beginning. It was *my* opportunity to educate. It was *their* opportunity to learn.

It has now been three years since that fateful meeting. I have been trained as an advocate through our state's Partners in Policy program. I have actively advocated not only for my own son, but also many children in many school systems. Through my own advocacy for my son, we found out that he has a non-verbal learning disorder (NLD). He is currently a senior, and soon is going to a local university for his psychology degree. The social worker who spoke to me that way so many years ago has since retired. Unfortunately, his replacement shared his same vision of their job function. No one from

continues...

within our AEA advocates unconditionally for parents or students. I am still committed to filling that void. And I realize that my life will be forever involved in social policy, social activism, and sharing my story with as many people as will listen until the system I am trying to change finally does!

For more information on non-verbal learning disorders, go to http://www.NLDline.com.

Printed with permission of Jamie Paige.

International Analysis

In policy planning, equal in importance to a journey across time is the journey across space. There is so much to learn of innovative practices and of possibilities that never would have been imagined without an international exchange of information. Due to the impact of globalization, the issues that one country is wrestling with, for example, the AIDS crisis or the influx of refugees, are the issues of other countries as well.

For productive problem solving (or better yet, prevention of problems) and for generating ideas, the broad view is clearly the most fruitful. Critics who so often use the strategy of disregarding a progressive idea as unworkable can be enlightened with evidence from elsewhere that indeed such a practice, for example, integrating openly gay and lesbian recruits into the military, works quite well where it is done.

An awareness of varying global arrangements reveals not only possibilities but also barriers due to differences in funding sources and cultural attitudes concerning the source of the income. Where there is a solid nationalized health care system in place, for example, open-door, harm reduction treatment offerings may be readily available. Emulation may be stifled elsewhere, however, without the necessary government supports.

To study the major value orientation of other lands is to realize the uniqueness of our own—the indomitable American work ethic, the impetus for privacy and individual rights over the public good, the elevation of nuclear family ties far above extended family obligations. And lurking beneath all these issues is a boundless optimism that success is ours if only we try.

Contained in the Universal Declaration of Human Rights (United Nations, 1948) are principles germane to the alleviation of oppression and injustice. (Refer to the Appendix to read the Declaration.) These principles, which are described in detail in Chapter 6, provide a template for how the state should treat its citizens socially, culturally, and economically. As backing for proposals within our area of interest, challenging economic or social oppression, there is an article of general tolerance. A proposal for a county-funded, ethnic-sensitive substance abuse program, for example, is in keeping with Article 25, which endorses the right to medical care and necessary social services, Article 27 pertaining to participation in the cultural life of the community, and even Article 16, which is directed toward protection of the family. A proposal to reduce school violence through anti-oppressive education can be guided by the principle found in Article 26, which states that education should be directed to the promotion of tolerance and to the furtherance of activities for the maintenance of peace.

We are talking here of domestic policy as viewed from the global perspective of international law. Some policy actions, as Healy (2001) suggests, have a direct transnational impact; laws and regulations pertaining to immigrants and foreign child adoptions are examples. Globalization has the potential to transport traditional social policy analysis into an ever-widening international arena, even to the extent of striving to influence their own governments to consider human rights issues and economic oppression in foreign relations.

Economic Analysis

Money talks, both in the ability to get a policy instituted and to allow for subsequent evaluation. Anti-oppressive proposals, if they are not cost-effective, will not see the light of day. Sadly proposals initiated by the states that are of a punitive bent can be tremendously costly and still receive widespread support due to their appeal to unconscious motives in the masses (fear of crime, displaced aggression) such as were discussed in Chapter 2. Policies geared to help "your tired, your poor, the huddled masses," however, must prove their economic viability and even then face an uphill battle in "the reluctant welfare state." The strengths-based perspective, so integral to social work practice and policy planning, is often less politically feasible than politically correct.

A critical area of need in these times of cost-saving and budget-cutting measures is for more and better research by social workers. Collaboration between social work researchers and practitioners in developing evidence-based treatment and services is the most critical issue for the future (O'Neill, 2000). The data that derive from such research are vital to social policy advocacy on behalf of our clients. Such data are also necessary tools in negotiations with insurance companies over the coverage that they are willing to provide for certain disabling conditions. Promising developments are occurring today with the awarding of federally funded research grants from the National Institute of Mental Health and the National Institute on Drug Abuse to research centers at schools of social work. Such research involvement boosts the status of the profession while providing the opportunity to document the effectiveness of social work policy innovation.

Social problems carry costs; these costs, which are often hidden, are seldom if ever shared equally among citizens (Chambers, 2000). The costs may be direct (drug users sentenced to prison) or indirect (taxpayers bearing the expense of incarceration). A monetary value can be assigned to this example. A RAND corporation study, for example, found that providing treatment to all addicts in the

United States at a price of $21 billion would save more than $150 billion in social costs over the next 15 years (Firshein, 1998). Estimates in costs and savings are available for each state. Access to such systematic research data provided in the RAND study is the single most effective argument in support of a policy change. The huge expense of the death penalty, when it was publicized, for example, became a highly persuasive argument against its use. The desire to see despised criminals die, however, overrode rationality in many cases.

Dollar costs of medical care can be calculated and compared to the costs of non-treatment inasmuch as untreated conditions develop into serious diseases. Sometimes such social problems incur costs that revolve around long-term losses in addition to or instead of immediate costs (Chambers, 2000). For example, the parents of a mentally disabled child or child living with AIDS may be deprived of help in their old age that otherwise might have been provided to them had they had a child who was able to provide care. The old saying, "an ounce of prevention is worth a pound of cure" can be validated through a computer search of various public health care sources.

Some examples of propositions that lend themselves to cost-benefit analysis are initiatives to provide home health care to disabled seniors instead of nursing home care; a gay/lesbian high school to offset their drop-out rate and subsequent unemployment; health care benefits to single mother-headed families leaving the welfare rolls; affordable housing for homeless families; and free English language instruction to immigrants. These examples are all geared to reduce oppression of one sort or another and to enhance full participation of vulnerable groups in the community.

Cost benefit analysis is often not possible, however (Einbinder, 1995). How can policy analysts, for example, give a precise dollar amount for saving a life, strengthening a family, or reducing depression? One option, Einbinder recommends, is to merely focus on the costs of the proposed program to achieve the desired result (such as reducing the number of suicides) without trying to quantify the benefits entailed.

Barriers to the introduction of social change must be anticipated to be offset or compensated for. Rental property owners, for example, can be expected to oppose the building of public housing, labor unions the growth of prisoner industrial work, tobacco companies the elimination of sports sponsorship activities, and gun manufacturers to oppose tightened gun-control legislation. These vested interests need to be exposed to the general public because any research data their representatives present are apt to be biased and therefore unreliable.

The issue of who will pay for a given initiative is crucial. A major barrier to its adoption is apt to come from the public if citizens must pay through property, sales, or income taxes for programs that do not appear to benefit them personally. It is important therefore to show how a proposal such as an after-school enrichment program will keep kids out of trouble and thereby benefit everyone in the community.

Central to anti-oppressive policy analysis is, of course, a consideration of the extent to which particular policies address issues of oppression. Economic oppression occurs when the scarce resources of society (wealth, educational advantages, etc.) are distributed unfairly. Proposals to raise the minimum wage to a living wage clearly qualify as anti-oppressive and reduce the need for people to rely on "welfare" or to work two jobs to the neglect of their families.

Means-tested programs, in contrast, such as supplements to the income of poor people are undesirable in the sense that they are invariably stigmatized and eventually resented by non-beneficiaries (Karger & Stoesz, 2002). The Congressional support for a means-tested program like Medicaid or food stamps can be anticipated to be less than support for a social insurance program such as Social Security or Medicare. A clever strategy that politicians commonly use to destroy a popular program is to make it available only for persons below a certain income level. Canadian politicians did this when they reduced the universal family allowances to a means-tested program.

Political Analysis

Policy analysis, at every step of the way, is a political activity. Power and oppression go hand in hand. Anti-oppressive policy then means recognizing power imbalances built in the social system and actively working toward the promotion of change to redress the balance of power (Dalrymple & Burke, 1995). Empowering policy is built on understanding of what life is like in the absence of choices and in exclusion from the source of decision making. At the macro level, as Dalrymple and Burke point out, empowerment is seen as a process of increasing collective political power. One cannot really challenge oppression without challenging at least some aspects of the power structure, and therein lies the difficulty.

The *political analysis* aspect of policy analysis refers to power relations, laws, and political legislation affecting disadvantaged populations. Political lobbying on behalf of clients is a vital and unique social work activity essential to influence the legislative process. Through consciousness-raising efforts, social workers work to mobilize public opinion against legislation that is hurtful to clients, for example, in Iowa where drastic cutbacks have been made to victim-assistance programming.

Resistance to change is inevitable; there are always stakeholders with vested interests in the status quo. Central to policy change efforts is an assessment of their power base, financial resources, political clout, and access to the media. Corporations and companies, through their advertising in the local newspaper, may have an inhibiting effect on news reporting; newspapers rely on businesses for their source of revenue. When corporate interests are involved and their control of the media pronounced, a good strategy for reformers may be writing letters to the editor. Often the press will take an interest in an issue if the community is affected and if public opinion becomes aroused. In-depth stories such as an exploration of scandals involving nursing home mistreatment of residents or of local homeless families can attract the attention of local politicians. Policy analysts can then send a fact sheet of community needs related to the topic to interested politicians for legislative action.

Knowledge of the political context is vital so that we do not exhaust our political connections and discourage social activists at a time when efforts will be wasted. Events of September 11, for example, put a damper on incentives to provide an amnesty to undocumented Mexican workers. As a war fever grips a nation, initiatives for peacemaking such as programs to teach conflict resolution in the schools are apt to be "put on a backburner" until the war fever subsides. Fortunately, however, the legacy of generous federal funding following the Columbine High School shootings in Littleton, Colorado, and contagion-generated shootings elsewhere continues to finance safe-school, anti-bullying programs.

What is the NASW position on the involvement of social workers in the political arena? In *Social Work Speaks,* under the entry "Electoral Politics," (NASW, 2003), we learn that social workers have been actively involved in lobbying the legislative and executive branches of government since the early part of the 20th century. Whenever the political participation of the profession is diminished or absent, as the NASW statement tells us, the quality of public policy deteriorates. NASW endorses and actively contributes to the campaigns of politicians whose platforms are consistent with NASW policy statements. The social work association gains clout with politicians through its endorsements of progressive candidates. In hopes of gaining power for the profession, NASW now has its headquarters in Washington, D.C., and the 1993 Delegate Assembly made support of social worker candidates running for public office a priority.

Ballot measures present another way to exercise electoral influence at the state level, both opportunities for the passage of progressive initiatives and to oppose oppressive (for example, anti-gay) pieces of legislation. In recent years, NASW has taken a public stand against state and city initiatives imposing welfare restrictions on single mothers and immigrants and anti-gay/lesbian proposals to restrict human rights. As the federal government increasingly turns over more responsibility for the delivery of social services to the states, the opportunity for influential lobbying by practitioners in the local community is now enhanced. In recognition of the fact that decisions about our clients are now made at the state level, schools of social work all over the country are organizing students and faculty to talk to legislators on lobby day and throughout the year. Social workers can acquire influence through their expertise derived from close contact with their clients, knowledge of community resources, and acquaintance with the research literature. Developing fact sheets of treatment effective studies and cost saving remedies can be highly effective with legislators. For example, my students and I developed fact sheets on the effectiveness of substance abuse treatment in reducing recidivism rates of offenders suffering from addictions problems; we mailed the fact sheets to interested legislators who utilized the material when the issue of reducing state expenditures arose. The material summarized data from other states on results of sentencing reform legislation. An excellent resource for learning the steps for influencing state policy is *Social Work Advocacy* by Schneider and Lester (2000). (You will find the website for influencing social policy at http://www.statepolicy.org.)

Putting It All Together

As a guide to the presentation of a policy proposal, whether for students in a policy analysis class or for research practitioners engaged in policy advocacy to consult, I have organized the material presented in this chapter in outline form. I used the following outline in teaching a course on social work policy. Groups that consisted of four to six students divided up the sections, collectively produced a 10–15-page paper, and later produced a brief fact sheet to present to state legislators. Among the topics chosen were advocacy for a state-assisted suicide bill; prison sentencing reform; legalized marijuana; the case against school consolidation; expanded funding for drug courts; and establishment of mental health courts. See Box 4.2, "Outline for Anti-Oppressive Policy Analysis," for the framework that was used for the policy analysis as discussed in this chapter.

Box 4.2   Outline for Anti-Oppressive Policy Analysis

I.   Description of the Social Condition/Problem
    A.   What is the social condition that is oppressive?
    B.   What are the facts (from official and unofficial reports) concerning the social condition?
        1.   What does documentation through review of the literature show?
        2.   What do we know from agency records, surveys, interviews with key experts?
        3.   What are forecasts for future problems, expenses related to the problem?
    C.   To what extent is the social condition perceived as a social problem?
        1.   How is the problem defined at the various levels of society?
            a.   What value biases are implicit?
            b.   To what source is the problem attributed?
        2.   For whom is the situation in question a problem?
II.   Historical Analysis
    A.   What were the relevant social conditions like in the past?
    B.   How did the social condition (for example, child beating) come to be defined as a problem?

continues...

     1. How was the problem later defined in terms of changing social values?

     2. How was the problem dealt with?

  C. Which influential groups were involved in supporting and opposing proposed remedies? Are the groups the same today?

  D. What are the precedents for the ideas and values being used to correct the situation?

  E. To what extent were the approaches to the problem effective or ineffective?

  F. How did the manifest goals differ from the unstated or latent goals of potential solutions?

  G. Comment on the lessons of history relevant to the present issue.

III. Policy Formulation Overview

  A. What are the goals (manifest and latent) of your proposed policy?

  B. What can we learn from people's (clients') narratives about the need to strengthen resources?

  C. What are the pros and cons of various ways of dealing with the problem?

     1. How does each of these competing policies meet the criteria of self determination, empowerment, adequacy, feasibility, and efficiency?

     2. How is your proposal superior to other remedies?

  D. To what extent can public opinion be mobilized in support of your proposed policy?

  E. In general what do the research findings tell us about the problem?

  F. What are anticipated barriers to policy change?

IV. The Global Context

  A. What can we learn about alternative policies or approaches to meet the same need?

  B. Discuss differences in funding sources and levels of support.

  C. How is your proposed policy integrated within the cultural values of one or more other countries?

  D. Could we advocate a similar policy for the United States given U.S. traditional values?

  E. Relate the policy under consideration to the relevant section of the Universal Declaration of Human Rights.

V. Economic Analysis

  A. How much will the proposed initiative cost?

     1. How does this expense compare with present or other proposed offerings?

     2. How will the proposed program be funded?

continues...

    B.   What will be the projected cost savings (the benefits) to the state, county, or agency?

    C.   Which groups benefit financially from the social problem (for example, landlords from housing shortages)?

    D.   Discuss the initiative in terms of its bearing on economic oppression.

    E.   If relevant, measure the economic benefits in terms of the impact on the physical environment. Is the policy consistent with environmental sustainability?

    F.   If the initiative entails an economic benefit, is the benefit means-tested?

VI. Political Analysis

    A.   Who are the major players involved in the policy innovation or policy to be changed (politicians, professionals, populations at risk)?

    B.   Who are the major stakeholders who have vested interests in making/resisting the proposed change?

        1.   Assess the extent of opponents' political backing, clout, and media access.

        2.   Assess the extent of the supporters' political backing, access, clout, and media access.

    C.   What is the political context within which the policy initiative has been conceived? Is political/racial/gender oppression an issue of public concern?

    D.   What are the major political arguments used by opponents against the proposal? Draw on research data to refute or acknowledge the truth of these arguments.

    E.   What are the NASW Code of Ethics standards (1996) and NASW policy statements (see *Social Work Speaks* [NASW, 2003]) relevant to the policy?

    F.   Describe any lobbying efforts and any relevant legislative bills introduced.

    G.   Which profession (lawyers, psychologists, managed care bureaucrats, etc.) controls the territory? How does this influence affect the policy's acceptability?

    H.   Gauge the likelihood of having the policy implemented and anticipate possible unintended (positive and negative) consequences of the initiative's enactment.

Policy Implementation

Reformers who see their policies implemented or programs instituted will not want to let their guard down. Opponents of the changes enacted may passively resist the changes in ways that undermine the intent of the measures introduced. In the case of protections given to physically handicapped persons in the Americans with Disabilities Act of 1990, for example, many employers were slow to comply, such as with building accessibility requirements (Jansson, 2001). When affirmative action programs first recruited women to work in male-dominated fields, fellow workers and employers often made life very uncomfortable for them; as a result many of the token hires left.

Additionally, many of the policies that were well conceived failed to work out because of unintended consequences. A well-known historical example is when the Quaker ideals of prison reform were adopted and prisoners were placed in solitary cells to help them repent, and many of them became psychotic. And in World War I, orphaned infants placed in a germ-free environment and therefore never touched had severe developmental problems and one third died (Spitz, 1945)

Follow-up research and evaluation are vital to redress unanticipated problems and to furnish data for objective decision making to either discontinue the program/policy or to perfect any flaws in the design. When the results are shared with other professionals, successful programs/policies might be adopted elsewhere. Model programs offer all kinds of grant-writing opportunities to assess treatment effectiveness or service utilization, or to develop similar pilot programs for empirically based program evaluation studies.

Kirst-Ashman (2003, p. 189) has introduced the Five-E framework for the evaluation of an existent policy. The Five-E model asks the following questions:
- How *effective* is the policy? (Does it accomplish its basic goals?)
- How *efficient* is the policy (in terms of money and time)?
- Is the policy *ethically* sound?
- What does *evaluation* of potential alternative policies reveal?
- What recommendations can be *established* for positive change? (How can it be improved?)

A different kind of evidence needs to be gathered when the policy change is a matter of *judicial* process. Figueira-McDonough (1993) compares judicial policy-making with other forms of policy development. This process is often initiated by the aggrieved party and the case must be made in terms of legal doctrine and legally recognized rights. Because this is a lengthy process, its success requires building a coalition that can lobby for a sustained period of time, as Figueira-Mac-Donough indicates. It is often very difficult, I might add, to obtain legal representation in cases of this sort, involving oppression and/or discrimination. Chapter 6 explains the role of the courts in protecting the rights of citizens against excesses by the state.

To conclude this chapter, see Box 4.3, which presents a useful consciousness-raising exercise that shows the links between discrimination and the role of policy initiatives in confronting this form of oppression.

Box 4.3   Small Group Exercise

Oppression Through Discrimination

1. Describe to other group members an experience in which you person-
    ally encountered discrimination because of your "status" (age, sex, eth-
    nicity, occupation, appearance, sexual orientation, beliefs, marital status,
    etc.). Describe your involvement in discriminating against a person of
    another status.
2. After each group member has described the experience, discuss the fol-
    lowing questions (as a group) and make a composite list of responses
    for each question.
    a. What feelings and thoughts did the experience evoke in you?
    b. What do you think were the feelings and thoughts of the other
        person(s) involved in the experience?
    c. What were (1) the underlying causes of and (2) the value(s) being
        expressed through the discriminatory act?
    d. In what ways could social policy play a role in helping to eliminate
        each type of discrimination identified?

Summary and Conclusion

Policy analysis for anti-oppressive practice differs from the traditional approach of analyzing policy in its emphasis on structural barriers rather than
individual pathology. The policy formulation scheme presented in this chapter
was informed theoretically by Chapin's (1995) inclusive, empowerment approach.
This approach underscores the need for client perceptions of the situation to be
clearly understood and incorporated in the research design. Social policy development, from this perspective, is a powerful tool for helping people attain social
and economic justice.

However sympathetic social workers might be with their clients' problems,
there is only so much that they can do to help them on a one-on-one basis. Often
the source of the problem is external. In order to operationalize social work values
we need to get involved (whether directly and indirectly) in the formulation and
modification of public policy. As it is, decision making is often from the top down
with more input from the business community than from the recipients of the
services under consideration or their representatives.

Policy analysis is highly political, and the anti-oppressive framework introduced in this chapter is unabashedly so. It is by no means value free but infused
with social work values. Central to this framework is a challenge to the social
structure itself, a social structure in which forces of oppression are institutionalized to the extent that persons in positions of power can maintain their control
of scarce resources. While promoting ideologies that deflect criticism away from

them onto other groups—criminals, terrorists, welfare recipients—and keeping the level of mass anxiety at a high pitch, the members of the ruling class can maintain their political control and leadership. Recent revelations concerning corporate greed and irregularities that were not so irregular at all have created a climate of distrust among the general population regarding corporate ideology. The widespread cynicism, hopefully, will have a positive effect in the long run.

So how can social workers and their supporters confront the enduring social discontent and help redress the balance between the haves and the have nots? Although fraught with difficulty, getting involved somehow in the policymaking endeavor seems a logical way to begin. In collaboration with the users of services and equipped with an understanding that all the oppressions have a common source, social workers as policy analysts can find themselves actively involved in the political process. The research effort, especially in a time of across-the-board budget cuts of social services, is pivotal to the social work mission. In the generation and analysis of data concerning treatment and program effectiveness, social work researchers can assume innovative and influential roles. Work toward effecting social change can be immensely satisfying and professionally empowering, as we will see in the chapters following.

Five
The Empowerment Tradition in Social Work

But from the ashes of destruction, mayhem, and oppression may emerge the human spirit, the capacity for the heroic. So we can never dismiss the possibility of redemption, resurrection, and regeneration.

Dennis Saleebey

In her research on battered women who managed to escape the battering, Schechter (2002) found three factors that made a new start possible. The factors were someone believed her; she felt safe; and the violence against her was taken seriously. Studies of rape survivors, similarly, showed that the initial reaction by friends or authorities has more impact on the victim's eventual recovery than anything else (Schwartz & DeKeseredy, 1997). Crucial in overall recovery was not hearing that she was a good person (despite what happened) but hearing the words, "It wasn't your fault." Together these two examples capture the essence of personal empowerment in a situation of degradation and self-doubt.

The discussion of these examples of encounters between crime victims and agencies created to help them suggests that to meet the client's needs, agency representatives need to choose their words carefully. They need to empathize, not criticize. The case of the battered women could have been life threatening to many individuals. In the situation involving rape victims, the risk was in reinforcing a severe self-blame that could be long lasting. In contrast, responses of empowerment can promote healing and be highly effective in a wide variety of circumstances in which people encounter violence or some other form of oppression.

Just as oppression may take place at the individual level, so members of historically denigrated groups collectively may have little sense of their self-efficacy in overcoming adversity. In contrast to disempowerment, which is about not being believed, about not being respected as a competent and capable person, empowerment is about feeling someone is there with you, providing support. To be empowered means to feel a boost in one's sense of personal power. The notion of empowerment is nothing new; whatever the terminology, empowering practice has been a consistent theme within the social work profession for more than a century (Simon, 1994). Central to the empowerment framework is a focus on promoting critical awareness or social consciousness to navigate the system and work toward personal or social change or both.

Whereas the focus of Chapter 4 was on the intellectual process of confronting oppression through policy analysis, a process which entailed the study of structural arrangements regarding power imbalances, this chapter is concerned with the social work mission as stated in the Code of Ethics, which is to attend "to the needs and empowerment of all people who are vulnerable, oppressed, and living in poverty" (NASW, 1996, p. 1). Theoretically, this chapter follows Simon's conceptualization of empowering practice as engendering collaborative partnerships with clients; a focus on client strengths; a dual focus on individuals and their environments; and a channeling of energies toward historically disparaged groups.

As our starting point, we examine the empowerment tradition in social work from across the last to the present century and discuss the process of empowerment on three levels—the individual, interpersonal, and institutional. Basic assumptions of this chapter are that with help most people can gain power over their own lives, that the helping effort must be collaborative both in terms of relationship and purpose, and that the highest level of empowerment involves taking action, speaking out in some way, on behalf of socially disadvantaged groups. Empowerment theory transcends all dimensions of the human condition—personal, social, political, and global—wherever there is power imbalance. These realms are viewed not as disparate entities but as interconnected interactively: The personal is political and the political personal, in other words. Change must be directed, as Gutiérrez and Lewis (1999a) suggest, toward both large and small systems. The simultaneous focus on individual and political change distinguishes political empowerment from standard policy practice, as Gutiérrez and Lewis further indicate.

Historical Context

In her rigorously documented history, *The Empowerment Tradition in Social Work*, Simon (1994) locates the origins of modern empowerment theory in cultural "forces that converge in which they (the actors) have lived" (p. 46). These cultural forces that existed beside other less progressive strains sprang out of revolutionary religious developments of the 16th and 17th centuries. The variety of religious sects within the Protestant Reformation mandated eventual coexistence while Protestantism itself introduced the democratic notion that the faithful need no longer turn to religious "experts" such as priests to find Truth. Quakerism, as Simon further suggests, added still another democratizing premise "to the storehouse of ideas that gave rise to the tradition of empowerment" (p. 35). Quakers, unlike Puritans, taught that there was that of God in every person and that decisions should be based on consensus.

An opposing cultural force to empowerment and tolerance of differences, *moralism* was to combine with the capitalist or Protestant work ethic to legitimate class differences and to blame many of the poor themselves as undeserving of aid. Of the two opposing strains, the one for compassion and social equality, the other for harsh competition, the former strain was the forerunner of what we know today as empowering social work.

An overview of the history of the social work profession is a proud history, the story of strong women and gentle men in many ways ahead of their time who worked for social reform or to help individuals in distress. There were, of course, some low moments—conformity under Hitler's Germany and under McCarthyism in the United States, and the dominance of psychoanalytical theory in the 1920s and 1950s (Reisch & Andrews, 2001). The New Deal of the 1930s was a high point, as social workers advised President Roosevelt on ways to rebuild the society following the collapse of the economic system. Canada experienced a similar paradigm shift from attention to personal attributes as a cause of poverty to putting the "social" back in social work.

The history of the development of the social work profession and of its educational institutions reveals that evolution is circular rather than linear and occurs in rotating shifts (van Wormer, 1997). These shifts tend to reflect the ideological rhythms of the wider society. Historically, the movement has alternated between the two seemingly opposing forces: personal troubles and public issues. Franklin (1990) has revealed how social work responded to the ideological influence of the times by offering interventions—community action, social casework, group therapy—that were compatible with the popular currents. We have to remember there was much overlap between the interventions, until one or the other won out, and that countervailing forces were always present simultaneously. Shining through all the periods were vestiges of resistance when resistance was called for. (So it is today, as the leaders of the social work profession relentlessly and forthrightly confront the conservative onslaught on the social welfare state.)

The profession got its start as a movement to alleviate poverty and help people cope with the stresses and displacements associated with urbanization, industrialization, and the large-scale influx of immigrants. Seeking to improve living conditions and address discriminatory practices, social workers such as Jane Addams and Julia Lathrop were social reformers and community workers. Working against oppression in the environment, these early social reformers provided a leadership that was consistent in many ways with empowerment-oriented practice (Robbins, Chatterjee, & Canda, 1998). During what is now known as the Progressive Era, social work leadership was provided in the areas of peace activism, efforts to reduce poverty, and work to eliminate oppression against minorities, women and children. As Shulman (1999) reminds us, however, many in the settlement house movement made little effort to actually organize the poor for their collective empowerment, but rather simply advocated on their behalf. The piece that was missing was true collaboration in organizing efforts. Moreover, the focus singularly was on the acculturation of the poor and immigrants to the values and beliefs of mainstream society. Still, as Shulman acknowledges, the early roots of the group work and community organization methods can be traced to these energetic early pioneers.

Levels of Empowerment Practice

We will remember from Chapter 1 Dalrymple and Burke's (1995) definition of anti-oppressive practice as practice that recognizes power imbalances and works toward the promotion of change to redress the balance of power. Central to this formulation is the imperative to challenge "institutional practices that oppress and so systematically disempower those with whom we work" (p. 15). Anti-oppressive practice, as Dalrymple and Burke inform us, is built on the model of empowerment. Following their logic, I am using both terms, empowerment practice and anti-oppressive practice, as synonymous. My thinking is that, inasmuch as empowerment practice addresses power imbalance as a form of oppression, and anti-oppressive practice is geared toward the empowerment of oppressed persons and populations, the difference is one of syntax rather than meaning. Payne (1997), however, perceives that empowerment is a more positive approach to social work than either the traditional or radical anti-oppressive approach, which regards oppressed groups as "powerless in the face of structural oppression" (p. 276). I agree that empowerment is a more positive term on the surface but solely because of the terminology rather than usage. To anti-oppressive theorists like empowerment theorists, social work practice requires far more than listening skills; the worker becomes a change agent in the political meaning of that term.

Dalrymple and Burke's (1995) formulation incorporates a model for the understanding of the process of empowerment; this model is informed by the belief that power can be imparted to those who feel powerless, that a person can take hold of his or her own life at the personal, cultural, and institutional levels. Their model, accordingly, is three-pronged. Empowerment practice takes place on three levels: the levels of feeling, ideas, and action.

The *feeling* level begins with the personal reality of people's lives and their emotional response to that reality. GlenMaye's (1997) description of the personal dimension of women's consciousness raising would be relevant here. Such consciousness raising begins with the identification of feelings and perceptions from the vantage point of one's own experiences and expressing these feelings in one's own language. For women oppressed by cruel circumstances, the power to name their own experience often previously has been denied them. Many, such as rape survivors, whom GlenMaye had counseled as clients, found it difficult to express their feelings. These only were able to do so in consciousness-raising sessions where they shared with other women the commonalities of oppression.

How can we engage people in the problem solving process? Dalrymple and Burke (1995) provide the following answer: "By making visible their personal experiences of oppression" (p. 50). In this way, participants begin to value themselves and to understand their emotions. The lack of an outlet for such emotional expression, conversely, can make troubled people obedient and malleable, susceptible to being used by others (Bishop, 1994). In her elegantly written book, *Becoming an Ally*, Bishop provides the example of abused children who have learned to suppress their feelings as a mode of survival. Such suppressed emotion can make a person with too little power even more vulnerable, Bishop explains.

In his photographic essay, *Transcending: Reflections of Crime Victims*, Zehr (2001) places us, through photographs and personal narratives, in the world of survivors of horrendous crime (for example, the mother's loss of her children to murder by their father). In this book, survivors share their stories, recounting their journeys toward healing. "Our truths are embedded in our stories," Zehr observes. "We must create new or revised narratives that take into account the awful things that have happened.... The recreation of meaning requires the re-shaping of our lives" (p. 189).

The *idea* level of which Dalrymple and Burke speak is closely, almost seamlessly, bound to the feeling level of empowerment practice. The idea level involves a new evaluation of self and situation through acquiring new insight. Sometimes the acquisition of knowledge is gradual; sometimes there is an "Aha!" moment of realization that what seemed to be so is not so. Examples of such lightbulb experiences are the battered woman who learns of the power games that were played to put her down, the rape victim who realizes it was not her fault, or the boy who comes out to himself as gay. The counseling relationship can serve as a powerful tool in helping such clients chart a new course toward self and societal awareness and self-love. Consider the following description of an awakening into Black consciousness, provided by journalist Kaplan (2001):

> I borrowed my father's old handbook copy of *Black Rage* hoping only for a side comment or two about the black psyche, some incidental insight that might prove useful in writing about race and depression... But when I started reading it felt not quaint at all but immediate, devastatingly relevant. Here were the million points of connection among ethnic/social, and individual dynamics that I saw daily but, despite the vast array of media outlets at my disposal, never heard or realized in words. This was analysis, epiphany, prophecy... I wasn't alone. (p. 90)

Such insight, as illustrated here, can be sociological, psychological, or personal. The therapist, group leader, or leader can elicit such a meaningful response by helping the survivors of oppression place their seemingly unique experience in context, give meaning to the feeling. As an active listener, the therapist listens to the client's story and offers new meanings and new interpretations. Above all, practitioners must be willing to listen, hear, consider, and affirm each person's act of naming and defining his or her own reality (GlenMaye, 1997). Such active listening can liberate the strength and energy of disempowered persons as they gain a glimpse of the unfair and oppressive conditions of their lives. Liberation is a journey that begins and ends in feeling. The final emotions are tempered with new insights and a redefinition of the situation as one that moves from the personal to political realm.

Because a major theme of oppression is the concept of power, the idea level logically would include attention to the negative consequences that arise from powerlessness. Power imbalances in relationships, and the need to make choices about one's life or livelihood, would also be addressed. Through consciousness raising and the realization that those among us who are victimized are not responsible ourselves for our own victimization, feelings of self-blame can be replaced by self-acceptance. Problem analysis at the macro level often reveals the need for structural change so one's needs can be met. The subordination of women is a factor that may lend itself to violence, whether institutionally (for example, against women in prison) or within the family system. From a positive standpoint, power can be a liberating force. Gaining a sense of personal power can be a first step in assuming personal responsibility for change in moving, as Gutiérrez (1991) puts it, from apathy and despair to positive social actions..

Methods used at this consciousness-raising level include education in the form of workshops, small group formats, mutual aid efforts, and sharing of interactive email and exposure to other mass communications. As support networks in which individuals can discover mutual strengths and insights, ongoing small groups are ideal mechanisms for altering consciousness about the self and others (Parsons, 2002).

At the *action* level, the individual moves into the political realm. The advances may be manifest at the interpersonal level, such as joining a self-help or advocacy group to support and advocate for others in the same situation. We should never underestimate the efficacy of self-help groups. As Schneider and Lester (2000) confirm, self-help groups are some of the most effective groups available to consumers. Such organizations rely on their own members' efforts and skills as primary resources. Typical examples are groups that meet to cope with shared family problems such as debilitating and addictive diseases, single parenting, and bereavement. At the broader level, social action can take the form of organizing to work for new legislation in hopes of wider impact. This social action stage involves working with others to change social institutions. We will discuss feminist organizing and welfare rights activism later in the chapter.

Empowerment, according to Fleming and Ward (1999), is the dominant social work term of the present day. "Empowerment," they write, "is the process by which power is developed or taken by the powerless themselves" (p. 370). They equate empowerment, in other words, with social action. Social action as a theoretical perspective draws on several strands of thought, among them that found in the women's movement and the disability movement, and more recently, in the writings of Black activists such as bell hooks, herself inspired by the radical pedagogy of Freire (Fleming & Ward, 1999). The radical empowerment pedagogy of Freire is an underpinning of empowerment practice in social work, notes Lee (2001). The use of dialogue is central to both the liberation teachings of Freire and social work.

Freire's Influence

To learn of the kind of resourcefulness that exemplifies the social work imagination in the form of collective field activities, we can look to Latin America. There, grassroots organizations, often with little or no help from their official leaders, have formed to work among the poorest and most needy groups of society to try to bring social development to their countries. Chilean social work education, in particular, was revolutionized as a result of the pedagogical instruction of Paulo Freire, an exiled Brazilian educator living in Chile. From 1965 to 1973, when a military dictatorship intervened to suppress the program and the social workers who were organizing across the countryside, a real participatory democracy characterized social work education. Today, while human rights are being restored (to some extent) in Chile, there and throughout Latin America, schools of social work are training their students in this collectivist form of organization. Let us hear from Freire (1973) himself who described his emancipatory pedagogy as follows:

> The critically transitive consciousness is characterized by depth in the interpretation of problems; by the substitution of causal principles for magical explanations; by testing of one's findings and by openness to revision; by the attempt to avoid distortion when perceiving problems and to avoid preconceived notions when analyzing them; by refusing to transfer responsibility; by rejecting passive positions; by soundness of argumentation; by the practice of dialogue rather than polemics; by receptivity to the new for reasons beyond mere novelty and by the good sense not to reject the old just because it is old—by accepting what is valid in both the old and new. (p. 17)

Social work in industrialized countries and in other parts of the world still has much to learn from the methods advocated through Freire's charismatic leadership (Johannesen, 1997). Empowerment strategies adopted by Latin American social workers enabled socially excluded groups such as migrant workers and other marginalized persons to be agents of their own inclusion. Ramanathan and Link (1999) look to Latin America for inspiration as well. Mexican social workers, they inform us, have turned away from what they see as the predominant focus in the United States on individual adjustment of persons with problems to a broader focus on organizing communities. Through global exchange, as Ramanathan and Link have found, the model of shared learning and consciousness raising articulated by Freire can have a profound influence on social workers and social work educators. Although a national survey of self-identified radical social workers conducted by Reisch and Andrews (2001) determined that most radicals are pessimistic about the future of radicalism within the field, the belief in the liberatory potential lives on within radical social work, and most especially within radical feminist social work.

Feminist Social Work

The purpose of feminist practice is in keeping with social work—helping people help themselves. However, its concern is more uniquely in helping women deal with the sexist oppression in their (our) lives. In the 1980s and early 1990s, The Women's Community for Feminist Social Work, or Fem-School, organized a summer training session to develop and teach methods of practice that advance feminist worldviews. The annual gathering of women-oriented women engaged in mutual consciousness-raising activities as a process of enhancing both awareness and commitment. As participant Bricker-Jenkins (1991) described the process, it was cerebral as well as emotional. "It is a search for meanings, and how those meanings were derived" (p. 294). Freire's theory of critical pedagogy and approach to knowledge where the students are active participants is the chosen paradigm for the Fem-School. The goal is individual and collective growth; the means is feminist education designed to engage all participants in the process of personal and political transformation.

Feminist educator hooks (1994, p. 202), similarly articulates Freierian premises in terms of "teaching/learning to transgress," and critical thinking as "the primary element allowing the possibility of change." Related to critical thinking is, of course, cultural competence, an indispensable ingredient for working in a multiculturally diverse and complex environment. Diversity is not merely tolerated, it is welcomed and celebrated. The challenge to social work, for example, is to recognize the strength in difference, sexual and otherwise. We can learn from Lorde (1984) of this challenge:

> In our world, divide and conquer must become define and empower... Racism and homophobia are real conditions in our lives in this place and time. *I urge each one of us here to reach down into that deep place of knowledge inside herself and touch that terror and loathing of any difference that lives there. See whose face it wears.* Then the personal as the political can begin to illuminate all our choices. (pp. 112–113)

In a later article on feminist issues in social work, Bricker-Jenkins (2002) presents a conceptual framework in feminist practice. Most relevant to empowerment theory are the conceptual components of collectivism (self-actualization as a collective endeavor), a pro-woman stance, personal oppression as political, and a focus on the mobilization of individual and collective capacities for healing, growth, and personal/political motivation. Given the societal barriers that obstruct one's vision and keep women and other oppressed groups from achieving their potential, all practice is necessarily political. In work with lesbian, gay, and bisexual clients, for example, attention would be focused not merely on the dynamics of heterosexism in particular but on the dynamics of oppression and scapegoatism generally.

Just as empowerment practice has enriched feminist theory, so has feminist theory enriched empowerment practice theory, especially insofar as women's issues are concerned (East, 1999). The feminist and empowerment perspectives both view power and powerlessness related to race, gender, and class as central to the experiences of women in poverty and women of color. *Empowerment theory,* sometimes called the *strengths approach* because of its positive approach in helping people, sees individual problems as arising not from personal deficits, but from the failure of society to meet the needs of all the people (Gutiérrez, 1991). Empowerment theories explicitly focus on the structural barriers that prevent people from achieving such needs. These barriers include the unequal distribution of wealth and power inherent in post-industrial economies as well as the effects of prolonged powerlessness on oppressed groups (Robbins, Chatterjee, & Canda, 1998).

Theories of gender oppression bring our attention to the basic structure of dominance and social control of the patriarchy and sexism latent in society. While having a realistic awareness of the barriers facing women who are disadvantaged in our society, social workers of the feminist school seek to uncover coping strategies used even in the most difficult of circumstances.

To identify and understand the strengths needed to overcome the multiple oppressions of racism, sexism, and homophobia, Icard, Jones, and Wahab (1999) conducted focus groups of lesbians of color to discuss their experiences. In later reviewing their recorded comments, four overlapping prerequisites to nurturing strengths essential to survival emerged. These prerequisites are self-liberating dialogue; the ability to transform dehumanizing experiences into something empowering; solidarity with others; and love and mutual trust. Most importantly, conclude the authors, knowledge is essential for empowerment. One woman from the focus group summed up her experiences with this observation: "I've been doing some reading. You're not going to beat me down with that. You know, that 'you're a homosexual and you can't be Christian' stuff; I'm just not going to have it cause I've done a lot of reading on that. I guess strength is just knowledge for me" (p. 225).

Based on my work with female offenders and substance abusers, I developed a Five-Stage Empowerment Model. A phase approach, the model is built on a composite of different activities in which clients progress from total absorption in their own stories, feelings, addictions, to making a contribution to others. The theory behind the phase approach is that a course of treatment, like life, is a journey and that progress, if it occurs, is an outgrowth of identifiable although overlapping processes. The five identified processes are dialogue, awareness, motivational and feeling work, healing, and generativity. From the client's point of view, the stages are relate, absorb, work, heal, and reach out (see van Wormer, 2001).

Assessing Client Strengths

Feminist therapy is highly political; it is built on the simultaneous view of women as independent beings and as members of an oppressed gender class. Proponents of the *new school of feminism* accept the first but not the second premise, which some perceive as too negative—so-called "victim feminism" (Robbins, Chatterjee, & Canda, 1998). In any case, feminist therapy involves counseling clients (whether men or women) both individually and in groups to help them locate the sources of their pain. Hill and Ballou (1998) summarize the principles of feminist therapy as follows: a recognition of the reality that the personal is political, that much of the stress that brings people into therapy is structural; an awareness of the forces of classism, racism, heterosexism, and disablism as well as gender as they impinge upon the life of the client; and a belief that therapists should see themselves as change agents in the wider society.

A concept that Hill and Ballou omit, but without which feminist therapy would be relatively meaningless, is the utilization of a strengths perspective. By the same token, many of the strengths theorists do not place gender (or race or class) at the center of their discourse. An underlying premise of this book, however, is that gender is at the center of many of the most explosive and divisive issues of our time, issues such as welfare reform, reproductive rights, and anti-drug policies. My personal impression based on a familiarity with the literature is that proponents of empowerment theory tend to focus more on political realities of coping while proponents of the strengths perspective are more focused on helping clients build on their own resources. Strengths-based therapists, however, are often politicized in their encounters with bureaucratic constraints both from the government and their own agencies that limit their client-centered proclivities. My approach here, in this book, is to consider the notion of strengths as an essential component of empowerment theory and practice. This conceptualization is consistent with that of three popular social work textbooks, for example, *Social Work: An Empowering Profession* (DuBois & Miley, 2002), *Empowerment Practice in Social Work* (Shera & Wells, 1999), and *The Empowerment Approach to Social Work Practice* (Lee, 2001). All these texts show us how to effectively incorporate strengths into each phase of the helping process.

The Strengths Perspective

Within the social work practice literature, a focus on client strengths has received increasing attention in recent years. Unlike related fields, moreover, social work has come to use the term "the strengths perspective" or "the strengths approach" as standard rhetorical practice. The strengths perspective, as Kirst-Ashman and Hull (1997) note, assumes that power resides in people and that social workers should do their best to promote power by refusing to label clients, avoiding paternalistic treatment, and trusting clients to make appropriate decisions. A presumption of health over pathology and on self-actualization and personal growth are key tenets of the strengths approach.

Although the literature consistently articulates the importance of a stress on clients' strengths and competencies, practitioners will be cognizant of the reality of standard clinical practice built on a treatment problem/deficit orientation, a reality shaped by agency accountability and the dictates of managed care. Third-party payment schemes mandate a diagnosis based on relatively serious disturbances in a person's functioning (e.g., organic depression or suicide attempts) and short-term therapy to correct the presenting problem. Furthermore, the legal and political mandates of many agencies that shape the professional ethos may strike a further blow to the possibility of partnership and collaboration between client and helper (Saleebey, 2002).

What you have in social work, in short, are two contradictory elements. On the one hand is the thrust to help people and, to paraphrase William Faulkner (1950), to help them not merely to endure but to prevail. "It is writer's privilege," declared Faulkner, "to help man endure by lifting his heart." We could consider this the social worker's privilege also. Social workers are members of a profession that aspires to help people become more loving and less embittered, more trusting and less competitive, more responsible and less irrational.

Countering the idealistic element in social work is the on-the-job, gut-level reality—the resistant clients, cynical workers, and tediousness of problem-oriented case management. (The British use of the term, *care* management, carries more positive connotations.) As novice social workers and students become socialized into professional norms, they often are inclined to try to separate theory from practice, all too willingly moving from what they perceive as the academic ideal to the demands of the real world. Years later, invariably, they will attend a workshop oriented around some aspect of client engagement only to momentarily get reconnected with social work's roots and calling. And, for the moment, once again they will see, following Lewin, that "there's nothing so practical as good theory" (cited by Polansky, 1986). Several years ago in Iowa, for example, intensive strengths-based assessment training was provided to all the child welfare workers in the state.

The strengths perspective has been applied to a wide variety of client situations, to work with mentally ill persons and their families; coming out gays and lesbians and their families; child welfare clients; homeless women in emergency rooms; the isolated elderly; addicted drug users; and troubled African American families (Saleebey, 2002; van Wormer, 2001). The concept of strength is also part and parcel of the growing literature on family-centered practice, narrative therapy, the client/person-centered approach, the ethnic-sensitive programming, and gender-specified counseling. In his comprehensive overview of social work theory, Turner (1996) identified two common threads unifying contemporary theory. These were the person-in-the-situation conceptualization and the holistic understanding of clients in terms of their strengths and available resources.

Filtering out the major themes from the strengths perspective relevant to practice with vulnerable persons, I offer the following guidelines for empowering practice.

Seek the positive in terms of people's coping skills, and you will find it. Look beyond presenting symptoms and setbacks and encourage clients to identify their talents, dreams, insights, and fortitude. A key point that strengths theorists emphasize is that assigning labels to clients is fraught with negativism. The problem is often not in the diagnosis itself but in the manner in which the label is applied. Rapp

(1998) warns us about the process of naming that belongs to the professional, not the client, and a problems-deficit orientation that can develop a life of its own. The person suffering from schizophrenia, for example, *becomes* a schizophrenic (Saleebey, 2002). Once a client has been given such a label, all other facts about a person's character and accomplishments, as Saleebey suggests, recede into the background. The difference between "I am illness" and "I am a person who has an illness" is profound. Hope is engendered in the latter but not the former.

Cowger (1994), similarly, states that use of diagnosis is incongruent with a strengths perspective. In response, I will make the case that, when done with sensitivity, the naming of symptoms can actually alleviate blaming. As we learn more and more about how brain chemistry affects our moods, cravings, and other behavior, such knowledge, far from being destructive, can be liberating to the individual. Clients need to know, for example, what form of depression they have or whether or not their problems at school stem from a hyperactivity disorder. In any case, the process of assessment should be a collaborative, explorative process; it should not be imposed from above. I am not talking, of course, about the use of negative, catch-all labels such as antisocial, borderline personality, and histrionic. The term *codependent* as used in the substance abuse treatment field, similarly, is widely criticized for its negative connotations (see van Wormer & Davis, 2003).

Listen to the personal narrative. Hearing the client's story, the client's personal and family history, is an excellent source of data for discovery of latent strengths. Through entering the world of the storyteller, the practitioner comes to grasp the client's reality, at the same time attending to signs of initiative, hope, and frustration with past counterproductive behavior that can help lead the client into a healthier outlook on life. The strengths therapist, by means of continual reinforcement of positives, seeks to help the client move away from what Van Den Bergh (1995, p. xix) calls the "paralyzing narratives." Through the self-expression of narrative therapy, clients can be helped to reauthor their lives, reframe the essence of their existence (Kelley, 1996). In introducing alternative ways of viewing reality, the therapist may provide hope.

The concept *suspension of disbelief*, borrowed from studies of ancient Greek literature and adapted by Saleebey (2002) as one of the key concepts of the strengths perspective, has special relevance for work with offenders. In contradistinction to the usual practice in interviewing known liars, con artists, and thieves, which is to protect yourself from being used or manipulated, this approach would have the practitioner temporarily suspend skepticism or disbelief and enter the client's world as the client presents it. To the extent that involuntary clients may "have us on," as Saleebey acknowledges, this should be regarded as a reaction to their loss of freedom, a form of resistance that may be abandoned once trust is developed. A willingness to listen to the client's own explanations and perceptions ultimately encourages the emergence of the client's truth.

Validate the pain where pain exists. Reinforce persistent efforts to alleviate the pain and help people recover from the specific injuries of oppression, neglect, and domination. Consider, for example, the degree to which loss and pain and, in all probability, anger are staples of the offender experience. Typical losses include loss of freedom of varying degrees, court sanctions, relationship adjustments, and forced abstinence from use of alcohol or other drugs. Strengths-oriented treatment helps clients grieve their losses and achieve some degree of acceptance of things they cannot change. The therapy process engages the client and helps the client find ways of coping that are alternatives to chemical use or destructive behaviors. The focus is on enhancing the client's sense of control and ability to make decisions in a situation of legal constraints and entanglements. "To heal our wounds," as hooks (1993) tells us, "we must be able to critically examine our behavior and change" (p. 39). As clients begin to take responsibility for their lives, the healing process can begin. Generally, this involves recognizing how past events influence present feelings, thoughts, and behavior. Women's and men's healing may involve a journey back in time to childhood or early adulthood where trauma has occurred. Healing may require a working through of guilt feelings, feelings that are real whether there was any actual guilt or not. Inner change often comes through identifying irrational thoughts, understanding how thinking and feelings are intertwined, and learning to reframe unhealthy assumptions and beliefs (van Wormer, 2001).

Goodson (2003), a youth social worker and himself an ex-convict, says it best:

> I deal with a lot of cultural pain. The same issues come up again and again, and the issue of race always comes up, the issue of Who I am. Who am I as a black man? In a lecture I heard recently, the speaker said the only thing that keeps people clean is the fear of dying of an overdose. But in my work we have to go beyond that and acquire a love for life, a love for yourself, a love for your family, and so on. Sometimes we preach a message of running from rather than a message of salvation. My point is we have to go beyond fear to the positives. As black men we have to view this (drug use) as self-destructive behavior due to cultural self-hatred.

Similarly, in her book on Black women and self-recovery, hooks (1993) connects the struggle of people to "recover" from suffering and woundedness caused by political oppression/exploitation with the effort to break with addictive behavior. "Collectively, Black women will lead more life-affirming lives," she writes (p. 111), "as we break through denial, acknowledge our pain, express our grief, and let the mourning teach us how to rejoice and begin life anew."

Mental health counselors, addiction workers, and correctional counselors often find themselves in a position of extreme power imbalance that, if handled incorrectly, can be the death knell of a therapeutic treatment relationship. Workers can minimize this imbalance by stressing the importance of the client's perceptions and meanings. The fundamental social work value of self-determination is reified as practitioners entrust clients with rights and responsibilities to make decisions in each phase of the treatment process. To be effective, the process must redefine traditional roles, insofar as is possible, to reflect the status of clients as active partners (Miley, O'Melia, & DuBois, 1998). The long-standing social work principle "begin where the client is" has profound implications for the path that individual therapy will take. In partnership, workers and clients map out an area of where to go (the goals), how rough a road to travel (issues to address), and the means of getting there (intervention and exercises). Instead of a philosophy of the treatment guide as the expert and teacher, the notion of this joint venture is simply that two heads are better than one to figure things out.

Related to the concept of collaboration is the notion of *interactionism*. Interactional relationships are reciprocal exchanges in which the teacher is the learner and the learner the teacher. The opposite of interactionism is the model of cause and effect, a linear concept in which an action at point A causes a reaction at point B. The added dimension here is that A affects B and B affects A simultaneously. The effect is not merely additive but synergistic, for when phenomena, including people, are brought into interrelationships, they create new and often unexpected patterns and resources that typically exceed the complexity of their individual components (Saleebey, 2002). The whole is more than the sum of its parts, in other words.

In a relationship, because of the synergy involved, moods are transmitted, often unintentionally. The effect is as much on the therapist as it is on the client. Thus, the depression of one becomes the depression of both and likewise with joy.

Draw on every ounce of your social work imagination. Social workers need to be intermediaries, to open up the world to another, even as they gain a new or altered perspective from the same source. The energy of mutual discovery feeds on itself, recharges itself. Social work imagination makes it possible "to perceive the congruities in the incongruities, to discern the false dualism between the private and the public, to experience the beauty of social work against the bureaucratic assaults, and to see the past in the present" (van Wormer, 1997, p. 205). To have a new vision of the future, so important in work with court-ordered clients and other offenders, it is helpful if not absolutely necessary to have a new vision of the past. The mind is a refuge of ideas and images, many of them unhealthy, some distorted.

In counseling oppressed people, the worker can begin by entering the world of their oppression—hearing the pain, anguish, and confusion and drawing on the client's own language and concepts to become the dominant mode of expression. An understanding of how sexism, racism, and class oppression affect a person's outlook on life is essential to effective work with him or her. Be prepared to find a history of victimization in abusive relationships, addiction, inadequate support systems, and severe economic problems in alternation with glimpses of inner resourcefulness, daily survival skills, concern for children, and family loyalty. Through reflective listening and reinforcing revelations of strength, the social worker can seek pathways to possibility when even the most convoluted life stories are offered. The strengths/empowerment approach is especially effective in helping people reclaim a degree of personal power in their lives if indeed they ever had any, and in helping them gain a sense of it if they did not.

Organizing Groups and the Community

For individuals who are oppressed and overwhelmed by their situations, consciousness-raising groups are the optimal medium for empowerment. For other individuals who are not overwhelmed but working to end oppression, group solidarity in collective action can be highly productive. One should never underestimate the power of an approach based on strengths and possibility rather than probability. It may not do much to change people. But in the final analysis, it is the only thing that will. Morale, affectional ties, exchange of views, and commonality of interests in a group enhance learning (Lee, 2001). For special populations such as gays and lesbians, support groups are extremely helpful in the coming-out process. For racial and ethnic minorities, who similarly may face issues of pervasive oppression in their lives, empowerment groups are the intervention of choice.

The task for group workers is to help members develop the knowledge and skills needed to recognize and affect political processes (Robbins, Chatterjee, & Canda, 1998). The explicit purpose of such a group is personal/political empowerment. Group members determine what external barriers to achieving their goals exist and areas of internalized oppression that need to be addressed. Even if no policy changes come about, the group experience itself can be extremely powerful; some of the friendships that develop may last forever. Lee describes, with sample dialogue, appropriate interventions for both the beginning phase of groups work with oppressed people and the work phase that takes place when trust has been established and goals of action set.

Read Box 5.1 to learn how group empowerment can be reinforced in the unlikeliest of places—an Indiana women's prison.

Box 5.1   Social Worker Incognito: Empowerment Behind the Wire

By Ardyth Duhatschek-Krause, MSW, PhD

Even though I am a social worker by profession, the women I work with do not think of me as a social worker. Instead, I am known by the titles of "Director" and "Professor." Conversely, my students are not solely students to me. Since the university program in which I administer and teach is in a state prison for women, I must also view my students as "offenders."

A metal fence topped with circles of electrical barbed wire surrounds my students and me. Even though I am lucky enough to go home each night, my students and I are still literally and figuratively behind this wire together

continues...

when it comes to our freedoms. My students have certain limitations on their basic freedoms of speech and action. For example, they cannot refuse the orders of authority figures, and there are strict limitations on what they can do, wear, or own. I, too, am limited by the procedural requirements of the prison in both my power to make educationally focused decisions in my formal university roles and in my ability to incorporate social work principles and values in my work with the students. For example, I am required to place "security" as the highest priority in my educational programming. Although crucial to prevent escapes and maintain order for the 1,000-plus people living and working within the prison, security is also in direct opposition with one of the most cherished social work principles, that of self-determination. Thus, if a student is planning a class presentation or research paper, I must restrict her from certain topic choices that might in any way promote prison violence, a proclivity toward gang activity, or facilitate an escape or a prison uprising. Or, if a student would rather miss class and sleep in with a scratchy throat on a blustery morning, unless she has been formally "laid in" by the medical department, I must "call out" that student and insist that she come to class immediately.

With these limitations notwithstanding, I still manage to insert social work principles into my work insofar as it is possible. Drawing on Wilson and Anderson's (1997) five dimensions of empowerment (educational, economic, personal, social, and political), I will briefly show how I shape my instruction and programming accordingly.

Educational and economic empowerment come into play as my students work toward the goal of earning a college degree. Often on graduation day, the students shed the tears of a very special joy. One student seemed to speak for many when she said: "I'm so happy! I have finally done something right!" When she said this, I realized that walking down that aisle of the prison chapel to "Pomp and Circumstance" might be the first time ever for some of the women to achieve societal accolades for an accomplishment.

In my role of instructor in courses on psychology and sociology, I have multiple opportunities to facilitate *personal empowerment*. Keep in mind that these inmates, battered as they have been by life's cruelties and any regrets they may feel at their own behavior, typically have low self-esteem. The degrading treatment they receive as prisoners compounds this phenomenon. This low self-esteem is evidenced in inmate writings for class assignments. Whether due to earlier substance abuse or personal trauma or poor education, many of the writings are strikingly superficial. In my psychology class, one strategy to help students realize they are special is to have them choose

continues...

from a list of adjectives to describe their individual interests, views, and characteristics. A second strategy is to elicit group affirmation. For example, if we are discussing group membership and a student says: "I tend to keep to myself until I know people pretty well," I might ask the class something like: "Why might that be a good idea?" If another student then pipes up in and says: "I'm different—I like to ask lots of questions to get to know people on my own," I might then ask the class: "How is asking questions another good way to fit into a group?" Finally, I try to further reinforce the students' sense of competence (as well as the value of individuality) by observing: "Isn't it neat how we can have two entirely different styles, and yet both of them are equally effective ways to relate?"

As both a teacher and an administrator in this environment, I try to provide as many choice-making opportunities as are practical. I do not just say, "It is your choice," when I present these opportunities. Instead, I advise the student that a part of the process of deciding whether or not to drop a class or to put extra work into a research paper, for example, involves a careful consideration of the pros and cons of all options, plus acknowledging the potential short- and long-term consequences of a choice.

The fourth form of empowerment identified by Wilson and Anderson (1997), *social empowerment,* involves a sense of group identity as a platform from which to impact upon mezzo and macro systems. Group identity is already well developed within the walls of a prison. The women are very cognizant of their common identity as "offenders." Even though this label seems at first blush to be kinder than the older terms of "prisoner" or "inmate," in my opinion, it is more abhorrent. Being called an "offender" is being told that you continually offend. Most of the women are painfully aware of how they have harmed society with their criminal offenses, or rather how they have "offended." Accordingly, I refer to the women simply as students.

My favorite method of social empowerment is therefore to insert content from feminist and women's studies literature into my course content whenever appropriate. Helping these women to develop a group identity as women serves two purposes. First, as opposed to their group identity as offenders, being "women" places them in membership of a group that is in many ways viewed positively by society. Second, women as a group also share oppression as a commonality with offenders. By creating an awareness of the meaning, impact, and coping strategies for the social injustices experienced by women as a minority, I hope to simultaneously instruct them in ways to deal with their other minority group status, or that of "offenders."

continues...

The final type of empowerment is *political*. This type is actualized by knowledge of and participation in the democratic system. My Senior Seminar, a course that prepares students for life "outside the wire," includes material on the major political parties. I tell my students that I would like them to understand the political system so that when they get out, they can have an impact on it. I impart my desire that when they are legally able, at the very least, that they will vote. (Our state, Indiana, is one of a limited number that eventually allows ex-felons to resume this right.)

A second way that I attempt to facilitate power is to give the students an opportunity to participate in an actual democratic system. Recently, we held an election for a Student Advisory Committee. The students voted for which self-selected candidate they wanted to represent their degree program. The function of this committee is to advise our university program in the self-study that we are doing for accreditation purposes. We are hopeful that if successful, this committee will become an ongoing opportunity for our students to have a voice in their educational experience.

In summary, it is true that the wire boundary that reduces the liberty of the ones who I serve also partially incarcerates the social worker in me. But what I tell my students, and what I remind myself daily, is that a fence is only a fence. Once we have tapped into the power of our internal wings, we are free to soar together to the remarkable heights of our own potentials.

Printed with permission of Ardyth Duhatschek-Krause.

Based on the premise that it takes empowered social workers to relinquish some power inherent in their positions in order to empower clients, Abram, Schmitz, Taylor, and Bartlett (2001) team-taught a feminist social work practice course. Vital to the process was the development of a learning environment conducive to group decision-making. Strategies used were the development of a non-hierarchical teaching/learning model; a team approach; and validation of the contributions of women, their ways of knowing, and female "voices." Pre- and post-test results revealed that on completion of the course, students had significantly higher perceptions of their personal and professional power.

Work with Battered Women

Helping others is a major source of empowerment for the helper. Most students of social work volunteer their time and energy on behalf of others less fortunate than themselves. Volunteer work at a crisis line or at a local women's shelter to help battered women and their children is typical. Such students, upon graduation, may get jobs in affiliation with such shelters such as the Family Service League in Waterloo, Iowa. Whether as volunteers or staff, part of their work may involve one or more of the following: working to improve community resources;

organizing public news events to share research on the numbers of women beaten and killed by their partners; participation with concerned members of the community and shelter supporters in "bring back the night" (anti-rape) marches or on victim impact panels; and engaging in fund-raising efforts for expanded shelter services.

To appreciate the importance of such activities, we need to think back to the time before the establishment of shelters, when abused women were whispered about and generally within families regarded as a source of embarrassment. When shelters were opened to provide safety to endangered women, they ended up providing a good deal more. Shelters, as Schechter (1982) observed, offered the supportive framework through which thousands of women turned "personal" problems into political ones, rid themselves of self-blame, and called attention to the sexism that left millions of women violently victimized.

The empowerment philosophy characteristic of women's shelters centers today on an awareness of oppression based on race, class, sexual orientation, and gender. Shelter life is woman-centered, chaotic with so much coming and going, emotionally charged, and guided by women who have an agenda, and it overwhelms normal adaptive processes (van Wormer, 2001). In group sessions, the process of empowerment takes place as women fully acknowledge their vulnerability to male violence. The emphasis on self-protection, on finding one's voice, the sharing and listening to others in a similar plight. frees up the mind to contemplate the forbidden (escape) and prepares the way for progression from feelings of self-blame to anger and maybe to the realization that "I deserve better than this."

A three-part model of empowerment for women in situations of abuse is presented by GlenMaye (1997) as follows:

1. Development of consciousness of self as a woman.

2. Reduction of shame and self-blame, and acknowledgement of anger as a catalyst toward change.

3. Assumption of personal responsibility for changing self and society. (p. 36)

Effective organizing for community action often begins with the formation of small groups (Gutiérrez & Lewis, 1999a). Helping a woman develop critical awareness and personal safety may ostensibly end the effort for that particular women and the organization. Many of the women, sometimes years later, return to the shelter to volunteer their services or return to college with plans for an internship at the local women's shelter.

Mutual Aid

Effective organizing requires breaking down societal barriers to build alliances across racial and ethnic lines (Gutiérrez & Lewis, 1999a). Many African-American women, Latinas, and other women of color have been active in mutual aid societies within ethnic communities. Recognition of the contributions of women of color to feminist and civil rights causes can help to break down the barriers and difficulties that exist in cross-cultural organizations, as Gutiérrez and Lewis indicate. I have chosen three unique examples to illustrate how diverse groups of people, people with vastly different ethnic and class backgrounds, came together with common cause. These are (1) the Kensington Welfare Rights Union in Philadelphia, (2) the community-building work with the Maori people in New Zealand, and (3) the Peace Power anti-bullying initiative.

The Kensington Welfare Rights Union

The following description is based on a chapter contained in *The Strengths Perspective in Social Work Practice* by Saleebey (2002). This chapter, by Jones, Bricker-Jenkins, and members of the Kensington Welfare Rights Union (2002), is titled "Creating Strengths-Based Alliances to End Poverty."

The Kensington Welfare Rights Union (KWRU) has been actively building a mass movement to end poverty since 1991. It was created by a small group of welfare mothers in the multiethnic, economically impoverished Kensington section of Philadelphia. The values and visions underpinning this mass movement are those contained in the U.N. Declaration of Human Rights (see Appendix)—the right to economic and social security and to an adequate standard of living for health and well being. In the words of the authors, Jones, Bricker-Jenkins, and associates, "We see the war on the poor in broader terms—as a tactical assault on one segment of the larger class of people who do not have control over the means and mechanisms to meet their basic human needs" (p. 191).

Social workers involved in the movement see themselves not as advocates but as allies, seeking collaboration in all dimensions of the necessary work in organizing to end economic oppression. KWRU is conceived by all participants as a fight for economic rights, for giving poor people a voice. To accomplish this end, leadership was developed from the ranks of the poor. General themes of the movement are as follows:

- Education and collective action as opposed to social service delivery.
- Healing through struggle.
- Changing hearts and minds.
- Mobilizing the skills and strengths of members and allies.
- Connectedness rather than individualism.
- Common cause between social workers and people in need as mutual targets of current economic policies.

As Jones, Bricker-Jenkins, et al. describe their framework in Saleebey (2002):

The framework is especially consonant with some implementations of strengths-based, feminist, empowerment, structural, and generalist models, and it evokes Bertha Capen Reynold's famous dictum—that the best social work is done "on the highways and byways of life." (p. 210)

KWRU's "New Freedom Bus Ride" was highlighted in Lee's (2001) chapter on community and political empowerment practice. In 1998, this now historic bus ride visited more than 30 towns and cities across the country. At each stop along the route, local groups who were assisted by members of the radical social work organization Social Welfare Action Alliance (SWAA), formerly, the Bertha Reynolds Society, organized rallies and teach-ins to focus on ways the United States was in violation of the U.N. Universal Declaration of Human Rights. The tour ended with a tribunal at the United Nations headquarters in New York, in which representatives of America's poor people made their case. In that moment, local, national, and international interests were one.

Empowerment Work with Indigenous Populations

Mutually reinforcing and supportive gatherings working toward tangible social change link the personal and political and help overcome the internalized oppression that is characteristic of marginalized people. Approaching cultural heritage as a kind of sacred realm, family therapists in Greater Wellington, New Zealand, allow only Maori staff to work with Maori clients (the Maori are a native people originally from Polynesia), and European staff with European clients (Markowitz, 1994). According to their approach, therapy and community building are synonymous. As a result of the family center's work, clients have created tenants' unions and unemployed people's unions, and they have fought for better housing and welfare laws. The team insists, according to Markowitz, that there is no healing in isolation and that the root of the clients' problems is in their disconnection from a vitalizing sense of belonging and meaning. Similar ways of healing are being employed in North America where First Nations people are developing their own traditionally based, ritualized programs. In Canada, the principle of self-determination is interpreted to mean that the indigenous people alone can reaffirm their traditional beliefs and customs, that they must educate their own people in their own schools of social work, accordingly. In turn, Natives are educating non-Natives in aboriginal folk knowledge about the art of healing (Mawhiney, 1995).

In her work on breaking the cycle of oppression, Bishop (1994) finds that anger, sharing grief, and above all, friendship are sources of power. People linked in a joint struggle, as Bishop suggests, lose their sense of society-induced shame. They are able through consciousness raising and healing to move beyond oppression and become allies to other oppressed groups.

Social workers are looking closely at New Zealand's family group conferencing model as a community-based response to crime. This model, a form of restorative justice (see Chapter 8), is a key element of community justice in New Zealand where it is used for most juvenile offenders. Many of the cases involve decisions concerning abuse of children as well. The conferences were initiated to give (extended) family members and indigenous communities a voice in what could be done to protect children. So successful were these conferences as measured in follow-up surveys that in the Sentencing Act of 2002, New Zealand expanded official recognition of restorative justice practices for the entire justice system (PFI Center for Justice and Reconciliation , 2002). See Chapter 8 for more details on restorative justice practices.

Peace Power Initiative to Reduce School Violence

In *Peace Power for Adolescents: Strategies for a Culture of Non-Violence,* Mattaini (2001) introduces a community-centered initiative to reduce school violence. The model, inspired in part by Native American traditions for sharing power, teaches that there are non-coercive ways to influence the world of youth and help them contribute to the community. Prevention of bullying and the growth of exclusive school cliques, and the teaching of acceptance of youth who are different, are among the goals of Peace Power programming. The broader goals are ambitious: to produce cultural change that constructs and maintains a new way of life for everyone involved in a child's world.

Central to all the Peace Power initiatives are the following basic principles: the selection of a project that is tangible and doable; a strong educational component including social workers not as experts but as collaborators; general agreement concerning the structural origins of oppression and injustice; the use of small, task-oriented groups to facilitate readiness for action; a shift away from a problem focus to a solution focus; and a willingness to address racial, class, and gender conflict up front while keeping members of the community action focused on the external goals.

Implicit in all these initiatives is the spirit of hope and belief in the human spirit. In *Sisters of the Yam,* hooks (1993) graphically captures the essence of this belief in the story of an African American midwife, Miss Onnie. Miss Onnie shared memories passed down in her family history of the pain of slavery. Although she named their sorrows, she always evoked the need for Black people to let go of bitterness. In their historical role as caretakers, Black women, as hooks notes, practiced the art of compassion and knew that forgiveness not only eased the pain of the heart but also made love possible. "When we feel like martyrs," hooks observes, "we cannot develop compassion" (p. 168). Moving from the micro to the macro realm, hooks leads us into the highest level of empowerment. If we genuinely desire to change our world by cultivating compassion and the will to forgive, as hooks explains, we should be able to resist oppression and exploitation, "to joyfully engage in oppositional struggle" (p. 172).

Summary and Conclusion

In the 19th century, before social work got its name, the seed for the profession as we know it today was sown. It was the seed of empowerment.

The empowerment tradition in social work remains alive and well. What we have today is empowerment practice that is more grassroots-derived and less paternalistic (maternalistic) than the historic formulations of social helping that preceded it.

A multi-level construct that is applicable to individuals as well as to groups and community organizations, empowerment is both a process and an outcome, both a model and a method. Empowerment describes both the means and ends of treatment. To facilitate empowerment, social workers integrate strategies at the personal level with parallel interventions within the interpersonal and political realms. Consistent with the strengths perspective, the focus is on people as possible heroes of their own lives, not its victims. Celebration of human diversity, the maintaining of a critical perspective, and promotion of social justice are all themes of empowerment, as of social work practice generally.

The personal is political and the political is personal. This, in a nutshell, is the underlying theme of the *feminist empowerment* approach. Central to the feminist empowerment approach is the view that humans are unique, multifaceted beings with the potential to make a contribution to their community (Kelley, 1996). This contribution can be made quietly or through public consciousness raising and networking, for example, through membership in self-help groups or specialized professional associations. Sharing in writing and receiving newsletters is an example of *educational* empowerment. *Political* empowerment can occur through activities such as lobbying politicians and mass media campaigns. Issues relevant to women in the throes of political and personal oppression include such activities as lobbying for victims rights, working toward legislative changes to protect single mothers on welfare from losing their benefits, and working to enhance affirmative action programs to increase the female-to-male ratio in male-dominated fields of employment.

In recent years, activist social workers have moved from advocacy of clients on a case-by-case basis to the more holistic and radical *cause* advocacy. The description of the KWRU mass movement encapsulates this development most memorably. At the time of the present writing, this movement continues to expand.

Part Two
Injustice and
Restorative Justice

Injustice and oppression are inextricably linked, as we learned in Chapter 1. There is no "shifting of gears," therefore, as we proceed to a discussion of themes of injustice in society. Compared to the concept of oppression, justice relates to the law and, therefore, to institutionalized forms of treatment. In exploring the roots of injustice then, we will be concerned with the institutionalized component of oppression. Unjust or unfair treatment by the system engenders the kind of oppression that has been the subject of four of the five previous chapters.

The three chapters that comprise Part II of this volume take us into the realm of social justice and human rights and the denial of the same. In Chapter 6, the War on Drugs was shown for what it is—a war on the poor and people of color. Social inequality is reflected too, in the erosion of social spending, an erosion that can be regarded as a denial in meeting citizens' rights to fairness and justice. For an international perspective on American human rights traditions and violations, we turn to United Nations documents, especially the U.N. Universal Declaration of Human Rights (see Appendix) and the U.N. Convention on the Rights of the Child. For a view beyond U.S. borders, a boxed reading describes the social conditions faced by the children of Romania. Chapter 7 takes as its framework the radical policy analysis of existing programs in need of restructuring. Various means of initiating change are discussed; these include working within the system, whistleblowing, and protecting the system from the outside. The role of nongovernmental organizations in publicizing injustice is highlighted. The book ends on a positive note with Chapter 8, "Restoring Justice Through Restorative Justice." The case is made that the social work profession should be at the helm rather than at the stern of this exciting social movement. As a potentially revolutionary way of responding to both personal and social injustice, restorative justice is making inroads in reconciling victims, offenders, the community, and, occasionally, nations. In concluding the book, this chapter puts it all together in contemplating the oft-noted link between personal troubles and political issues.

Six
The Nature of Injustice

> The ultimate weakness of violence is that it is a descending
> spiral begetting the very thing it seeks to destroy. Instead of
> diminishing evil, it multiplies it. You may murder the liar, but
> you cannot murder the lie, nor establish the truth. You may
> murder the hater, but you do not murder hate, nor establish
> love. Returning violence for violence multiplies the violence,
> adding deeper darkness to a night already devoid of stars.
> Darkness cannot drive out darkness. Only light can do that.
> Hate cannot drive out hate; only love can do that.
>
> Martin Luther King, Jr.

Structural violence related to human rights violations is the concern of this chapter. Structural violence is mistreatment of citizens by the society; it is violence ingrained in the social structure. Key components of structural violence and injustice are domination and constraints on liberty. Dehumanizing, "development-inhibiting conditions of living," as Gil (1998, p. 10) informs us, such as slavery, serfdom, exploitative wage labor, unemployment, hunger, unaffordable housing, homelessness, and inadequate health care and education, are examples of injustice imposed by the lawmakers and legislators in society. As enunciated in the U.N. Universal Declaration of Human Rights, all the above injustices represent denials of human rights. The human rights focus of this chapter is in keeping with recommendations contained in CSWE's (2001) accreditation standards, which state that studies on social and economic justice be grounded in an understanding of "human and civil rights" (see Section IV C).

In any given society, without strong values of social and economic equality, powerful interest groups write the laws and set the punishments for violation of the laws. In the criminal justice system, gender, class, and race are interlocking forms of social oppression related to the unjust social order. Gender, class, and race represent power hierarchies in which one group asserts power over another, securing a position of domination and assuring control over such material and nonmaterial resources as income, wealth, and access to healthcare, corporate welfare benefits, and the mass media. Control of the mass media is especially useful in mobilizing a nation for war, in whipping up the sentiment that would allow for a huge military–industrial defense budget. No one captured the essence of media control better than Orwell (1949). In the following passage from *1984,* the party official instructs:

"There is a Party slogan dealing with the control of the past," he said. "Repeat it, if you please."

"'Who controls the past controls the future, who controls the present controls the past,'" repeated Winston obediently. (p. 204)

Internationally, as well, control of the media by commercial enterprises is crucial to the selling of Western products as tickets to the Western lifestyle. Markets are created, in this way, for products for which there is no need. Through consumerism in a continually globalizing economy, strong nations come to dominate the weak, debt-ridden nations and the gap between rich nations and poor is exacerbated. The counterpart to White, middle and upper class, male and heterosexual privilege is seen in the privilege enjoyed by the nations of the Global North. In their control of the world banking system, and backed by unprecedented military might, the nations of the Global North are in a position to extort wealth, including access to resources, from economically dependent states, and they do so. Injustice is thus an *inter*national as well as an *intra*national phenomenon. As with all oppression, the possession of power is key to the wider social structure.

In this chapter, we view the nature of social injustice within the context of international law. Inequities ingrained in the law and in social legislation are considered. The book concludes with the U.N. Universal Declaration of Human Rights, the "gold standard" in the human rights literature (see Appendix).

Patterns of Injustice

Social injustice is ubiquitous in contemporary (as in traditional) society. It has been a major concern of every social science discipline from sociology to political science and of many professions including law and social work. Singularly, social work has as its ethical imperative that social workers promote social justice and that they challenge social injustice wherever they find it (NASW, 1996, p. 5).

Although NASW does not provide a definition of injustice, we can deduce from the social work literature that the existence of poverty and discriminatory legal treatment are indicative of unjust social conditions. Whereas the former aspect of injustice may stem from too little interference by the state, the latter may stem from an excess of interference by the state. Social workers, whether engaged in individual practice or community organization work, deal on a daily basis with the personal and social problems that are rooted in structural or societal violence. Such system-level violence, as Gil (1998) argues, obstructs the fulfillment of individual human needs; such violence is endemic in institutional systems built on domination and exploitation.

Over the past decade, social workers and others in the helping professions have witnessed the impoverishment, harassment, dehumanizing drug testing, and even prosecution of their clients. Miller and Schamess (2000) cite as recent examples of repressive legislation the so-called "welfare reform" act which forces single mothers of small children to work long hours for below a living wage; legislation stripping immigrants of their civil rights; and the incarceration of alarming numbers of African Americans, most for non-violent offenses. To this list of repressive legislation, I would add the military–industrial build-up, the preparation of the American and British economies for war, and the passage of the Patriot Act for tighter surveillance of the American people. All five of these repressive trends—welfare reform, anti-immigrant legislation, mass incarceration, build-up for war, and emergency security measures—are politically and economically motivated. All have important implications for social work in terms of the profession's historic commitment to social justice.

Welfare Reform

Injustice and economic oppression are inextricably linked. We explored this interrelationship in Chapter 2. Let us now contemplate the backlash in our society against persons who are underprivileged and who had previously been entitled to some special consideration, whether by means of affirmative action, welfare benefits, disability compensation, or general assistance. What happened to the ethos providing for their support? Although it is hard to pinpoint the exact reason for the ideological conservatism that began in the late 1970s, two factors can be singled out as likely culprits. The first was what Reisch and Andrews (2001) describe as a backlash against the tumultuous movements of the 1960s and against the progressive programs of that period, even the once-popular anti-poverty initiatives. The second major development was the shift in political/economic ideology of the 1980s, now known as Reaganism.

Politicians alone cannot effect a major paradigm shift in the public's thinking. Control of the media, of course, can be an asset—necessary but not sufficient for mobilizing the society toward change. Essential also is a scientific rationale, preferably from a prestigious academic source. Conservative think tanks finance studies from the social sciences for just this purpose.

The work of Charles Murray, much of it financed by the American Enterprise Institute, provided a strange twist on victim-blaming, blaming the victims of poverty themselves for causing the situation or situations that gave rise to their impoverishment. Ignoring many of the root causes of poverty, for example, technology, politics, and the free market economy, Murray, in *Losing Ground* (1984), blamed government aid itself and the progressive programs of previous decades for a host of social problems associated with persistent poverty. He continued that argument in a much-talked-about essay published in the *Wall Street Journal* (Murray, 1993). In Murray's words, "Illegitimacy is the single most important social problem of our time—more important than crime, drugs, poverty, illiteracy, welfare, or homelessness because it drives everything else" (p. A12).

Coercive welfare measures were introduced through a series of laws proposed by the Republicans under President Ronald Reagan (Dominelli, 2002b). A unique phenomenon of the blaming-the-poor rhetoric of the 1990s was the success in enlisting the lower-middle classes in the service of the upper-class establishment in targeting the poor as society's scapegoats. What a contrast this was to the period of the Great Depression, when it was those who had amassed great fortunes who were put on the defensive and attacked by the politicians and the press. Although the nation and states spend only a minuscule portion of tax revenues on welfare (i.e., aid for the poor), the reason for the national budget deficit is pinned on the poor and their purported lack of morality. The tacit assumption that benefits have been too generous is belied by an actual 40% decline in welfare recipients' "real" dollar purchasing power since the early 1970s (van Wormer, 1997).

The emphasis on workfare and the development of job skills in welfare recipients implies it is the individual's (usually a single mother's) unwillingness to work that is the problem. The realities of the global economy and technological revolution, however, point to the limited supply of jobs and high costs of affordable health care as key factors in the need for welfare assistance. For most long-term welfare recipients, the barriers to employment are considerable. Based on a review of welfare-to-work evaluations, Popple and Leighninger (2001) list health problems, drug abuse, low ability level, and lack of job experience as contributing factors to low employability. In a pattern familiar to those with knowledge of U.S. history, masses of powerless workers are now pitted against each other in a "race to the bottom" with regard to wages and working conditions.

While the media largely applauded the success of welfare reform, this success was in terms of the large numbers thrown off the welfare rolls rather than in the alleviation of poverty. A study conducted by the University of Wisconsin–Milwaukee exposes the true facts concerning the first and most restrictive of the new welfare policies in Milwaukee County, Wisconsin (Scherrer, 2000). With a big drop in the numbers of families receiving food stamps and state-sponsored medical care, the children in these families have suffered the worst of all. As the gap between the haves and have-nots has been widening (in the United States, the richest 1% owns 40% of the nation's wealth; 50% of the total income is earned by the top 20% of households), there is hunger in the land (see Food First, 2002). Providing a digest of U.S. government data, the "Food First Fact Sheet" reveals that in 2000 nearly one in five American children went hungry on a regular basis.

The market economy, social services cutbacks, and conservative ideologies have prepared the groundwork for the return of public welfare responsibilities from the state to the families themselves (Dominelli, 2002b). Women's independence from men has been threatened thereby. Women escaping domestic violence may end up on the streets. In fact, the most rapidly growing contingent of homeless people are families in desperate need of social services and affordable housing, neither of which is available.

A human rights perspective teaches that for the protection of vulnerable groups in society such as single mothers, a focus simply on equality for that group is not enough. Structured change is necessary; such change has to do with the distribution of wealth and power and safety net protections for all the people, not just for those at the highest echelons. Any theory of social justice and injustice must identify as a central concern core resources such as income and wealth, jobs and educational opportunities, child care, and health care (Miller, 2000). So-called welfare reform, the aim of which is to remove social protections for the most vulnerable people, represents a social injustice every bit as much as the denial of civil and political rights. In an international context, it is a denial of rights, the rights to having one's needs met.

The media and the politicians have constructed the myth of the "welfare queen" (term coined by the Reagan administration) to disparage stay-at-home mothers, and as Dominelli (2002b) argues, to provide a cheap source of easily exploitable labor. Indeed, the country had gone from viewing poverty as the result of economic conditions over which the needy had little or no control (for example, ill health, unemployment, etc.) to blaming the poor and the nation's public welfare programs for their problems (Tice & Perkins, 2002). The passage of the 1996 Personal Responsibility Work and Opportunity Act took place under the Democratic Clinton Administration. This act, which abolished the Aid to Families with Dependent Children entitlement, effectively reversed six decades of social policy designed to protect families with children from the throes of poverty. Welfare reform thrust the welfare burden upon the states but with inadequate budgets to do so. Because of the absence of affordable child care or health insurance, coupled with the fact that the minimum wage is far below a living wage, large numbers of families have been thrown into dire poverty. The government's historic role in instituting social justice has been replaced by a role in institutionalizing injustice.

Because large numbers of the children whose mothers have been forced off the welfare rolls are children of color (and so perceived by the public), the attack against welfare, as Tice and Perkins indicate, is preeminently a racial attack. "The same racial agenda," as they further suggest, "is behind both welfare cutbacks and affirmative action, often coded in language of 'no special rights,' as if people of color were currently equal and asking for privileged treatment" (p. 314).

The welfare cutbacks represent not only injustice, in that they are aimed at one segment of the population only, but they also represent a violation of human rights. People who are forced off welfare by time limits or who are excluded because of their status as immigrants are being denied their human rights (Pearce, 2000).

Economic Rights Are Human Rights

It may come as a surprise to some Americans that human rights include social and economic as well as legal rights (Wronka, 1998). Part of the reason may be because, as Gil (1998) informs us, the Bill of Rights of the U.S. Constitution guarantees civil and political rights only. The U.N. Universal Declaration of Human

Rights, in contrast, provides for civil and political rights within comprehensive economic rights.

Remarkable for its time, the Declaration, born out of the waste and carnage of World War II, remains the most far-reaching of all U.N. declarations. As champion of the Human Rights Commission, Eleanor Roosevelt was instrumental in bringing this universal document to fruition even against opposition from the U.S. Department of State (Cook, 2001). The U.N. document consists of two covenants: one for political and civil rights: another for economic, social, and cultural rights. Characteristically, the United States signed the former covenant but not the latter.

By 1990, the Declaration had become customary international law. The Declaration's significance is in that it gave the world, for the first time in history, international principles to which sovereign nations could be held accountable. This human rights document goes beyond social justice to transcending civil and political customs, in consideration of the basic life-sustaining needs of all human beings, without distinction (NASW, 2000c).

In 1977, then U.S. President Jimmy Carter signed the U.N. International Covenant on Economic, Social, and Cultural Rights. Nevertheless, this document, which has been signed by 145 nations, still awaits U.S. Senate ratification (Food First, 2002). The wait may be a long one.

As a global profession, social work is concerned with economic and social rights as well as with civil rights. (When people are hungry, in fact, their concern with personal liberties is apt to be slight.) As a global profession, social work can be expected increasingly to look to human rights documents such as the Declaration as a blueprint for policy practice. The standard is there. Consider Article 25, for example:

1.   Everyone has the right to a standard of living adequate for the health and well-being of himself and of his family, including food, clothing, housing and medical care and necessary social services, and the right to security in the event of unemployment, sickness, disability, widowhood, old age or other lack of livelihood in circumstances beyond his control.

2.   Motherhood and childhood are entitled to special care and assistance. All children, whether born in or out of wedlock, shall enjoy the same social protections.

Three categories of rights are provided in the Declaration: economic and cultural rights; protection against discrimination based on race, color, sex, language, religion, and political opinion; and civil and political rights against the arbitrary powers of the state. Those articles of the Declaration concerned with economic, social, and cultural rights range from the less urgent rights of "rest, leisure, and reasonable limitation of working hours and periodic holidays with pay" (Article 24) to the more fundamental rights of food, housing, health care, work, and social security (Article 25). The fact that these rights are included nowhere in the U.S.

Constitution (but in many European constitutions) has hindered the American people in their claims to basic social and economic benefits.

The principles of social and economic justice as enunciated in the Declaration closely parallel the values practiced by the founding mothers of social work since the earliest days and those more recently spelled out in the 1996 NASW Code of Ethics. Unique to social work among the helping professions is the emphasis on social justice in the social environment. Merely putting band-aids on clients is never, can never, be enough. Because of the close interconnectedness of the personal and political realms, the artificial split between macro and micro is just that—artificial.

A timely addition to the social work literature, Reichert's (2003) *Social work and Human Rights: A Foundation for Policy and Practice*, will have an impact in raising the consciousness of the social work profession with regard to human rights principles. The adoption of a human rights framework is increasingly relevant today, given the realities of the global market. A human rights discourse can provide a basis for awareness of, and alternatives to, the global regime that reinforces structures of disadvantage "through blatantly undemocratic processes which result in benefits for the few rather than the many" (Ife, 2001, p. 202). Should social work move in the direction of a human rights orientation, it inevitably will move, as Ife suggests, away from individualizing practice toward a universalist realm. Yet in all fields of social work practice, whether with individuals, families, or communities, social work must be grounded in human rights (NASW, 2000c).

Clearly tied to human rights, as Reichert indicates, is the social work notion of empowerment (2003). Empowerment requires living conditions conducive to the fulfillment of basic human needs, a social environment in which the individual has the opportunity to achieve social security, and access to the essential human resources including a clean environment and access to health care.

Although, as Reichert concedes, the NASW Code of Ethics does not use the term "human rights," the code bears an uncanny resemblance to important human rights documents, especially to the Declaration. One entire category of the Code of Ethics, Category 6, contains within itself, as Reichert notes, "a mini Universal Declaration." "No other helping profession," as Reichert further notes, "has a code of ethics that so closely matches the Declaration" (2003). Found in Category 6 are the responsibilities of social workers to the wider society, to engage in social and political action that seeks to ensure that all people have equal access to employment and resources, and to expand opportunity for all people with special regard for those who are "disadvantaged, oppressed and exploited" (NASW, 1996, Standard 6.04b).

Watkinson (2001), writing from a Canadian perspective, argues that the inclusion of human rights documents and legal decisions arising from them are an essential part of social work education. Human rights laws, moreover, as Watkinson indicates, "provide a valuable theoretical and practical base for assisting in social change" (p. 271). Because Canada was a signatory (unlike the United States) to the Covenant on Economic, Social and Political Rights, social workers in that country can use the document as a touchstone by which to examine social policy and to hold the government accountable. All the provinces in Canada, as well as the federal government, in fact, have human rights legislation that is administered by a Human Rights Commission. For Canadian social workers, as Watkinson argues, human rights laws can be a valuable tool for advocacy for social and economic justice within the era of globalization.

Economic globalization, or the macro-economic policies associated with the global economy, have important human rights implications. Such policies require that the non-industrialized nations reduce their indebtedness to the world banks through reducing social welfare spending and producing cash crops for export, which has dire consequences for the family farm. Relevant to economic inequities, women perform two thirds of the world's work but earn only one tenth of all income; women own less than one tenth of the world's property (Human Rights Watch, 2002). Presently, 70% of the world's poor (surviving on less than $1 a day) are women; also related to economics, more than half a million women die each year due to lack of prenatal and postnatal care (Aleman & Susskind, 2000).

Women's Rights Are Human Rights

NASW endorses the human rights of people as a universal value that takes precedence over cultural norms when cultural norms conflict with such values. Ritual genital mutilation of girls and women, for example, is condemned as a human rights violation. NASW supports the adoption of human rights as a foundation principle upon which all of social work theory and applied knowledge rests (Asamoah, Healy, & Mayadas, 1997; NASW, 2000c).

Although women in an unjust society may suffer the same political and economic abuses as men, many violations of women's rights are distinctly connected to women's gender. Traditional approaches to human rights violations were not concerned with women as women. Until the past decade, family abuses such as executions for adultery, for example, were seen as cultural or private matters and, for the most part, they were rarely publicized.

Through their participation in U.N. world conferences, women's groups have brought increasing attention to the United Nations as a key forum for advancing women's rights (Fried, 1997). "Human rights are women's rights" has become the motto of the international movement to protect women from abuse. In 1995, women linked up from Austria to Zambia at the United Nations Fourth World Conference on Women. The historic conference was held at Huaira and Beijing, China. Whereas at previous women's conferences, feminists from the westernized nations were reluctant to even appear to criticize traditions from other parts of the world for fear of being accused of lacking cultural sensitivity, this time women's voices were united on behalf of the many who are unable to speak. At the 1995 conference, the debate on health and reproductive rights was led primarily by delegates who were neither Western nor White. In demanding that women's rights should supersede national traditions, the Beijing accord marked a historic breakthrough (Chesler & Dunlop, 1995).

The Declaration had included women as an at-risk population since it was written in 1948. Yet, just as with the Civil Rights Act of 1964, which forbade discrimination on grounds of sex, little heed was paid to gender issues until women organized to demand it. After the Beijing conference, Amnesty International, the nongovernmental organization that has done so much to publicize human rights abuses worldwide, took up the call (van Wormer, 2001).

Around the globe, death by stoning in Iran and Nigeria, genital mutilation in 28 African nations, rape of young girls in South Africa in the belief that sex with a virgin will cure AIDS, dowry deaths in India and Pakistan, sexual slavery in Thailand, and wife abuse in all countries have shocked the sensibilities of humanists. The savage treatment of women by the Taliban in Afghanistan, of course, received the most media attention of all. It was only after September 11, however, that the American government, which had previously looked the other way, called for the liberation of these women. Today, under a new regime in Afghanistan, many women are still forced to hide their bodies in the burqa and girls' schools are subject to burning. The treatment of women in the United States, although strikingly better than their treatment in some parts of the world, is not exempt from international concern. According to an Amnesty International (2001b) investigation, *Broken Bodies, Shattered Minds*, a woman is raped every six minutes and battered every 15 seconds. You will read of human rights violations in U.S. women's prisons later in this chapter in Box 6.2.

In this atmosphere of international attention to women's maltreatment, how is it possible that the United States undermines its own stand on human rights? So asks Goodman (2002) in her column titled, "Surely This Country Can Sign a Women's Rights Treaty." Goodman's reference is to the lamentable fact that the United States is the only major democratic nation that has refused to ratify the International Convention on the Elimination of All Forms of Discrimination against Women. Jimmy Carter had signed this treaty for women's equality under his presidency. A total of 170 countries have ratified this document. By not joining the international community, as Goodman argues, America damages its authority to call others to account.

Children's Rights Are Human Rights

Adultism was a concept introduced in Chapter 1. Because children are often viewed as the property of their parents, the potential for rights abuses within the family is rampant. In many parts of the world, in fact, children have no rights at all. The individual states in the United States have laws protecting children from abuse and neglect, and in situations of adoption disputes, laws state that the child's interest must be taken into consideration.

In 1989, while I was working in Norway, the U.N. Convention on the Rights of the Child was passed by the United Nations General Assembly. This landmark document, which was almost immediately ratified across the world, provided for the child's right to due process in court, a right to be protected from violence and exploitation, and a right to health and nutrition. The passing of this document was historic in that this was the first human rights document to focus specifically on the rights of children. Norway, like many other nations, rapidly revised its policies to be in compliance with international law. (Norway's adjustments were in the area of tightening due process procedures in juvenile hearings.)

Norway and Sweden had previously outlawed all forms of physical violence against children. Article 19 of the Convention requires state parties to take legislative measures against such practices. In Canada, the provincial governments and members of Parliament have faced intensive lobbying to protect children, as adults are protected, from assault. Now the pressure has intensified due to the support of international law. Children's rights are gradually being expanded in Canada as a result of recent human rights cases in which the U.N. Convention has been a prominent feature in the deliberations (Watkinson, 2001).

To date, all nations have ratified the Convention except for two: Somalia and the United States. Former President Bill Clinton signed the Convention in 1993; it has never been ratified, however. Among the objections are fear of increased state interference in family life; the failure of the Convention to preserve the rights of the child "born and unborn"; restrictions on the government to execute children; the requirement for universal health care for children; the proscription against inflicting violence against children (hitting, spanking, etc.); and the proscription against recruiting children under the age of 18 into the military (Reichert, 2003; van Wormer, 1997).

Eloquently, boldly, the U.N. Convention on the Rights of the Child sets forth its underlying principles in its introduction ("Excerpts from the United Nations Declaration on Children," 1990, p. 1A):

Each day, countless children around the world are exposed to dangers that hamper their growth and development. They suffer immensely as casualties of war and violence; as victims of racial discrimination, apartheid, aggression, foreign occupation and annexation; as refugees and displaced children, forced to abandon their home and their roots; as disabled; or as victims of neglect, cruelty and exploitation.

Each day, millions of children suffer from the scourges of poverty and economic crisis—from hunger and homelessness, from epidemics and illiteracy, from degradation of the environment. They suffer from the grave effects of the problems of external indebtedness and also from the lack of sustained and sustainable growth in many developing countries, particularly in the least developed ones.

Each day, forty thousand children die from malnutrition and disease, including acquired immunodeficiency syndrome (AIDS), from the lack of clean water and inadequate sanitation and from the effects of the drug problem.

These are challenges that we, as political leaders, must meet.

The Opportunity

Together, our nations have the means and the knowledge to protect the lives and to diminish enormously the suffering of children, to promote the full development of their human potential and to make them aware of their needs, rights and opportunities. The Convention of the Rights of the Child provides a new opportunity to make respect for children's rights and welfare truly universal.

Leaving no stone unturned, the Convention (and this is its triumph) is all-encompassing. Its clauses provide uncompromising protection not only in the usual areas—health, education, and nutrition—but also in the less tangible areas of economic and sexual exploitation, torture and war, and homelessness.

To appreciate the remarkable qualities of this far-reaching document, read the entire Convention on the Rights of the Child (United Nations, 1989). Rights specified in the Convention cover three major areas: entitlements related to material provisions; protections (as from labor exploitation) to safeguard children's well-being; and affirmative rights related to privacy, culture, and religious and language rights. Having just returned from Korea where children who aspire to college education study from dawn to midnight, I was impressed with Article 31: "States recognize the right of the child to rest and leisure, to engage in play and recreational activities appropriate to the age of the child and to participate fully in cultural life and the arts" (United Nations, 1989). The young adults I met in Korea confirmed that although children are well cared for, there is little time for play or sleep in the harshly competitive environment.

Throughout the world, despite the promises and the nearly universal ratification of their treaty, children's rights are widely disregarded. Human Rights Watch (2001a), in the report "Children's Rights," lists the following violations as typical of child mistreatment worldwide: severe violence inflicted by adults; psychological trauma; children tortured in correctional institutions; children in schools assaulted by teachers (virtually all Southern U.S. states permit paddling); and execution of children for criminal behavior. To that list we can add sexual slavery (as in Thailand) and infanticide of female infants (as in parts of eastern Asia).

However unlikely this is at the present time, U.S. ratification of the Convention on the Rights of the Child would empower the social work profession to challenge unjust treatment of children by their parents and by society. NASW (2000c) urges promotion of the U.N. Convention in its book of policy statements, *Social Work Speaks*, and urges social workers to be vigilant about human rights violations of children, the providing of adequate safeguards for them in all settings, and the abolition of physical punishment of children at school and in the home. Human rights violations are pandemic throughout the world. Box 6.1 graphically describes the cruel legacy of injustice that was imposed upon women and children in Romania under an especially virulent form of communism.

Box 6.1   Lesson from Romania

Human Rights and Social Injustice
by Carol Cook-Roberts, LISW, University of Northern Iowa

During the spring semester of 2000, I taught a social work course on international social welfare in which the students conducted a service learning project to benefit a Romanian orphanage as well as enhance student learning of a society and its struggle toward social and political change. At some point in the semester, I decided to plan a summer trip to Romania to investigate firsthand the current state of social work education and human services. While an understanding of the broad societal structural needs is crucial in social work change efforts, it is equally important to gain an appreciation for the individual experiential realities of those we hope to assist. Indeed, this should inform our change efforts at every turn.

I wish to give you a quick view of why Romanian society deteriorated under the Ceausescu government and share with you a brief individual moment that held and, to this day, holds significant meaning for me. Simona, my translator and cultural guide in Romania, and I were expecting a taxi that seemed delayed or headed to a location other than the Child Welfare and Protection office in the coastal town of Constanta, where we waited outside in the hot, blistering afternoon sun. Romania was experiencing record-breaking heat caused by a Saharan wind pattern that found its way into southern Eastern Europe. I had concluded a meeting to discuss child welfare issues in Romania with the director of this county organization. The month was July 2000, and I had arrived in Bucharest, the capital city, two days prior to this time and was still experiencing the effects of jet lag coupled with the unique exhilaration that comes with the long-awaited arrival in a culture struggling to redefine itself.

Romanians had lived for over two decades under the reign of Nicolae Ceausescu, the idiosyncratic Communist leader executed after a brief so-called revolution in December 1989. Memories of the post-revolutionary newscasts that shocked the world concerning the plight of abandoned, orphaned, and handicapped children during Ceausescu's period as leader of Romania were

continues...

still fresh in my mind. Most of the children in institutions lacked adequate clothing, food, heat, medical attention, education, and furniture to support their fragile lives. Even scarcer was the most basic of human needs—loving human contact. More than most tragic stories from abroad and domestically, the images and accounts of abandoned Romanian children touched something deep within me.

The crimes attributed to Ceausescu seemed to be limitless. Chief among these was the creation of state-run orphanages that housed, or perhaps more accurately stated, warehoused, 150,000 children living in desperate circumstances by the end of his regime. Ceausescu had declared that: "The fetus is the property of the entire society. Anyone who avoids having children is a deserter who abandons the laws of national continuity." Birth control, abortion, and sexual education were forbidden by law. Along with encouraging women to have five children, Ceausescu abolished the social work profession—those charged with the obligation to ascertain the needs of children and families, provide direct services, and advocate for humane social policies. It is not perplexing to imagine why the social work profession posed a threat to the likes of Ceausescu and his most ardent followers. The regime craved control over almost every aspect of people's lives. And they attempted to hide the outcome of their oppressive aims from the global community by tightly controlling media sources.

I grew up in a large family and my youngest brother has a disability; he fits into the category referred to as "dually diagnosed." My brother was born in the United States during the time period of Ceausescu's rule. Had he been born in Romania by a "simple twist of fate," he no doubt would have been labeled "unrecoverable" by the state. Though thousands of non-disabled children were placed in orphanages, those deemed disabled were later found to be in the most deplorable ones. Romanian children are loved by their parents, but the government had not only forced harsh reproductive policies on women, in an unprecedented effort to rapidly increase the population to fuel a state goal for industrial labor, but its economic policies were disastrous. For most, the means to adequately support a large number of children had been removed. These political and economic realities collided in Romania to the great disadvantage of average citizens. My brother would probably have landed in an "orphanage." As a Romanian he would not have been without parents but rather would have faced abandonment by my parents, not because he was not loved but because the family was too large and poor to support him. One can imagine the bonding between mother and child broken by the social fractures in Romanian society.

continues...

What becomes of a society that loses its way? What becomes of large numbers of children left in the hands of underpaid and ill-trained state employees to be raised in overcrowded institutions? What drastic measures must women, who have lost legal control over their reproductive rights, take? A recipe for social disaster was created in Romania. Now, the European Union has applied its considerable weight to persuade the Romanian government to improve the lives of institutionalized children and establish policies and services to reduce the need for institutionalizing children.

Waiting during my visit to Romania outside the Constanta Child Welfare and Protection building, I saw a white Dacia, a car commonly seen on the streets of Constanta, pull into the parking lot. In the back seat of the Dacia a young woman was feeding a baby from a bottle. The woman and child both seemed young. The baby looked no more than six months old. Simona and I realized after a half-hour wait that the taxicab we called for was not on its way to return us to the coastal seashore where I was staying. We reentered the plain concrete structure of the Child Welfare and Protection building and made our way up to the third-floor main office to once again call the cab company. We were informed that it would be a quarter of an hour before the cab would arrive. Standing in the narrow hallway we heard the plaintive cries of a woman sitting around the corner from us. She was speaking and crying at the same time. Even though I did not understand the Romanian words she said, and could not see her, the sorrow expressed in her voice had a distinct universal quality. The voice expressed sorrow and pleading. Simona and I were silent. Simona looked around the corner and caught a glimpse of the woman. Outside of the building, I asked Simona what the woman had said. It turned out to be the same young woman I had seen arrive with a baby cradled in her arms, at the Child Welfare and Protection building, not over half an hour earlier. She was there to hand her child over to the county workers and her lament was: How can I go home without you? What can I do if I don't have money to support you? All the while the mother looked at and addressed her baby, though I suspect she was in actuality addressing a society that had abandoned her and her dreams. This was one mother's voice. It was painful to think of a chorus of Romanian mothers engaged in this sort of dirge.

I vowed to find a way to devote a portion of my professional life to assist, even if in small ways, in the improvement of social conditions for women and children in Romania. Perhaps I could arrange for social work students and colleagues to engage in an international change effort and work closely with Romanians striving to reestablish the social work profession. My motivation came primarily from many years as a social work community prac-

continues...

titioner and educator. It came from pondering what the life chances would have been for my youngest brother and parents had they been Romanians during the Ceausescu era. It also came from being a mother. What would my fate have been as a Romanian mother and social worker?

Printed with permission of Carol Cook-Roberts, Director of Field Instruction, Social Work Department, University of Northern Iowa

Injustice in the Criminal Justice System

Every society must preserve public safety and trust by prosecuting crime. Injustice enters the picture when the severity of the punishment is out of proportion to the offense and when there is inequity in how the laws are made and enforced. In the United States, both conditions apply. Mandatory minimum sentencing has removed judicial discretion and created a system in which drug offenders, in many cases, are serving more time in prison than violent offenders. And as always, race, citizenship status, and economic resources dramatically influence how different groups of people experience the American system of justice (Miller & Schamess, 2000). Once convicted offenders are behind bars, human rights abuses occur on a regular basis; most prisons are seriously overcrowded, and violence in men's prisons is rampant. In short, for persons convicted of a crime, the erosion of their constitutional rights is unceasing (Whitlock, 2001).

Punishment Severity

With more than 2 million persons confined in jails and prisons currently, the United States now has the highest incarceration rate in the world. The continued growth in the prison population despite years of falling crime rates reflects the impact of America's war on drugs (zero tolerance for drug dealers), imposed mandatory prison terms for drug crimes, abolition of parole in many instances, and "three strikes and you're out" laws in several states. The majority of the prisoners are minorities. Since 1995, the number of male prisoners has grown 24% while the number of female prisoners has increased 36% (Bureau of Justice Statistics, 2002b). Fortunately, due to budget shortfalls in the states, moves are underway in many states to reverse some of the harsh sentencing laws.

During 2001, with more than 5,000 people executed worldwide, Amnesty International called on the U.N. Commission to take a strong position against the death penalty (Amnesty International, 2002). The United States remains the only Western country to still allow this form of punishment (Reichert, 2003).

In March 1995, the United Nations conducted its first-ever review of the human rights situation in the United States ("Human Rights in the USA," 1995). The United States is in violation of the terms of the International Covenant on Civil and Political Rights, which includes a ban on the execution of juveniles. U.S. law permits the execution of persons whose crimes were committed when they were under the age of 18. Article 5 of the U.N. Universal Declaration of Human Rights states: "No one shall be subjected to torture or to cruel, inhuman, *or* degrading treatment or punishment." This standard, which seems identical to that of the U.S. Bill of Rights, is in fact a higher standard due to the word "or." The application of the Eighth Amendment's "cruel *and* unusual" punishment, according to an article in *The Harvard Environmental Law Review* (Geer, 2000), requires that both elements apply at once—cruel *and* unusual. According to a recent Supreme Court ruling, the majority determined that if the cruelty is usual, then it is constitutional!

Behind Prison Walls

Today the treatment of prisoners regarding extreme overcrowding and limited physical activity, the death penalty, and Native American rights are among the human rights issues that are under international scrutiny for the first time. The use of chain gangs as a form of involuntary, unpaid labor could be challenged under Article 4's absolute prohibition of slavery. The U.S. Constitution, significantly, does not prohibit slavery in all circumstances (Refer to Box 6.2).

Few law-abiding citizens are aware of the brutalities that routinely take place behind prison walls. Male-on-male inmate violence, as mentioned earlier, is widespread. According to a recent empirically based survey, 21% of inmates in seven prisons had experienced at least one episode of pressured or forced sex within the prison (Human Rights Watch, 2002). Staff generally ignored such attacks. Violations by correctional officers include punitive use of electrical stun devices and confinement in total isolation for 23 hours per day in maxi-prisons. To learn of sexual abuse by male officers of female inmates, read Box 6.2.

Box 6.2   Human Rights Violations Against Women in Prison

by Katherine van Wormer

Research for the book, *Counseling Female Offenders and Victims: A Strengths-Restorative Approach* (2001) took me behind prison walls, inspired me to do a national survey of women's prison wardens, and got me in close touch with female inmates and their families across the country. What I discovered were violations of the human rights of women that were beyond anything I could have imagined.

The violation starts with the criminal justice system. Actually, it starts with involvement with drugs and with men who often mistreat them. Consider the following scenarios: Cindy, aged 35, is serving 10 years for mailing a package containing crack; she had to serve the maximum because of her inability to provide sufficient information about higher-ups. Tangela, aged 22, was sentenced to 10 years for counting money for her boyfriend, a crack

continues...

---

dealer. Cindy and Tangela's boyfriends, who got them started on drugs in the first place, are serving four and five years, respectively. This situation is typical. Women drug users often wind up with longer sentences than the drug-dealing men they are involved with because they lack the information about the drug trafficking operation that the prosecutors seek, or because they are unwilling to go undercover or snitch on family members. The men turn in their girlfriends as the only way they have of getting their lengthy sentences reduced.

This brings us to the criminal justice system and today's gender equality laws that are now being applied in situations in which the woman was an unequal partner; possibly the female partner was even operating under a threat. These gender equality laws which benefit women at the higher echelons are being applied against women at the lower echelons with a vengeance. This failure to take individual circumstances into account, combined with the zero tolerance, anti-drug laws, is responsible for the situation you see today. According to the Bureau of Justice Statistics, between 1990 and 1997, the number of female inmates serving time for drug offenses has nearly doubled, while the number of males in prison increased by only about 48 percent. Almost half of the women in prison today who were sentenced under the new mandatory laws have been convicted of conspiracy.

Two documents of relevance to the harsh sentencing of women are the U.N. Universal Declaration of Human Rights and the U.S. Constitution. Under international law and the U.S. Constitution, the rights of prisoners and of women are enunciated. Article 5 of the Declaration, which states: "No one shall be subjected to torture or to cruel, inhuman or degrading treatment or punishment," is the most relevant in its reference to torture and to cruel, inhuman, or degrading treatment. This clause is used to argue for protection of battered and other mistreated women worldwide.

In 1994 the United States ratified the Convention against the Torture and Other Cruel, Inhuman or Degrading Treatment or Punishment. The U.S. government only signed this treaty with the stipulation that individuals would be given no more rights than those provided by the U.S. Constitution. This restriction has important implications for prisoners who are mistreated in the custody of the state.

U.S. resistance to international human rights commitments was even more pronounced in the failure of the Senate to ratify the Convention on the Elimination of all Forms of Discrimination against Women. The Convention was adopted in 1979 by the U.N. General Assembly. At the time of this writing,

continues...

this treaty is due to come up for the second time for a vote before the full Senate. Of particular relevance to incarcerated women are this treaty's provisions of the right to adequate health care services and protection against gender-based violence. Because it affirms the reproductive rights of women, its passage is problematic.

Other relevant documents of the United Nations are standards that carry less legal weight than treaties but which nevertheless have moral power. Relevant to women who are imprisoned is the U.N. Standard Minimum Rules for the Treatment of Prisoners. Rule 53(3) provides that women should be attended and supervised only by women officers. In the United States, however, nondiscrimination guidelines have removed most restrictions on women working in men's prisons. Accordingly, more often than not, women incarcerated in the United States are guarded by men; uniquely in this country, men are sometimes placed in contact positions over female inmates (van Wormer, 2001). Violations in the form of sexual harassment have been reported in virtually every state (See Amnesty International, 1999). The worst violations have come from privatized prisons; these prisons are staffed by poorly trained and poorly paid correctional officers.

The stories of rape, revenge deprivations, forced nudity in lockup, pregnancies in a closed system where the only males were the guards, forced abortions, and solitary confinement of complainants and witnesses to the abuses barely received notice until seven or eight years ago. It was thanks to the facts revealed in a string of lawsuits that organizations such as Amnesty International were able to run investigations of their own.

A major setback to the civil rights of inmates came in the form of the passage of the Prison Litigation Reform Act in 1995. This act limits judicial supervision of prisons and thereby reduces the civil rights of inmates. The difficulty of litigation notwithstanding, substantial settlements have been awarded in a number of high-profile cases.

Labor exploitation is another area of human rights concern. In 1979, to ensure a cheap labor pool, Congress began a process of deregulation that allowed private corporations to exploit the captive labor market for profit. Modern-day prison labor bears a frightening resemblance to slavery that few people acknowledge. With wages as low as 11 cents an hour in some places and no benefits or vacations, the prisoners must choose between taking low-paying jobs or serving longer sentences, because "good time" policies subtract days from one's total sentence for good behavior and days worked. Such prison labor practices bear a striking resemblance to slavery,

continues...

and this is more than coincidental. In fact, involuntary servitude as punishment for crime is *legal* under the U.S. Constitution (13th Amendment), but not under the Universal Declaration of Human Rights (United Nations, 1948) which, as a more comprehensive document, outlaws slavery of all forms.

Female immigrants, including refugees in detention, are another group of women who have suffered serious human rights violations. Even before the war on terrorism was declared, brutal treatment of detained political refugees was the norm. Yet because the detainees are not U.S. citizens, they are considered to be outside the jurisdiction of the protections of the U.S. Constitution. They are not, however, outside the scope of international law.

Are there any positive developments relevant to women and the criminal justice system? Yes, there are drug courts that send women addicts to treatment instead of to prison, and there are restorative justice programs that focus on restitution rather than retribution. And, according to my survey of women's prison wardens, tighter restrictions are quietly being placed on male officers.

The War on Terrorism and the Thirst for Power

Under the U.S. Patriot Act of 2001, the U.S. attorney general was given unprecedented powers to detain non-citizens on national security grounds. Under this act, non-citizens suspected of terrorist acts could be held in custody indefinitely (Human Rights Watch, 2002). New orders by the President permitted military jurisdiction over non-citizens and military commissions to hear cases that were not subject to the rules governing due process safeguards required at regular military court-martials. Such safeguards as presumption of innocence, protection against forced confessions, and the right of appeal would no longer apply. By November 2001, more than 1,100 people, mostly Arabs or Muslim men, had been detained in this fashion. These steps taken after September 11 were an erosion of key values including the rule of law, according to the *Human Rights Watch World Report*.

Following September 11 in the United States, a war mentality ensued. Customary adherence to international law gave way to a new ethos that was made palatable to the American people by a constant media bombardment of reports concerning terrorism and the possibilities of far worse horrors to be inflicted upon Americans. In the war against "evildoers" and "an axis of evil," in President George W. Bush's terminology, the relinquishment of human rights protections seemed a small price to pay as did the shift in government spending away from the public welfare and health care onto "national security" and defense. Recently, Nobel Prize recipient Jimmy Carter (2002) expressed his concern in an article titled "The Troubling New Face of America."

Fundamental changes are taking place in the historical policies of the United States with regard to human rights, our role in the community of nations and the Middle East peace process—largely without definitive debates (except at times within the administration). (A 31)

Plans got underway for expenditures of up to $100 billion for a full-blown war against Iraq that ideally would result in "regime change." The "pre-emptive strike" concept (attack a country *before* it becomes a threat) represented an altered model for conducting foreign affairs as did the acceptance of assassinations of leaders of enemy states.

Human Rights Watch has been at the forefront of efforts to promote the International Criminal Court, a permanent tribunal to investigate and prosecute individuals accused of genocide or other wars against humanity. Such a truly international court would hold all countries accountable. The United States, under President Bush's leadership, however, "unsigned" the United States from the U.N. treaty establishing the international court. Special arrangements were then made with the United Nations to protect U.S. "peacekeepers" from accountability to the international community for human rights violations.

Civil liberties do not count for much in a warfare state; the rights of people who look like the enemies count for little as well. Just as peace and social justice are interdependent (NASW, 2000c), so the impact of war is brutalizing on all those who are caught in its web. Not only the tragic loss of life and traumatized lives, but also the enormous drain on the world's dwindling natural resources, are antithetical to global social welfare and security (NASW, 2000c). For the sake of the welfare of all people and the balanced economic and social development of nations, the United States should consistently emphasize cooperation in its foreign policy, as NASW urges in its policy statement on peace and social justice.

Social work and the peace movement have a longstanding connection. Jane Addams, the founding mother of social work, was a pacifist who saw herself as a citizen of the world. She believed that violence was used because people lacked knowledge of other ways to fight injustice (Farrell, 1967). Social work has continued to have a strong peace movement within its ranks. Social workers, as Verschelden (1993) tells us, have a moral responsibility to work toward a redirection in federal spending—away from militarism and globally toward the creation of a safe and just environment. "Promoting peace and social justice and resisting nuclear war are consistent with the central values of the social work profession, which stress self-determination, human rights, and social equity" (Van Soest, 1995, p. 1814). Interestingly, the resolution that Congress recently passed, to back the president's request for authorization to use the U.S. forces against Iraq if Iraq did not relinquish weapons of mass destruction, failed to acknowledge our own role in acquiring and selling such weapons ("Nonviolent Solution Backed on Iraq," 2002).

War, in its preparation and execution, has a strange, almost addictive attraction to people. It is associated with bonding, pride, patriotism, and a sense of purpose.

Only in hindsight does the futility of war come to light. The cartoon book, *Addicted to War: Why the U.S. Can't Kick Militarism* (Andreas, 2002) graphically illustrates the history. Taking the long view, Moyers (2002, October) similarly grasps this strange attraction: "Ah, the glories of war, the adrenalin that flows to men behind the desks at the very thought of the armies that will march, the missiles that will fly, the ships that will sail, on their command."

Much of the radical commentary about the military preparation to invade Iraq concerns the need for oil. However, logically speaking, conservation of resources would make more sense. Instead of the ongoing construction of highways, the building of urban and rural mass transportation systems would be more to the point. Working *with* rather than *against* the Middle Eastern countries would make more sense as well.

Upon hearing one of President Bush's "call to arms," I went, almost as if compelled, to my bookshelf and picked up a book I had not fingered through since the 1960s. The book was *The Arrogance of Power* by then Senator William Fulbright (1966). Fulbright, who was chair of the Foreign Relations Committee, had written the book to express his dismay at American foreign policy. My eye hit upon passages that I had underlined 35 years before. I then reread how America, caught up in the mire of the war in Vietnam, was in danger of losing its perspective on what exactly is within the realm of its power and what is beyond it. Above all, as Fulbright had noted, America was showing signs of that "arrogance of power" that had destroyed nations in the past. Lack of assurance tends to heed an exaggerated sense of power or need for power, he explained.

But the part that really took me aback was his review of the history of war and his gripping conclusion:

> Many of the wars fought by man—I am tempted to say most—have been fought over such abstraction (Who has the best religion? To prove they are bigger, better, stronger). The more I puzzle over the great wars of history, the more I am inclined to the view that the causes attributed to them—territory, markets, resources, the defenses or perpetuation of great principles—were not the root causes at all but rather explanations or excuses for certain unfathomable drives of human nature. (p. 5)

What this explanation says to me now is that there are psychological motives that underlie much of this international competition and rivalry that have more to do with irrational aspects of human behavior than with the control of the market or balancing the national budget. I have always thought the amount of oil consumed in warfare, supposedly to gain access to oil, was far disproportionate to any possible gain. Fulbright's study of power is an important reminder to search for the irrational as well as the rational motive in human affairs.

Whether or not we accept Fulbright's arrogance-of-power thesis, we can certainly make the case that capitalism, globalism, and military industrialism have combined to provide a war on terrorism in the absence of any scientific study of whether dropping bombs on a people effectively will combat terrorism or conversely (as in the Gulf War) plant the seeds for hatred and further terrorist attacks. We can certainly make the case, as did Martin Luther King (1967) in the quote that introduces this chapter, that "the ultimate weakness of violence is that it is a descending spiral begetting the very thing it seeks to destroy" (p. 62).

Summary and Conclusion

This chapter has shown the inextricable links among social and economic injustice and the use of raw power in our nation's "welfare reform" enactments; the mass incarceration of drug users and, following September 11, of "enemy combatants"; the official harassment of citizens from nations of the Middle East; in our national repudiation of the dictates of international law; and above all, in the preparation for war, militarily and ideologically. Central to all these issues is an injustice related to the denial of human rights. The human rights creed, as set forth in the U.N. Universal Declaration of Human Rights, is as relevant today as it was in the post-war world in which it was conceived. Freedom from fear and freedom from want are the twin aspirations of this remarkable document. Social workers will find many of its principles incarnated in our NASW (1996) Code of Ethics, especially under Standard 6, "Social Worker's Ethical Responsibilities to the Broader Society." This standard internationalizes social work and relates ethical standards to the broader environment.

Injustice stems not only from economic inequities but also from an inequitable power structure that divides the races and ethnic groups within their class. To challenge such oppression, a human rights value base is essential as an organizing framework. When considered through the lens of human rights, personal problems can be seen more clearly as political problems. Because of the universality of human rights, women and indigenous peoples from all over the world can hold their nations accountable to a common standard. Moreover, they can organize. The next chapter will move us from the study of injustice to direct social action.

Seven
From Policy Analysis to Restoring Justice

> Where after all, do universal human rights begin? In small places, close to home—so close and so small that they can't be seen on any map of the world. Yet they are the world of the individual person.
>
> Eleanor Roosevelt

> Human suffering anywhere concerns men and women everywhere.
>
> Elie Wiesel

On the road to restoring justice, a good starting point is radical policy analysis: *policy analysis* to relate to the intellectual aspect of the venture, *radical* to remind us of the structural component in social injustice. Our journey will be informed by the thought-provoking work of Gil, whose book *Confronting Injustice and Oppression* (1998) spells out the concepts and strategies of radical policy analysis. The model provided by Gil is primarily heuristic, or designed for the student/ activist to discern the path for himself or herself. Accordingly, discussion of this framework will lead us to a consideration of the teaching/learning process itself. What is "education to be an ally"? How can a social justice and/or human rights perspective serve as the organizing framework for social policy evaluation? These are among the issues to be addressed in the opening pages of this chapter.

Effecting social change toward a just society—this is the basic theme of both these final chapters. In light of the fact that they most directly deal with society's ills, social workers often see themselves as change agents. The role of change agent, whether working within the system or without, can be quite frustrating. Sometimes it takes drastic measures such as "whistleblowing" to bring about change in the organization. (Later in the chapter we will explore this phenomenon in some depth.) A less painful way to bring about desirable change is to work toward progressive reform through lobbying or maybe writing op-ed articles in the local newspaper. Advocacy for social justice might take the form of work to increase funding for a women's shelter or to establish drug courts to help keep people who suffer from drug addiction out of prison and into treatment programming instead.

From *outside* the system at the grassroots level, typical activities that change agents might pursue range from waging informational campaigns through establishing radical listservs and websites on behalf of a particular cause or causes; to involvement in welfare rights marches and other forms of direct action; to involvement in antiwar or anti-World Trade Organization demonstrations. From an international perspective, the work of nongovernmental organizations (NGOs) is of vital importance in the protection of civil and minority rights. Armed only with access to the printing press, Internet, and media sources, NGOs such as Amnesty International have aroused the consciousness of the world. Many social workers and social work students and educators are members of such organizations, and we would be remiss to ignore their contributions to social reform.

On multiple levels, much exciting work is being done by social work practitioners and educators in the interests of social justice. To capture the special quality of the various change efforts described, this chapter makes extensive use of the personal narrative. Thus we will hear from heroes in places as diverse as at a city council, on the "new freedom bus," at a Southern church, and in a Midwestern prison. Common to all these accounts is the refusal to be silenced in the face of injustice.

David Gil's Radical Policy Analysis

Policy analysis, as we learned in Chapter 4, is a strategy for studying a particular policy and assessing the possibility of introducing progressive change. Engagement in the analysis of policy is an exercise in critical thinking as we weigh existing standards of social welfare against a higher standard such as that contained in the United Nations Universal Declaration of Human Rights (see Appendix). A human rights focus provides a meaningful standard in that it takes social work out of the realm of pathologizing and directs our attention to systemic roots of social injustice. A human rights focus, moreover, provides us with a valuable theoretical basis for assisting in social change (Watkinson, 2001). The starting point to even contemplate meaningful social change is radical policy analysis.

Radical policy analysis is defined by Gil (1998) as a didactic exercise designed to enable the student or scholar to "discern changes in the relative circumstances and power of people, social groups, and classes, and in the relations among them" (p. 121). The focus of Gil's analysis is twofold: to study the power arrangements in society and to gauge the possibility of significant change to help people realize their basic needs thereby.

In a tightly structured, capitalistic system such as exists in the United States, as Gil reminds us, the consequences of tampering with one aspect of that system can have a rebounding effect on the whole system. Imagine the consequences of a successful proposal to make the minimum wage a living wage, for example, or to remove the burden of health care provision from the employer. To learn the intended and unintended consequences of a given policy proposal, Gil recommends that we conduct a comparative examination of alternative policies that are all geared toward the same end.

How does radical policy analysis begin? The effort, according to Gil, begins with a shared assessment of the fundamental causes of social injustice. Such an assessment necessarily brings us into the realm of power arrangements and social and political imbalances in society. Addressing these imbalances in the power relations might imply the need for revolutionary change. Here is where the *radical* aspect of Gil's formulation enters the picture. The revelations that likely would unfold in the study of the power relations among the various social groups and classes in the society might evoke a desire for some sort of rectification to set things right. (We discuss the restorative process of reparations in Chapter 8.)

The framework for Gil's radical policy analysis consists of five seemingly innocuous questions:

1. Which societal domain (for example, health care allocations) does the policy address?
2. How would the policy affect this domain (for example, a government reimbursement scheme) in concrete terms?
3. How would society's institutions and policy system, and the extent to which people can meet their basic needs, be affected by the concrete effects of the policy?
4. What effects may be expected from the interactions of the policy with various forces within and outside the society?
5. What alternative policies could be formulated concerning the same and different objectives, and how would they compare? (pp. 121–122).

Although the questions addressed here are no more radical in their implications than is our anti-oppressive policy analytical scheme presented in Chapter 4, Gil's theoretical scheme is focused more on the root causes of issues and on major systems change and less on progressive initiatives. The root causes of a lot of social problems today, as Gil accurately notes, are ingrained in global capitalism. Real change of the social realities, accordingly, can be "assumed to require transformations of entire policy systems rather than marginal adjustments of specific policies" (p. 119).

The ethical goal of Gil's policy analysis is to take us beyond single issues, then, and into the arena of collective political action; the pursuit of social justice is best accomplished through the building of social movements. In fact, policy analysis itself might be carried out in cooperation with community organizations that confront injustice and oppression. Social work education from this perspective should be offered in a non-hierarchical, non-competitive context; social work education should be primarily social justice education.

Teaching/Learning Concepts of Justice

Last year at a national social work conference I attended, the presenters reported on an informal survey they had taken of their American students of social work and then of their Albanian counterparts (Downey & Romano, 2001). How many had read the Universal Declaration of Human Rights? Surprisingly, only a minority of the Albanian students had read the document, but twice as many of the Albanians as American students had done so. Upon my return from the conference I posed the same question to my advanced-standing graduate class. A few had heard of the Declaration, but none had read it. I then proceeded to pass out copies of this document which, though written in 1948, is equally relevant today. Our class project was to compare the articles of this universal document with the ethical standards contained in Section 6 of the NASW (1996) Code of Ethics. Both documents, as we found, have a great deal to say about social justice and the standards toward which we, as social workers and citizens, should aspire.

Teaching social work from a human rights perspective entails a paradigm shift as we move from a framework based on needs—the quest for what clients need to live productive lives—to a notion that to have one's needs met is a basic and intrinsic right. In this era of global market politics and welfare constraints, the teaching of human rights becomes a journey of discovery for professor and student alike.

Following Van Soest (1995), social justice can be presented in terms of three components: *legal* justice which is concerned with what a person owes to society; *commutative* justice which relates to what people owe each other; and *distributive* justice, which is what society owes the person (p. 1811). To consider one policy, for example, eligibility requirements for nursing home care, is to understand a myriad of regulations, acts, norms, and obligations as they are integrated into the larger pattern of our culture that we have come intuitively, if not uncritically, to know.

What kind of teaching philosophy is the most suited to the study of social justice/human rights concepts? Pedagogical expert Palmer (1998) puts it best: The classroom he envisions is "neither teacher-centered nor student-centered but subject-centered" (p. 116). The ideal learning community, in Palmer's conceptualization, is one in which less is more. Drawing on the metaphor of Blake's poetic line, "to see a world in a grain of sand," Palmer asks, "Why do we keep dumping truckloads of sand on our students, blinding them to the whole, instead of lifting up a grain so they can learn for themselves?" (p. 122). Teaching from the microcosm for in-depth understanding rather than a bombardment of multiplicity of facts is the Palmer method of education. As applied to social justice, a thorough analysis of one social policy will reveal its relation to the whole as well as its interconnectedness with other policies. These three components, the law, the customs, and the distribution of resources, as we have seen throughout this book, are tightly interwoven.

Educating Allies

Information provided in this section pertains not just to professor–student but also to clinicians who offer workshops on confronting injustice or on "becoming an ally," to use Bishop's phraseology. Bishop (1994) illustrates popular education in terms of a spiral that moves from personal experience (such as with discrimination due to a role or status) to reflection, to analysis, to strategy, to action, and then begins again with new experience gained from the action. Keeping in mind that we play the role of oppressor as well as the person oppressed, Bishop argues that, on the road of being educated as an ally, we first have a great deal of unlearning to do.

One exercise Bishop finds especially useful is to draw an imaginary line down the center of the floor and call out various forms of oppression. People cross over the line as their identity category is called out. One side is privileged (for example, men) and one side is oppressed in each category. Participants discuss their experiences as a way of impressing upon them the basic concept of oppression.

In her workshops, Bishop uses flipcharts to generate awareness through provocative questions such as, "What do White people (politicians) gain from racism?" Participants work on the questions in small groups. No course or workshop is complete, according to Bishop, without action planning. Small groups work out strategies, then present these back to the large group. Bishop sums up her experience as follows:

> Educating allies is…a very satisfying form of education. Bridges are being built on the spot, good will and risk taking are being exercised, communication is taking place across the barriers of centuries, and experiments are initiated which have immediate importance in the process of building a new, more cooperative society. (p. 118)

Relevant to social work's person-in-the-environment configuration, Miller and Schamess (2000) take us into the arena of social psychology. How do we perceive things? How do we reconcile discrepancies in perception? What we are talking about is a situation of *cognitive dissonance*, the need to reconcile contradictions in reality, to explain, for example, how poverty can exist in a society rich with opportunity for success. To resolve the dissonance, our tendency is to redefine our perception of reality to fit notions that are comforting and consistent with principles of justice. Miller and Schamess write:

> One way in which white, middle and upper class citizens can resolve dissonance between societal myths of equal opportunity and the systematic pattern of inequality that exists in American Society is to target an oppressed subgroup and blame it for the adversity it suffers as a result of discrimination, prejudice, and/or inequality.(p. 49).

Understanding this natural tendency is essential to education for self/cultural awareness. If we are engaged in "teaching to transgress" (in the words of hooks, 1994), understanding the psychological forces we are up against is a crucial first step. This tendency is related to the blaming-the-victim concept described in Chapter 2.

Within the college classroom setting, Nagda et al. (1999) utilize a format of intergroup dialogues as a means of providing theoretical insights into the causes of dehumanizing conditions; such an approach, they argue, can help lessen the gap between social work's commitment to social justice and the actual practice of challenging social injustice. The intergroup dialogue format involves a brief lecture followed by small group-facilitated discussion in homogeneous racial/ ethnic identity groups engaged in dialogue around heated issues such as advantages based on racial group membership and affirmative action. In dialogue with the multi-group setting, students share their thoughts and feelings. Preliminary results showed that the intergroup dialogues helped participants gain insights into the impact of oppression and privilege and develop a commitment to greater personal and social change. It was clear that identity groups knew of their own oppression, but not of that of others.

In social work education, as Miller and Schamess (2000) suggest, the artificial gap between clinical and policy practice is reinforced by rigid educational structures. The work requirements of agency practice compound this false dualism. Policy and practice are inextricably linked, and human rights issues transcend them both. Accordingly, Downey and Romano (2001) of Colorado State University argue for teaching human rights concepts *throughout* the social work curriculum—that instructors advocate, teach, and model action that promotes full human rights. Similarly, in my course, "Social Welfare: A World View" at the University of Northern Iowa, students are assigned to form groups for class presentations on countries of the group's choice. In panels, students then present data on the various countries to show compliance or non-compliance with the Universal Declaration. They are referred to Amnesty International and Human Rights Watch as well as relevant United Nations investigative reports for their critical analysis. Comparisons between the selected country and the United States are prompted by means of consideration of the following questions: How does cultural heritage in the country of choice interfere with the human rights of vulnerable populations? Does the nation's criminal justice system abide by the standards of civil and political rights? Which groups are discriminated against in that society? These are the guiding questions of the research.

Social work educators can expand the person-in-environment configuration to emphasize the importance of a safe and just environment and the detrimental nature of an unsafe and or unjust environment. The physical environment can be viewed as essential to safety and health. As stated in the Universal Declaration, "Everyone has the right to life, liberty, and security of person" (Article 3). (Article 3 is occasionally cited in reference to worldwide female abuse and the need for protection of victims of domestic violence.)

The barriers to human rights education in the United States are many. The absence of a human rights focus at the high school level as opposed to a focus on the representation of America as the "land of opportunity" creates a climate in which any notion of entitlement is perceived as alien, even un-American. Dewees and Roche (2001) list three major factors that challenge U.S. social work educators in teaching about human rights. These are (1) the international human rights principle of indivisibility and its points of incongruence with the U.S. mainstream values; (2) the principle of universality which sometimes conflicts with the social work focus on individualism and respect for cultural diversity; and (3) the political action implications of a commitment to human rights analysis and their underlying values. To effectively meet the challenge, Dewees and Roche assign students relevant United Nations documents, including documents unratified by the United States as well as ratified documents. Additionally, detailed case vignettes are provided in the form of moving narratives that describe circumstances of extreme oppression. Students then analyze the readings from a human rights and social work perspective. Compelling videos are utilized as well to provide an international context to the study of human rights. The instructors have found that students are able to relate the case material to the world of social work practice and to appreciate the commonalities across the lines of personal identity.

In another contribution to the learning experience, Chen-Hayes (2001) has devised a social justice advocacy readiness questionnaire with 188 items related to issues of race, sex, ethnicity, and sexual orientation to stimulate self-awareness. Practitioners and members of the community can evaluate themselves and their organizations to promote social justice knowledge and advocacy through use of this question-and-answer format.

Cultivation of a social change approach is a major goal of the unique, three-part social policy/human rights sequence of courses at Springfield College in Massachusetts. Students are given the option of monitoring governmental initiatives for implementing a program such as a violence prevention training curriculum in the schools.

Working Within the System to Change the System

Upon graduation, many social workers go to work in social welfare systems that are coercive, punitive, discriminatory, and bureaucratic (Pelton, 2001). In corrections, child welfare, and substance abuse treatment, in particular, social workers are obliged to work as agents of social control. Commenting on the contradiction between the lofty goals of textbooks framed by models of empowerment, and the agency focus on client rather then structural inadequacies, Pelton ponders the question, to what extent "social education itself has become an accomplice to unjust systems"? (p. 439). The answer, I believe, is found in the truism that the injustice ingrained in the system infects every part of the system. The best that social education can do is to help prepare students to change what they can in small ways while not losing sight of their broader ideals. The creative and committed social justice-oriented clinician can find ways to maintain his or her vision and practices, as Swenson (1998) assures us: Social justice-oriented clinicians can support service innovations and work to develop new structures in agencies to counter oppressive beliefs and practices.

There are many avenues toward reform, and the best place to be to provide or initiate reform is from a position of power, usually within the system. Workers at the supervisory or administrative level have clear advantages in crafting programs and providing public testimony. Yet the front-line workers, too, have certain advantages in terms of their familiarity with the day-to-day day struggles of their clients. They can provide testimony of an especially graphic sort. A social worker counseling battered women, for instance, may draw on his or her direct knowledge of the human rights violations of victims of battering as public documentation that seeks to end domestic violence (Asamoah, Healy, & Mayadas, 1997).

According to the first and most basic ethical standards spelled out in the NASW Code of Ethics (1996), social workers' primary responsibility is to promote the well being of clients (p. 7). In relation to social services delivery, this obligation encompasses activities that promote clients' access to social services, maximize their rights, and reduce obstacles to services (DuBois & Miley, 2002). With respect to social policy, social workers advocate changes or, in today's global economy, fight to maintain funding for the social services we currently have. Within the agencies themselves, social justice work entails working at the agency level to develop client-centered practices and the education of colleagues about social justice principles (Swenson, 1998).

Flynn (1995) explores opportunities for achieving social justice goals in the organizational arena. Such opportunities are found in common principles of administrative law such as due process, and in the organizational policies themselves. Staff members bent on change must work at developing credibility over time. Radical advocacy is contrasted with strategies built on the existing social order of today's social agency environment. Such strategies may involve institutionalized democratic processes such as standing committees to hear grievances, review agency policies at fixed intervals, and/or perform evaluations of policy decisions and of the decision makers themselves.

Grant writing is an excellent source for effecting progressive change for the betterment of our clients. This is change, moreover, that has the full blessing of the authorities in that it can bring in the much-needed revenue to provide badly needed services. Typical examples are obtaining funding for victims-assistance programs, women's shelters, and prenatal clinics for high-risk mothers, and conducting funded treatment effectiveness studies with a control group. Sometimes the cost of successful programming will get picked up by a more permanent funding source.

Sometimes, however, the individual practitioner finds himself or herself estranged from the behavior and even values of the human service organization. Then the individual, whether out of desperation or with some realistic possibility of change, may turn to outside sources—licensing (overseeing) organizations, the courts, or even the media.

Whistleblowing

Whistleblowing, or what Glazer and Glazer (1991) interestingly term "ethical resistance," can be conceived of as an activity of last resort in an unusual and extreme situation. Rarely studied in the social work literature or in schools of social work, ethical resistance is a contingency for which the public or private employee may want to be prepared. Without the knowledge of what whistleblowing entails—the dynamics of resistance and adversarial counter-resistance tactics—the individual may pay an unnecessarily high psychological price.

Whistleblowing is not defined or even listed in the NASW *Encyclopedia of Social Work* (Edwards, 1995). *Whistleblowing* is defined in some depth, however, in the *Social Work Dictionary* (Barker, 2003) as follows:

> Informing those people in positions of influence or authority outside an organization about the existence of an organization's practices that are illegal, wasteful, dangerous, or otherwise contrary to its stated policies. The informant is compelled to notify outsiders (investigative commissions, the media, ombudspersons, congresspersons, and others) because authorities within the organization ignore complaints. Some organizations, such as the U.S. government, encourage whistleblowing by maintaining toll-free hot lines for anonymous tipsters and by trying to protect employees from subsequent retribution from employers. (p. 463)

Terms such as whistleblowing seem to capture of themselves, in memorable vernacular, an experience that social workers would recognize in all its intricacies and even forbiddenness. Images that are generated range from "the lone crusader" and hero to the bitter worker bent on revenge. As a term, whistleblowing is vested with both positive and negative characteristics. The positive side is conveyed in the occasional brief *NASW News* announcement, "money available for job loss due to whistleblowing." The NASW (1996) Code of Ethics makes no mention of whistleblowing, however. The closest standard is under Commitment to Employers: "Social workers should take reasonable steps to ensure that their employing organizations' practices are consistent with the NASW Code of Ethics" (Standard 3.09d, p. 21). The British Association of Social Workers (BASW) Code of Ethics (2002), in contrast, is far more emphatic: "Social workers will...familiarize themselves with the complaints and whistleblowing procedures of their workplace, with the relevant provisions of the Public Interest Disclosure Act and with BASW procedures for complaints against members" (Section 4.3j). The Public Interest Disclosure Act of 1998 is a new law introduced in the United Kingdom to protect employees who blow the whistle on employers. It is said to be the most far-reaching whistleblower protection law in the world (Dyer, 1999). In the United Kingdom, a new draft code of conduct for social care staff is to include a clause requiring them to blow the whistle on colleagues who abuse or exploit clients and refer the matter to the appropriate authorities.

To the degree that the company or concern is viewed as a malevolent entity, the whistleblower becomes a hero. Thus Hollywood immortalized Karen Silkwood for her ill-fated attempt to expose conditions in a plutonium plant. In recent years, we have seen major corporations such as tobacco companies and Enron "brought to their knees" due to the heroic efforts of former top-level insiders. Read, for example, about *Time* magazine's "Persons of the Year" whistleblowers Cynthia Cooper of WorldCom who exposed its cover-up bookkeeping; Coleen Rowley, FBI attorney who exposed the FBI's refusal to investigate an accused terrorist; and Sherron Watkins, vice-president of Enron, who exposed Enron's ethical violations (Lacayo & Ripley, 2002).

The progress in perception of whistleblowing from a vice (disloyalty to the agency/employer) to a virtue is chronicled in *Whistleblowing in the Social Services* (Hunt, 1998). In this unusual book, social workers speak out about their own experiences of exposing system failures that placed children at risk in England and Wales. That social workers and related professionals require training for accountability so that the public can be protected is a major argument of Hunt's volume.

That whistleblowing as an act of resistance traditionally has been discouraged by the profession is borne out by even a cursory review of the social work literature. Consider the following statement by Levy (1976, p. 171): "It is the agency's policies that the social worker has committed himself to."

Levi (1991) even recommended that the social worker who cannot honor the policies leave the agency. Kurzman (1983, p. 108), likewise, suggested that social workers caught in an unresolvable ethical dilemma "retain the right to leave." Similarly, Pawlak (1976) stressed the importance of "going through channels" as opposed to using "radical tactics."

Whistleblowing becomes, in this framework, a radical and controversial alternative. In preparation to "blow the whistle," one may choose to continue to work inside to expose the violations and ethical irregularities to the outside. Yet secrecy is necessarily required—secrecy and some degree of deception. Such ethical compromise may be regarded as an acceptable means towards achieving some higher end.

There is some evidence that social worker whistleblowers against their agency are treated with greater respect today then formerly. In the past decade, *NASW News* contained a rare headline on the subject: "Member Blows Whistle on Rx Refills" (1990). Kathy Leddy was fired from Hackensack Medical Center in New Jersey two months after she complained to the state attorney general's office that social workers were ordering prescription refills—essentially they were practicing medicine without a license. Leddy was granted an out-of-court settlement and was later hired by another medical center in New York. The New Jersey clinic was reprimanded by the New Jersey State Board of Medical Examiners and was forced to end all illegal practices.

The public recognition of whistleblowers against corporations that were bilking citizens of their savings has helped create a climate of support for persons who do not "tow the line." A course offered at the University of Pennsylvania may reflect increased attention to ethical resistance as a viable, even perhaps the only viable, option for fighting agency injustice. Significantly, the course offering "Social Work Values and Ethics" includes the study of whistleblowing as an ethical concept (see http://www.ssw.upenn.edu/home/programs/msw-courses.html).

Whistleblowing, in social work terminology, is more than a mere slang expression in spite of the inherent clumsiness of the term. Whistleblowing is a direct act of exposure against an individual or the agency for violation of societal ethics or law. Typical grounds for complaint may be violations of labor laws, health violations, laws pertaining to business and delivery of services, anti-discrimination laws, and laws and rules protecting clients (e.g., confidentiality). For whistleblowing to be successful, the violation of the law or professional ethics must be concrete and provable. Then there must be official machinery for investigating the charges. In the final analysis, as an after-everything-else-has-been-tried strategy, whistleblowing can be considered effective if the offending behavior or practice is brought to a halt and appropriate changes are made.

Still, whistleblowing by the social worker against a social work agency is an exceedingly risky (career-wise) and unpopular act. But how about whistleblowing in the non-traditional and perhaps culturally alien setting, such as a corrections facility or a for-profit hospital? Here, given the social work focus on dignity and individual worth, the value dilemmas are rampant. While corrections prioritizes security, private health care providers prioritize profits. An ethical issue may arise when the company's violation of standards produces harm to the individual worker or consumer of services. In this situation, the social worker, as representative of the company or agency, becomes an accomplice in the wrongdoing. Here the impetus for whistleblowing may be unleashed.

Many professional workers may be inclined to sacrifice ethical standards for personal career goals. The employer generally has the upper hand because of personal power, network connections, and knowledge of personnel legal protocol (Kenyon, 1999). The way of whistleblowing is the way to loss of employment, friends, social isolation, and impoverishment (see Alford, 2002), the opening of the door to ridicule and predictable "How could you?" looks that can kill. More subjectively, I would place whistleblowing on a continuum somewhere between the noblest self sacrifice and an irresistible quest for revenge. I believe that the worker enters this course as an act of utter desperation, all other resources having been exhausted.

This section on whistleblowing has a special meaning for me due to a personal experience at a private for-profit treatment center in Norway. In an article about my experience (van Wormer, 1995b), I presented my transition from company public relations advocate to betrayer of trust. The stages of this transition can be reconstructed as follows (see also van Wormer, 1997, Summer):

- Beginnings of distress; working through channels.
- Clinging to professional ideology and mixed loyalty to the company.
- Transitional stage from defender of the organization to spy.

- Reliance on strength of personal belief system.
- Seeking help from outside inspectors.
- Finding allies in the struggle.
- Most allies fired or quit.
- Publishing exposé article in widely circulated social work journal.
- Company retaliation; ostracism by staff.
- Resolution and settlement through social work union legal support.
- Failure of agency to change internally or of outside bodies to take action.
- Forgiveness and understanding by most earlier critics.
- Reclaiming one's professional life.

Seeking Change Through Legal Channels

The legal structure, as we have seen, plays a significant role in creating and perpetuating social injustice. The law can exclude certain groups from protection afforded to others. Consider, for example, the failure to grant gays and lesbians civil rights protections or to provide certain immigrant groups the same legal rights as citizens (Criminal Justice Collective of Northern Arizona University, 2000). See Box 7.1 to read of one effort (this one unsuccessful) that is illustrative of a national, city-by-city campaign to pass inclusive anti-discrimination ordinances.

As a member of the Cedar Falls City Council and a social worker, Elaine Pfalzgraf presented the following speech. As hers was the only vote in favor of the motion, this was very much a dissenting opinion. The issue was the need for a non-discrimination ordinance to protect the rights of sexual minorities within the city. This speech was given and televised before a packed audience of mostly gays and lesbians and their allies. A number of opponents, including a Boy Scout troop, were present in the audience.

Box 7.1   Sexual Orientation Motion

by Elaine Pfalzgraf, MSW, Member of Cedar Falls City Council

I feel very strongly that the committee should support the addition of sexual orientation to our human rights ordinance as a basis of discrimination in Cedar Falls. These two words include discrimination against heterosexuals as well as gays, lesbians, and bisexuals—all legal sexual orientations.

Gays, lesbians, and bisexuals pay taxes and user fees. They provide city services and contribute significantly to our community. They should have the same legal right to be protected under our laws as do all other Cedar Falls Citizens. We have already set the precedent by protecting gay, lesbian, and

continues...

---

bisexual city staff members through city policy, and we need to extend that same protection to the full community.

Cedar Falls is currently in the process of developing a comprehensive plan for the year 2010 and we have included the language of equal protections for all legal sexual orientations in that plan. Cedar Falls is a democracy; it is a plurality; it is a secular community that prides itself on its inclusiveness, progressiveness, and belief in human dignity, uniqueness, openness, intelligence, and its desire for diversity. By adding sexual orientation to the list of those receiving equal rights in our city, we will be enhancing those community strengths.

In my other life I am an independently licensed social worker and the walls in my office have heard many stories of pain, fear, distress, social injustice, and courage as people have come in for therapy and consultations—many who are dealing with the issues we are faced with tonight.

I have a poster on one of the walls in my office that for me states very clearly why passing this ordinance change is so critical:

"In Germany they first came for the Communist and I didn't speak up because I wasn't a Communist—

Then they came for the Jews and I didn't speak up because I wasn't a Jew—

Then they came for the trade unionist and I didn't speak up because I wasn't a trade unionist—

Then they came for the Catholics and I didn't speak up because I was a Protestant—

Then they came for me and there was no one left to speak up."

I urge the committee to use their compassion, their fair-mindedness, their concern for their fellow citizens, and their democratic responsibility to add the words sexual orientation to our human rights ordinance. I so move.

Source: Pfalzgraf, 2001. Printed with permission of Elaine Pfalzgraf.

In confronting oppression and restoring justice, a logical starting point is through organizing a movement to replace unjust legislation with legislation that is humanistic and fair. Activists should consult the web site at http://www.statepolicy.org, which is operated by the Influencing State Policy (ISP) association. ISP was founded in 1997 to increase social work efficacy in influencing state-level policymaking and legislation. "Policy affects practice; practitioners affect policy" is the ISP motto (Schneider & Lester, 2000, p. 115). Given the new federalism which transfers responsibilities to the states, the states have vast authority to design programs that best fit their needs. Under the circumstances, Schneider and Lester utter a call for action for persons at all levels of social work to learn how the state policy process works and how to participate effectively in it.

Reform Through Legislative Advocacy

The NASW Code of Ethics urges social workers "be aware of the political arena on practice and advocate for changes in policy and legislation to improve social conditions in order to meet human needs and promote social justice" (1996, Standard 6.04 A).

Over the years, legislative advocates have played significant roles in improving legislation in the health and human services arena. Schneider and Lester (2000) urge social workers to take their legislative responsibilities seriously, especially today now that the states are being given greater authority over client benefits and treatment possibilities.

In its policy statement, "Electoral Politics," NASW (2000a) describes the social work profession's role in making endorsements of candidates for political office and contributing from a separate fund set up for this purpose to their campaigns. Participation in campaign funding has amplified the political influence of NASW. Support of social worker candidates today is a top professional priority.

As discussed in Chapter 4, lobby days at state legislatures are busy times for social work activists. Typically, on whatever the given day is (it varies by state), busloads of social work students and their faculty travel to the state legislature to hear addresses by key politicians. They then meet with legislators from their own districts or those with similar interests.

One pitfall that I have seen in Iowa is that social workers from various agencies will lobby for increased funding for their particular interest group (for example, substance abuse treatment, halfway houses for persons with mental illness). Often this amounts to playing one group off against another. A united approach, in contrast, might focus on sentencing reform and a concomitant end to prison expansion to free money up for social services provisions.

Indeed, lobbying for cost-effective alternatives to current policies can carry a lot of weight with legislators, especially in these times of fiscal belt-tightening. We will discuss one possible initiative closely related to social justice, one with a great deal of potential of widespread adoption: the "drug court."

Making the Case for Drug Courts

Advocacy for drug courts that mandate treatment and close probationary supervision in lieu of incarceration is an avenue social workers might want to consider as an effective, very doable change effort. In advocating for legislation to set up drug courts, social workers can demonstrate the cost effectiveness of treatment over imprisonment. The money saved thereby can be freed up for positive programming and health care offerings. But more importantly, from a social justice standpoint, drug courts offer a way around the insidious anti-drug laws that impose mandatory minimum sentencing with often tragic consequences for the whole family (van Wormer & Davis, 2003). Such laws are classist and racist as we have seen. Sadly, the criminal justice system attacks most harshly those individuals with the least power to defend themselves.

The injustice in the sentencing laws is especially evident in the disparity in prison terms meted out for powder cocaine versus crack cocaine (the difference here is an incredible 100 to 1) and the new laws against methamphetamine (meth). Crack cocaine is associated with inner-city Blacks; meth with poor rural Whites. Meth is called "the poor man's" cocaine. Actually it is widely used by women, often in conjunction with their boyfriends. Many of the women get hooked attempting to lose weight; the men to have the stamina to work ungodly long hours.

Today, drug offenders account for half of the increase of the total population of nonviolent state prisoners; they now comprise nearly 60% of all federal prison inmates (Drug Strategies, 2001). Children are the innocent victims of the war on drugs, according to a recent report from Human Rights Watch ("Children Are Collateral Casualties of N.Y. Drug Laws," 2002). In the United States, 124,000 children have lost a parent to prison. When a girl loses a mother to prison, there is a high probability she will get into trouble herself. Thus, in many cases, the cycle of state abuse is never ending (see van Wormer, 2001).

Because the cost of prison spending is now the fastest growing category in state budgets, exceeding the rates of increase in state spending on health, welfare, and education (Bureau of Justice Statistics, 1999a), this is the aspect of the state budget to which social workers might direct their attention. A highly feasible and popular-with-the-public alternative to incarceration for drug users is the intensive supervision provided under the auspices of the drug court.

Drug courts began experimentally in Dade County, Florida, as an intensive, judicial-supervised, community-based treatment for felony drug defendants designed to reduce the increasing recidivism rates. A counter-trend to the "lock 'em up" mentality of modern criminal justice, the drug court movement has created a large market for substance abuse counselors to work with offenders in the community.

Diverting nonviolent drug offenders from the prison system into treatment, the drug court experiment has demonstrated that addicts can be returned to work, family, and ultimately the American mainstream (Johnson, 1998). Today, there are just over 700 drug courts in 50 states. Knowing that jail time awaits them if they begin abusing drugs again, offenders have a strong incentive to change. The saving of approximately $14,050 per year offers a strong incentive to the county to keep offenders out of jail as well. A review of this diversion program by the Justice Department indicates a 75% graduation rate. (To graduate one must remain drug free.) Estimates are that, long term, 20% will relapse. Over a nine-year period, 2,500 parents have regained custody of their children. In a systematic evaluation of the drug court operations across the state of Florida, Mayfield, Valentine, and McNeece (1998) applauded the programs as a feasible and more effective alternative to adversarial procedures to combat nationwide drug problems. Such programs offer extensive, long-term treatment at little cost to the offender; many opportunities exist for professionally trained counselors to find employment with such diversionary, community-based programs.

In California, a rigorously designed study of effectiveness of substance abuse treatment showed that the state received a $7 return for every dollar invested, the largest savings of which were from reductions in crime and medical costs (Swan, 1995).

Graduates of a similar three-phase program in Delaware, extending from incarceration where inmates live in a therapeutic community to a 12-month work-release program and then to aftercare or parole, were found to be both drug free and arrest free at much higher rates than were released prisoners in the control group (Hooper, 1997). Meanwhile in Iowa, more than 90% of the defendants in drug courts are methamphetamine users charged with nonviolent crimes. Although about half of the users have relapsed, corrections officials consider the program a success in terms of the 50% who have reclaimed their lives (Zeleny, 1997).

According to a feature story written for the *Join Together Report* by Curley (2002), Wyoming has launched the most comprehensive anti-drug plan in the United States. Funded with proceeds from the state's share of the tobacco settlement, House Bill 59, which has been signed into law, provides for an integrated, statewide alcohol and other drug control plan expected to save money for the state in terms of reducing crime and prison costs. A statewide adult and juvenile drug court system is bolstered by a heavy investment in outpatient and inpatient treatment provisions. Prevention efforts are a major emphasis in this programming. A point to note: Casting the legislation as a child-protection measure was instrumental to its passage, as stated in the article.

But won't most politicians be wary of appearing to be "soft on crime" and refuse to endorse such remedies? Politicians need to be aware that, as registered in a recent opinion poll, public opinion is changing. As an ABC News survey found, most Americans (69%) are in favor of treatment over jail for first- and second-time drug offenders ("Americans Support Drug Treatment Over Jail," 2001). Women, Democrats, and the better educated were the most favorable to treatment options for drug users according to this survey.

Court Litigation

Since the landmark 1954 decision of *Brown v. Board of Education of Topeka*, the courts have become a significant avenue of policy reform (Figueira-McDonough, 1993).

Judicial litigation is therefore of vital importance in policy practice. Policy reform through this means relies on a challenge to the system in the form of a formal complaint on behalf of an individual whose rights have been violated. Social workers can play an invaluable role in gathering data and providing expert testimony, for example, to show a pattern of abuse and neglect by the nursing home industry. They can also refer complainants to lawyers as in the case of class action suits. The greater and clearer the evidence of the infringement of legal rights, as Figueira-McDonough indicates, the stronger the case. Judicial policy making is slow but can have far-reaching consequences over time.

Human Rights Measures

In a unique action, MSW students in conjunction with NASW's Pennsylvania Chapter and other organizations, helped usher in a resolution on economic human rights through the state's House of Representatives (Stoesen, 2002). The resolution, which passed the House, calls for a legislative study into the feasibility of incorporating universal human rights standards, as stated in the Universal Declaration of Human Rights, into the state's laws and policies. The hearings that have been held statewide have offered a vehicle for uniting people living in poverty with each other; it has familiarized people across the state with universal human rights concepts related to the provision of an adequate standard of living and medical care. The state of Hawaii, at present, is the only state that guarantees the rights to healthcare in its state constitution.

Member nations of the European Union have taken a major step in the passage of the 1998 Human Rights Act. This act, according to an article in the *British Journal of Social Work* (Williams, 2001), makes the European Convention on Human Rights directly enforceable by the individual nation's courts and tribunals. The implications for social work policymakers are vast. Service users (what we call clients) can now challenge decisions by social services departments; therefore, according to Williams, the practice of social work must clearly embrace the human rights principles outlined in the Convention. Representative groups can bring a case forward on behalf not only of victims, but also of potential victims. In the European Union, the infliction and threat of corporal punishment against school children thus becomes a clear violation against Article 3 prohibiting torture or inhuman or degrading treatment/punishment. Article 8, which provides the right to respect for private and family life, potentially includes protections on the basis of sexual orientation. The significance of the 1998 Human Rights Act, as Williams suggests, provides a benchmark for reviewing the actions of social service and other public authorities.

Grassroots Organizing

Activities at the National Level

From the late 1960s, the civil rights, antiwar, anti-poverty, and women's movements spawned other social movements as the public attention was drawn to the power that even a small body of committed people can have in shaping social legislation. One lesson learned was the extent to which a sympathetic mass media is essential for arousing mass concern and social activism. Today, reliance on the

Internet helps bolster social organization while sustaining commitment to a common cause, even against the dominance of a corporately owned press.

Social workers can confront social and economic injustice one by one in their counseling-advocacy roles, or they can organize to confront injustice collectively. The profession today faces awesome challenges; many workers are torn between pressures to maintain high standards of efficiency in an environment of ever-diminished levels of external funding and a desire to take a public stand. Many will become disempowered by the seeming futility of much of their work; others will seize the opportunity to build on the current dissatisfaction with the growing gap in the distribution of resources (between rich and poor) to contemplate some kind of social action.

As a grassroots method, social action is communitarian, but its goals are larger than that; social action seeks outcomes that are tangible and controversial (Figueira-McDonough, 1993). Social action strives to make the invisible inequities in society visible for all to see.

One strategy in organizing on behalf of the deprived and impoverished is to obtain the facts and figures on where the money in the federal–state budget is going. Verschelden (1993) articulates the connection among poverty, personal, and domestic forms of violence, social injustice, and the violence of militarism. A redirection of the national budget in which approximately 50 cents of every federal dollar is spent on the military (refer to the government spending "pie" in Chapter 3) from military to domestic priorities, as Verschelden notes, would transform the social environment that we see today. Verschelden's arguments on the negative impact of militarism have even greater resonance today in light of the mounting military–industrial build up.

Activities at the State Level

In common with the peace movement, because it also relates to lopsided government spending, is the prison reform movement. Grassroots organizing here is most often directed toward the states where the consequences of policy choices are more immediately evident (Drug Strategies, 2001). Throughout the United States, accordingly, bills are being introduced to expand treatment and rehabilitation services with varying degrees of success. In Idaho and California, strikingly, initiatives in favor of government-funded treatment in lieu of incarceration for low-level drug offenders have been successful. In California, however, the lack of adequate funding threatens to hinder the program's success.

The prison reform movement in the Canadian provinces has achieved notable success in terms of overhauling their women's prison system from a male-oriented to a gender-specific, regionalized model. Based on her personal organizing experiences, Faith (2000) offers lessons for prison reform activists. I have paraphrased her guidelines as follows:

• Let insiders speak in their own voices to get the word out that prisons as a response to street crimes are ineffective.

- Build a support base for the work through forums, held inside and out, to facilitate communication.
- As a form of social expression, music is at the heart of social change because it is a great unifier; most music is welcoming whereas rhetoric is often challenging and hostile.
- Because up to 80% of all imprisoned girls and women were victimized early in life, we need to work against the conditions that produce crime; to do this is to work against the inequitable political economies and patriarchal violence that victimize women and children.
- When appraising whether a project is merely reformist or revolutionary, the question to consider is, how significant is the change?

In Canada, as Faith informs us, the prisoners' rights movement continues to advocate, along with former prisoners and their allies, for prisoner rights and strong aftercare programming. There, of course, as here, there is still much work to be done.

Related to prison reform in its confrontation of societal injustice, is the anti-poverty, welfare rights movement. Poverty, as we know, is closely linked with crime, ill health, and poor sanitation. When a perceived discrepancy exists between the haves and have-nots, people feel they have no stake in the community. Within the context of dire poverty in Pennsylvania, the Kensington Welfare Rights Union is the preeminent example of a successful U.S. grassroots social activist campaign. This campaign, which was described in some detail in Chapter 5 because of its empowering and collaborative aspects, is closely aligned with the Social Welfare Action Alliance (SWAA). As a welfare rights organization, SWAA actively participates in such events as the New Freedom Bus Tours. Traveling across North America, bus riders take their message that poor people are worthy and capable to all who will listen. Other events in which SWAA members participate are presentation of evidence to the United Nations of the United States' violation of principles of the Universal Declaration through the implementation of "welfare reform"; joining in marches of homeless people to state capitals to demand affordable housing; conducting educational workshops on globalization and the economic roots of poverty; and writing articles on the New Freedom Bus Tours for the popular press and academic journals. (See, for example, the article on the New Freedom Bus Rides by Baptist, Bricker-Jenkins, & Dillon, 1999.)

Nongovernmental Organizations

Throughout this book, reference has been made to findings of human rights investigations conducted by Amnesty International and Human Rights Watch. Such nongovernmental organizations (NGOs) are effective crusaders for human rights; their methods are data gathering and the publication of periodic reports of human rights violations.

Founded in 1961, Amnesty International (AI) places its focus on political rather than on economic rights; in its massive outpouring of literature and annual reports, AI provides painstaking documentation of human rights abuses in each country where substantiated abuses have occurred. The organization has more than 1 million members and supporters in more than 140 countries and a staff of 350 (Amnesty International, 2001a). Representatives of AI testify before national legislatures and submit reports to the United Nations and other intergovernmental organizations. The basic strategy is to show that people from around the world are watching and that they care.

The United States always makes the list of countries in violation of human rights treaties due to its inhumane treatment of prison inmates and practice of the death penalty. The shocking and meticulously researched report on U.S. prisons, "Not a Part of My Sentence: Violations of the Human Rights of Women in Custody" (Amnesty International, 1999), revealed to the world the rampant sexual abuse of female inmates by male correctional officers that was little known before the report was made public.

With a staff of 180 regional experts, Human Rights Watch (HRW) operates in more than 70 countries around the world. HRW's blueprint for action is the Universal Declaration of Human Rights. Recent investigations have been conducted on the use of rape as a war crime; the impact of AIDS on children in Kenya; and the use of the war on terrorism by Russia, China, and others to curb legitimate dissent. Recently, HRW has been at the forefront of efforts to promote the International Criminal Court. Highlighted on its web site is HRW's strong statement of opposition to the Bush Administration's efforts to exempt Americans from the court's reach (see http://www.hrw.org).

The work of NGOs, such as the two organizations we have discussed here, is of significance to the social work profession because of success in uprooting instances of injustice, the international focus on human rights violations on the home front, and the model provided of bearing witness to human suffering as an effective form of human action. Social workers worldwide, in their own political efforts to effect social change, can use the documentation provided by respected NGOs such as Amnesty International and Human Rights Watch. Social work researchers likewise, may use these facts in their own writings to bolster the case for legislative reform efforts.

Social action begins where people say no to injustice, "in small places, close to home," in the words of Eleanor Roosevelt, quoted at the beginning of this chapter. To conclude this discussion on how we can make a difference, I have chosen to present two small-scale but powerful examples of defiant, personal heroism. The first narrative, Box 7.2, concerns a stand against racial territoriality within prison walls; the second, Box 7.3, concerns reactions to a tirade against gays and lesbians from the pulpit.

Box 7.2   Standing Up Against Racism

by David Goodson, MSW

As a former prison inmate, I recall a facet of prison life that is crucial to one's survival: *territory*. Prisons tend to be segregated from a structural (prison official procedures) and a practical (inmate's choice) standpoint. On a practical level, blacks chose to sit with blacks at meal times in the cafeteria, and Mexicans chose to sit with Mexicans, and whites chose to sit and eat with whites. This and other activities in essence involved *claiming territory*.

Personally, I never bought into it, although I did associate with predominantly black inmates at dinnertime and other activities.

However, on a couple of occasions I was confronted with a potentially costly choice. While in jail on one occasion, I was in a pod or cellblock with 98% black males when a white male was housed in our pod. A few of the brothers (black inmates) were going to take the white guy's food and not allow him to eat as long as he was in our pod. I confronted the brothers to defend the rights of the white guy, saying that he had done nothing wrong to any of us, and it's not right to take his food and that they were not going to take his food.

The brothers respected my position and the white inmate was allowed to eat. On another occasion when I was transferred to another prison and was the "new kid on the block," I went to the cafeteria to eat. I wasn't familiar with the territory, meaning I didn't know what section the blacks, whites, or Mexicans sat in. I happened to sit in the section where white inmates sat. A white guy walked up and demanded that I get out of his seat, but I told him that I don't play the territory game and I'll sit anywhere I choose to sit. It became a very heated and intense moment between the two of us, but eventually he backed down and found another seat elsewhere. I am convinced that I didn't play the "claiming territory game" because prior to transferring to this new prison, this situation happened to me (only in reverse). I was accustomed to sitting in a regular sort of seat for mealtime with the brothers, and one day a new white guy, who was not familiar with the territory, was sitting in the seat that I usually sat in. The brothers demanded that the white guy get up and find another seat, and as he (the white guy) began to get up and move, I told him to go ahead and sit there because "I don't own that seat." The brothers were a bit upset with me but I just don't play that game, and they respected that, and they (the brothers) got over it.

I am telling all of this to say that it takes courage and conviction to stand up for not only what you believe in but what you know in your heart to be the

continues...

right thing to do, even when it's in opposition to those closest to you (family, friends, coworkers, race, or fellow inmates).

I will further submit that this is the kind of courage and conviction that white America has to have to stand up against racism and change this world.

Printed with permission of David Goodson, MSW.

Box 7.3   No More Music Today

by Jonathan Wilson

For centuries, closeted gay and lesbian people have been implicitly protesting the false stereotypes about them, the blatant, even haughty, self-righteous discrimination and the hateful rhetoric. They have been implicitly protesting the isolation, the silence, the ignorance, and the indifference (the ultimate form of hatred).

Because gay and lesbian people have been taught the same misinformation about same-gender oriented people as everyone else has been taught, this implicit protest has traditionally been in the form of self-destructive behaviors. They have dropped out of school. They have abused alcohol and other drugs. They have engaged in promiscuous behaviors. They have committed suicide. And worse, they have lived entire lifetimes of lies and deceit. Every such self-destructive act has been an implicit protest. It has hurt the individual gay and lesbian person, and it has hurt society as a whole. It has resulted in endless days of anguish and sleepless nights for themselves and those who love them. It has resulted in the loss of their energy, their creativity, their productivity, their self-confidence, their taxes, and their intellectual and artistic contribution to society.

And it is changing, thank God Almighty.

It is changing with men who are willing to join and participate in a gay men's breakfast club that meets in broad daylight once a month with prominent community opinion leaders, the largest breakfast club in the state of Iowa. It is changing with men and women who do nothing more daring than drive around with a rainbow or triangle bumper sticker on their cars. It is changing with some businesses and some governmental subdivisions adopting policies assuring nondiscrimination employment environments for all persons regardless of gender orientation. As self-respect grows, there is daily less self-destructive implicit protest.

continues...

Recently, a black Baptist preacher in the South was waxing eloquent in his condemnation of gay and lesbian children of God. He was really getting into it in the tradition and spirit of Pat Robertson, Jerry Falwell, and our local version of Professor Harold Hill, Bill Horn. Suddenly, in the middle of the sermon, the gay choirmaster announced in a resonant voice, "There will be no more music today." He then walked out of the sanctuary and the entire choir and most of the congregation followed.

It happened. Things are changing, thank God Almighty. If every gay male church organist elected on the same Sunday not to "play," there would be very little music that day and a powerful point would be made.

Such explicit protest is healthy, productive, and utterly effective. It is a great improvement over implicit, self-destructive protest. It is where we are heading and it promises tremendous progress in the very near term for enlightenment, tolerance, personal empowerment, and equality.

Source: Wilson, 1997. Reprinted with permission of Jonathan C. Wilson, attorney, who retains the copyright and can be reached at 515.288.2500.

Summary and Conclusion

This chapter presented a strategy for policy analysis that was radical in terms of the underlying goals of effecting broad-based change in the pursuit of justice. From the academic exercise of asking the big questions about policy, we moved into the area of learning/teaching from a human rights perspective—various techniques for shaping awareness and promoting group solidarity were described.

Although policy practitioners might favor one type of intervention over another, all types have a role to play in confronting societal injustice. Working within the system to change the system carries the least risks and the highest possibility of effectiveness in most situations. Being co-opted by the system, however, is always a risk; sometimes as the innovator compromises to move up within system, the compromises take a psychological toll. The role of conformist becomes a self-fulfilling prophecy. Barring that happenstance, the closer one can get to the source of the decision-making, the better.

Sometimes the system (as represented by the agency) is promoting injustice itself and working through channels fails to bring relief. In such a situation, the worker may decide to go to a higher authority, choosing to be true to his or her ethics over loyalty to the organization. The whistleblower might go public at some point, perhaps to share information with the press in conjunction with an investigation or court case. In any case, whistleblowing may function as a precursor to change.

Other means of social action discussed in this chapter include legislative advocacy to influence progressive legislation (or counter retrogressive legislation), and reform through litigation—using the courts to right a wrong. The drug court movement was discussed as an innovative, cost-effective alternative to the war on drugs.

The human rights concepts that framed Chapter 6 provided the point of departure for this chapter as well. Here human rights were seen from a social action standpoint. Central to social actions such as the shaping of anti-discriminatory legislation, grassroots campaigning against poverty, and the investigative work of international NGOs is the notion that people are endowed with basic human rights, which we as citizens of the world are duty bound to protect. Increased interchange between the field of social work and human rights lawyers, progressive legislators, and NGO campaign members has the potential to contribute to the development of innovative approaches to promoting social justice. NASW strongly endorses the fundamental principles set forth in the human rights documents of the United Nations and, in their policy statement, "International Policy on Human Rights," urges that:

- Social workers must become partners with the United Nations in advancing human development and human rights, including economic human rights and closing the economic gap.

- In all fields of social work practice, whether with individuals or families, with groups, communities, domestic institutions, or nations, social work must be grounded in human rights.

- Recognizing that social workers who advocate on behalf of human rights can become subject to reprisal, NASW should ensure that social workers who are threatened are given full support of the profession.

The appalling prevalence of wars, genocide, ethnic cleansing; discrimination and social exclusion, gender inequality, battering, rape, and the sale of women; sweatshops, child labor, and enslavement; and the suppression of human rights demonstrates that the struggle for human rights remains a high priority for the social work profession in the 21st century. (p. 182)

To the extent that societal values can be translated into public dialogue and other forces of social action, injustice at the societal level can be effectively challenged. Through such political involvement, the debate within the field of social work relating to individual change versus environmental change will have moved one step closer toward the environmental side of the equation.

Eight
Restorative Justice

We have to build a society where it's easier for people to be good.

Dorothy Day

You don't have to look hard to find social workers involved in all sorts of innovative activities and social change efforts related to societal justice and personal empowerment. From program initiatives to welfare rights campaigning to the peace movement, as we have seen, social workers are there. One area of innovation in which the U.S. social work profession has been remiss, however, is in the burgeoning field of restorative justice. Significantly, neither the *Encyclopedia of Social Work* (Edwards, 1995) nor the *Dictionary of Social Work* (Barker, 2003) includes the term. A search on Info-Trac (as of October 2003) of *Criminal Justice Abstracts* listed 247 articles on this subject compared to a mere four for *Social Work Abstracts*. Much of the information for this chapter, accordingly, is drawn from U.S. criminal justice and international social work and religious sources.

At the risk of seeming too much of an optimist, my prediction is that this situation is likely to change. This prediction is based on three major developments. First, I am anticipating a heightened influence of Canadian social work on the U.S. profession, thanks to a first-ever collaboration between the two countries through joint membership in the North American section of the International Federation of Social Workers (Stoesen, 2003). Canadian social workers are well versed in restorative principles, which they utilize in practice with youthful offenders and school situations. The second major influence relates to social work's increasing attention to indigenous and international knowledge: family group conferencing is a restorative method from New Zealand that is being modeled worldwide. Thirdly, the most extensive evaluation research on victim–offender mediation is being conducted at the Center of Restorative Justice and Peacemaking, which is housed at the University of Minnesota's School of Social Work.

It is highly appropriate although unusual that the Center of Restorative Justice and Peacemaking has a social work connection because so many in the profession work with persons who are court ordered into treatment as offenders, not to mention all the persons victimized by crime who come into treatment to work on issues of traumatization. As well, training in social work prepares graduates for work in juvenile and adult correctional institutions to provide general counseling for personal issues and substance abuse treatment, and to teach social skills such as stress management and anger management. Nevertheless, compared to other areas of social work practice, the clash between social work values and societal values is at its most pronounced here, in the correctional system. Whereas the general purpose of the criminal justice system is to punish offenders and deter others from law-breaking behavior by setting a harsh example, social work's mission, as we know, is to help people help themselves and to challenge social injustice (NASW, 1996). Under the guidelines of the Council of Social Work Education (CSWE) (2003), social work programs integrate concerns of social and economic justice content grounded in "human and civil rights" within the curriculum (Section IV C). There is much social injustice in the criminal justice system; violations of human and civil rights are systemic.

Human rights, as we saw in Chapter 7, are not always provided to U.S. citizens in our courts of law and correctional institutions. Criticism from human rights organizations has been directed not only toward the treatment of accused offenders, but also toward the treatment of victims of crime. In the United States, the justice system has evolved into an impersonal system based largely on plea-bargaining agreements between the prosecutor and the lawyer for the defense. In the rare case of a full-blown trial, a winner-takes-all battle to sell one's case to the jury ensues (Zehr, 1995).

Imagine, if you can, a system of justice consonant with social work values. Such a system would be victim-centered and anti-oppressive. It would be empowering to all parties. Process would be as important as outcome: The six core values of social work would be honored: the opportunity for service to the community; social justice or fairness; dignity and worth of the person; importance of human relationships; integrity; and professional competence.

Such a system would restore rather than dispel justice. It would provide a completely different way of thinking about crime and victimization, one more concerned with restoring losses to the individual and the community and preparing the offender for reintegration into the community than in removal from the community for a long period of time. Participation in this process would be voluntary and operate with the sanction of the more formal judicial system. Such an alternative process might be called restorative justice.

In this chapter, we explore the philosophy and practices of restorative justice, and examine the modern restorative movement in historical context. At the heart of this discussion is the description of each of the four most popular models of this form of justice—victim–offender conferencing, family group conferencing, community conferencing, and community reparation. Included in our discussion of reparation, at the macro level, is the controversial issue of reparations for wrongdoing against whole ethnic groups, tribes, or nations.

What does evaluation of the empirical research say about the effectiveness of these varied approaches? To answer this question, we examine recent scientific studies from the social science literature. Our focus then turns to healing, an area of major concern to social work practitioners. The final section of the chapter shows how closely restorative principles relate to the core social work values. The strengths perspective of social work is joined with restorative justice into an integrative model—the strengths-restorative approach. From the framework of this model, we will explore the relevance of restorative justice for victims, offenders, and the community. Throughout these pages, exemplary initiatives from different parts of the world will be described.

A basic argument of this book will be that restorative justice, as a multidimensional approach, can take into account social factors in the backgrounds of people related to their wrongdoing without in any way diminishing the magnitude of the loss experienced by the victim. Far from a threat to the human rights of the participants, restorative justice initiatives protect individual rights by providing options that no mere legalistic resolution could offer; participation is strictly voluntary. With regard to the matter of reparations for violations of human rights to whole classes of people, the restorative process is the method of choice for addressing the wrongs that have been done, both by individuals and by the state.

What Is Restorative Justice?

- After several meetings with the facilitator–counselor, a woman visits her grandson in prison; the grandson is serving time for the murder of his father (his grandmother's son). As the youth cries at the pain he has caused, grandmother and grandson express their love for each other in a deep embrace.
- A woman who had burglarized her friend's home sat with her family members in a circle that included the victim and the victim's family; after the victim told her story of fear and anguish and the offender apologized, arrangements were made for restitution.
- A big boy, "the school bully," listens to his victims tell of their misery due to the threats and ridicule they have experienced from this classmate; shaken by what he has heard, the bully promises not to continue acting like that and to get help for his problems.
- In an Indian peacekeeping circle, members of the community open the session with a prayer and reminder that the circle has been convened to discuss the behavior of a young man who assaulted his sister in a drunken rage; an eagle feather is passed around the circle, held by each speaker as he or she expresses feelings about the harmful behavior.

Common to all these illustrations is an emphasis on face-to-face communication, truth telling, personal empowerment, and healing by all parties to the wrongdoing. Around the globe, such restorative processes are offering hope for more constructive responses to harm inflicted by humans on one another. A deep yearning for community and reconciliation and a desire to be free from fear of another are propelling this vision (Pranis, 1999).

What is restorative justice and how does it differ from the more conventional forms of justice? The varieties of initiatives that fall under this rubric have their roots in the rituals of indigenous populations from across the globe. This form of justice has as its purpose the repairing of the harm that has been done to the victim, community, and offender himself or herself. Restorative justice condemns the criminal act but not the actor and holds the offenders accountable to the community (Umbreit, 2000). The restorative process can take place either in addition to or instead of standard judicial proceedings. This three-pronged approach gives individuals and families most directly affected by wrongdoing the opportunity to be involved in the resolution process. Providing a possible antidote to punitive politics, restorative theory can apply to a wide variety of contexts ranging from the most extraordinary forms of injustice considered by the South African Truth and Reconciliation Commission to corporate crime to ordinary, petty theft (Roach, 2000; Braithwaite, 2002).

More often described in terms of what it is not, rather than what it is, restorative justice is deceptively simple. In fact, this is just one of its many paradoxes. Among the paradoxes, restorative justice is:

- In seeming opposition to the dictates of criminal justice, yet it often operates through criminal justice auspices.
- Visionary, yet highly practical.
- A new approach that goes back to ancient customs and traditions.
- A person-centered and kind way of dealing with crime in a "lock-'em-up" era.
- Victim-focused yet beneficial to the offender as well.
- Secular yet often with religious overtones.
- An indigenous approach that can be applied universally, this innovation has been borrowed from the non-industrialized regions of the world rather than from areas of advanced technologies.
- A beacon of light to shine in the darkness.

The Restorative Justice Movement

Early History

Throughout history, local communities and traditional cultures developed ways of managing conflict, of bringing the offender to accountability to the community. These means of righting the wrong were ritualized but based on communication among members of the community and families of both parties. These forms of justice were found in all cultures. In the Navaho tradition, for example, peace-making is a form of communal response to help people who have been harmed by another (Sullivan & Tifft, 2001). Community justice operated in early modern Europe, but the emphasis on vengeance became formalized in the Middle Ages as feudal lords and kings consolidated the response to crime through the power of the state (Bazemore & Schiff, 2001). This development was an advance in the sense of preventing family feuds, yet the role of the victim was now relegated to that of witness (Pollard, 2000). Anything that violated the king's peace was interpreted as an offense against the king. Thus was retributive justice born. Trials by ordeal were common throughout early history. Today's trial might well be considered the ordeal. The trial or adversarial process is another development that dominates

Anglo-Saxon justice today. This process harks back to the Middle Ages in England when hired combatants fought duels on behalf of accused individuals (van Wormer, 1997). Today's trial is thus the counterpart to yesterday's dueling, which was literally trial by combat. Then, as now, it was a case of "winner takes all." Crime eventually became defined as an offense against the state. The role of judge emerged as a sort of referee between the disputing parties.

Today, deliberation takes place according to a standardized, one-size-fits-all trial, or more often, as mentioned earlier, a plea-bargaining arrangement; victim input tends to be minimal in plea bargaining hearings (Van Ness & Strong, 2002). Families on one side of the law are torn apart from families on the other side. Such court processes hardly enhance communication and healing among family members (Morris, 2000).

The legalistic concept of guilt, as Zehr (1995) indicates, is highly technical and removed from real-life experiences. The process rewards the person who denies his or her guilt and the one who has an aggressive, even ruthless attorney. The attorney's ability to demolish the witness, often the victim, is the measure of a successful lawyer. Individual accountability—to the victim or community—rarely enters into the picture. If an accused person confesses to the police, for example, his or her possibility of "getting a good deal" from the prosecutor is minimized.

Origins of the Modern Restorative Justice Movement

In 1974, frustrated by a system that did nothing to reform offenders, two Canadian Mennonites (one a probation officer) hit upon the idea of having two vandals meet with their victims to pay them back. Reluctantly the judge agreed; the youths went from house to house of the 20 persons whom they had vandalized to make restitution, and the victim–offender reconciliation movement was born (Zehr, 1995). Historically, restitution was designed to benefit the offender by promoting integrity and truth-telling and in being more humane than imprisonment. This form of justice continued to be used in Canada and came to the United States in the 1970s. Feminist-inspired victims' rights activists played a role in raising consciousness regarding the need for victims to be heard in the criminal justice process. The victims rights movement, as Viano (2000) suggests, received considerable support from the "law and order" contingent; together these groups championed victims' rights under the framework of traditional justice.

The 1980s saw a great expansion in victim–offender mediation programs, a fact Bazemore and Schiff (2001) attribute to the impetus for restitution and community service programs in the juvenile court. Local alternative diversionary projects for juveniles proliferated.

The initial conceptualization of restorative justice was bolstered through the pioneering work of Howard Zehr of Eastern Mennonite University (Umbreit, 2001). The focus of the early research on this new paradigm was in North America and to some extent in Europe. The American Bar Association has played a major role in recommending victim–offender mediation in courts throughout the country (Umbreit, 2001). International interest soon began to surge, however. Today, mediation of conflict through conferencing is the most highly developed in New Zealand where it is institutionalized throughout the whole system. All delinquency cases, except for murder and rape, for example, are handled in community family group conferences (Bazemore & Schiff, 2001). The similarities between restorative and aboriginal forms of justice, coupled with the failure of the existing criminal justice system to deal with the problems of indigenous populations, has enhanced its enthusiastic acceptance in New Zealand as in Northwest Canada (Roach, 2000).

With the passage of the Sentencing Act of 2002, New Zealand enacted new legislation to make restorative justice processes that had formerly been used with juveniles and families in the child welfare system also available for adult offenders (PFI Center for Justice and Reconciliation, 2002).

I first learned of restorative justice while in attendance at a social work conference in Canada. There I learned from social workers how juvenile justice had adopted restorative strategies to help kids stay out of trouble. One youth who had burglarized the home of his neighbors was held accountable by the neighbors. Seated in a circle, surrounded by family members, the boy was brought face to face with the personal suffering generated by the crime. The impact of such a community encounter can be positive, eliciting sincere apologies and reconciling neighbors who may then lose their fear of each other. In contrast to court adjudication, the conferencing encourages truthfulness and creative ways of making amends. Social workers who had participated as facilitators in such proceedings expressed their gratification at the good feelings that often emerged from such dialogue. Just as calls for retribution often bring out the baser instincts in people, they said, a focus on restoration and empowerment also tends to bring out the best in human nature. Where did they learn such an approach? From aboriginal teachings, they told me. Although the United States is far behind Canada (and New Zealand and the United Kingdom) in this regard, some states such as Vermont and Minnesota have integrated restorative justice programming within their departments of correction. We will discuss their exemplary initiatives later in the chapter.

On the international stage, the thrust for a restorative vision has been embraced through the role of the United Nations. Following consultation with nongovernmental organizations, the United Nations, through its Commission on Crime Prevention and Criminal Justice, approved a Canadian resolution that encourages countries to use the basic principles of restorative justice and to incorporate restorative justice programming in their criminal justice processes. These principles or guidelines were formulated by representatives of the 38 countries who attended a special U.N. conference for this purpose (see "U.N. Crime Commission Acts on Basic Principles," 2002). Sadly, the United States did not participate in the drawing up of these guidelines.

We could evaluate restorative justice programs, as Braithwaite (2002) suggests, in accordance with how well they meet the standards for human rights as spelled out in the U.N. Universal Declaration of Human Rights (see Appendix). Relevant articles of the Declaration for restorative programming include the right to protection, to ownership of property, to life, liberty, and security, even to health and medical care, and for the right not to be subjected to torture or cruel, inhuman treatment. The U. N. Declaration could provide guidance and a consensual foundation to cover many of the things we look to restore and protect in restorative processes. Above all else, restoration of human dignity to both victim and offender should be primary.

Worldwide, restorative justice has come a long way since two probation officers first pushed two tentative offenders toward their victim's homes in 1974 in Ontario. The criminal justice literature, indeed, is almost exclamatory regarding this new development. Restorative justice has variously been called "a new model for a new century" (van Wormer, 2001), "a paradigm shift" (Zehr, 1997), and "a revolution" (Barajas, 1995).

Introduction to the Four Models of Restoring Justice

Following Bazemore and Umbreit's (2001) typology, I have chosen to describe in this section four of the most popular forms of restorative conferencing. These include victim–offender conferencing, family group conferencing, community conferencing, and community reparation. Although Bazemore and Umbreit's (2001) typology was developed within the juvenile justice context, the models may easily be adapted to the needs of adult offenders as well. All four models take place within a community-based context and seek, in a non-adversarial setting, to bring victims, offenders, family, and community members together so that they may come to terms with the dimensions of pain and violation caused by the offender's actions. Keep in mind that these models are neither mutually exclusive nor are they complete in and of themselves. They are "ideal types" in the sociological sense of reconstructions of reality.

Restorative conferencing stresses offender accountability and the need to try to repair injuries to victims and to the communities in which these crimes have taken place. Whether these conferences occur before, during, or after adjudication, they promote education and transformation within a context of respect and healing. In implementing a particular model, one would adopt the various elements to the specific situation at hand. Consistent with the most fundamental principle of social work, we must attend to the caveat, "First do no harm."

Because of the complexity of the process, standard practices vary considerably with the local customs and particular circumstances. Victim–offender sessions, for example, may take place in "the free world" where material reparations are stressed or in prison where the focus is on information sharing and communication of regret. At any of these types of gatherings, any number of things can happen or fail to happen due to the emotional intensity of the occasion. By the same token, the impediments to evaluating outcomes are many, due again to the turbulent nature of the interchanges and the many variations in format (Presser & Van Voorhis, 2002).

Refer to Table 8.1 (p. 215) to compare the administration and process of each of the four basic restorative models to be discussed here.

Victim–Offender Conferencing

The most popular of the restorative models of providing justice, victim–offender meetings have a respectable 20-year track record (Bazemore & Umbreit, 2001). As suggested by its name, this model, introduced formally into the criminal justice arena in the 1980s, encourages one-on-one victim–offender reconciliation facilitated through a mediator. Key issues still to be resolved include the utilization of co-mediators; the nature and duration of follow-up victim–offender meetings; the use of victim–offender mediation for more serious and violent offenses; and the implementation of victim–offender mediation in multicultural and prison settings. Successful victim–offender programs have been implemented in places as diverse as Canada, England, Australia, and South Africa (Umbreit, Coates, & Roberts, 2000). Currently there are approximately 320 victim–offender mediation programs in North America and more than 700 in Europe (Bazemore & Umbreit, 2001).

A central feature of victim–offender conferencing is the presence of a trained facilitator. Although this intervention is often called victim–offender mediation, the mediation model to which feminists have raised considerable objection (and rightly so) is not the model I am referring to here. Presser and Gaarder (2000) carefully differentiate legal mediation between disputants and dialoguing between victims and offender. Furthermore, unlike the legal model, restorative justice is victim-empowering rather than victim-blaming. The protocol in this form of mediation is for victims to be given the opportunity to speak first.

In contrast to the traditional criminal justice procedures, restorative justice measures success not in terms of clearing the court docket or years in prison for the convict. The basic concern of what Brasswell, Fuller, and Lozoff (2001) term "real social justice" is concerned with healing relationships and with reclaiming stability and goodwill in the community. In victim–offender conferencing, crime victims and offenders are not placed in a passive role but are actively involved in a process to resolve personal conflict (Umbreit, 1993). Because the primary focus is on dialogue, my preference is for the term *conferencing* rather than mediation.

A case of unusual magnitude that shows the healing potential of this form of conferencing took place in Halifax, Nova Scotia. This was one of more than 2,500 cases in which parties to an incident met face to face with an offender to share the consequences of an act. Auld (2002) provides this report:

> Halifax (CP) – Passengers injured in a massive train wreck last year confronted the boy who caused the derailment, telling him in an emotional meeting

Thursday how the violent crash permanently altered their lives. A group from the Via Rail train that hurtled off the track in Stewiacke, N.S., sat down with the 15-year-old to find out why he removed a lock on a train switch and sent several cars plowing into a feed store.

"It was awkward, it was uncomfortable, but I'm glad I had the opportunity," said Paul Poirier, who was in the train's dining car with his wife, Jackie, when it derailed in April 2001. Twenty-three passengers and crew were injured and some were left with permanent disabilities.

"He expressed his regret and remorse."

First and foremost, victim–offender conferencing is victim-centered. What it offers to victims is the chance to meet offenders in a safe, trusting environment surrounded by family members and key players in the event. With the assistance of a trained facilitator, the victim is able to tell the offender and others about the crime's impact and question the offender about lingering aspects of the crime (Bazemore & Umbreit, 2001). There may or may not be a plan for financial restitution.

For the offender, such conferencing has the advantage of offering diversion from prosecution or the provision of the possibility of eventual parole. Psychologically, the opportunity to "come clean" as in cases of drinking and driving offenses, can be a step toward personal rehabilitation and healing. Participation by family members of the offender can enhance communication by formerly estranged relatives and create a climate of compassion and reconciliation all the way round.

Social workers can play an active role in case referral and intake, preparation of all parties for the encounter, conferencing, case follow-up, and research evaluation. Key issues for social workers to resolve include the utilization of co-facilitators; the nature and duration of follow-up victim–offender meetings; the use of victim–offender conferencing for more serious and violent offenses, including behind prison walls; and the implementation of victim–offender sessions in multicultural settings.

Exemplary Programs

Successful victim–offender programs have been implemented in Ontario and Manitoba, Canada; Valparaiso, Indiana; and Minneapolis, Minnesota, as well as Belgium, France, and England (Umbreit, 1999).

Minnesota stands out among the states in its infusion of restorative justice strategies within its Department of Corrections and for the gender-specific programming it has developed within its juvenile and adult institutions. The Minnesota Department of Corrections, furthermore, employs restorative justice planners to train people at the county level for diversionary conferencing (Pranis, 1999). The spirit of dialogue and healing is the defining factor within its programming.

In Minneapolis, the Central City Neighborhood Partnership has begun using panels of neighborhood residents to meet with offenders charged with soliciting prostitutes. If the offender cooperates with the residents' panel, the criminal case will be dismissed. At the conference individuals in the neighborhood tell the offender about the effects of prostitution on the neighborhood. Typical sanctions would be for the offender to contribute to an organization helping women escape prostitution, writing a letter of apology, and helping with construction on a halfway house (Knapp, 1999).

Deserving of special mention is the AMICUS program in Minneapolis. AMICUS is not an acronym; it translates simply as friend. This program for girls in trouble with the law combines gender-specific concepts with the principles of restorative justice. A major challenge of this approach is to counter what the girls, hardened by experiences with the criminal justice system, have learned: don't trust anyone, don't look anyone straight in the eye, the victim is the enemy. Now they are asked sit in a circle—along with the victims, victims' family members, their own family members, and their probation officers—and to trust the truth that will emerge from the circle. Individuals tell the offender how her behavior has caused harm with an emphasis on feelings; a spirit of empathy, dialogue, and healing prevails (see Goodenough, 2000).

Exchanges with Violent Offenders

Within prison walls and without, members of victim-impact panels speak to inmates and probationers. The purpose of such exchanges, which originated with Mothers Against Drunk Driving (MADD), is to confront persons convicted of drunk driving with the gravity of their behavior. A secondary purpose is to enable offenders to empathize with victims and/or family members for their loss. Attendance at such panels is generally required of the offenders. Panels typically consist of three or four victims who present their stress of grief and loss due to a car accident with an intoxicated driver (Office of Justice Programs, 1998). The format of the panels does not allow for dialogue but for listening and the growth of awareness.

Some individual victims are arranging meetings with convicts for the purpose of communication, to get questions answered about the crime. Meetings are arranged with the help of a victim liaison. Sometimes the offender uses the occasion to make amends and ask for forgiveness. A kind of spiritual healing may take place, a healing involving both offender and victim. A Texas program focused entirely on victims has a waiting list of 300 victims wanting to meet their offenders (Morris, 2000). About half are the friends and family members of murder victims, another 25% the survivors of violent crimes such as assault and rape.

A moving description of the Transformation House program at Lexington, Kentucky, is provided by Tereshkova (2000). Remarkably, the goal of the program is to bring together death-row inmates with their victims' families to promote healing for both parties. To learn more about the remarkable work that was being done at the women's prison in Kentucky, I went to Central Kentucky to interview Linda Harvey, social worker and founder of Transformation House. Harvey's work is solidly family-focused. Joining with a team of trained volunteers, Harvey offers interactive seminars to provide opportunities for healing for victims/survivors whose lives have been wrecked by violent crime. Seminars are offered in local prisons, as well, to help inmates face the impact of their crimes on surviving family members. Uniquely, Harvey's program operates outside the judicial system but in cooperation with prison professional staff.

Roche (2001), a victim liaison for the Iowa Department of Corrections, describes how she herself in 1993 went through the process. Her young husband had been killed by a drunk driver, leaving her the sole parent for their two-year-old son. As she relates her story:

> I very much wanted to have a voice at the trial and express my feelings to him, the man who had taken my husband's life. A lot of people wouldn't feel that way, but to me I needed to see him, to talk to him. And I felt he needed to hear this from me. I called the Department of Corrections. They said, "You're the victim, you can't do that."

> After several years of therapy I decided to give the Department of Corrections a call. This time I was referred to Betty Brown in Des Moines who is now the administrator of restorative justice for the state. Betty met with Robert Clay (who had killed my husband) at the prison in Fort Madison. At first he said there was no way. Robert's counselor had not wanted him to participate so Betty had to speak with her. Once he agreed, we both went through months of preparation.

> What do you want? This was the question I was instructed to work on. This was a serious crime, so the meeting was about dialogue, not restitution. I wanted Robert to make amends, to make amends so that he would not drink because of what he had done. I wrote out questions I wanted the answers to so when I met we'd know each other's responses.

> Arrangements were made through the prison system. The warden was suspicious, however. "I have no idea why you want to do this," he said.

> The meeting lasted three and a half hours. I was seated first, while the security guard looked on. When Robert walked in, I had a strong physical reaction. Betty was with me and Robert's counselor, and within a period of time, we were dialoguing. I played a tape of my son, Sam, now 6, during this meeting. Was it cathartic? Yes. And did Robert open up? Prior to the meeting, Robert was very quiet. This is what his counselor said; "He expressed no emotions. This meeting had an effect on him; now he's smiling for the first time."

Family Group Conferencing

We have the Maori people and social services authorities of New Zealand to thank for the introduction of this innovative programming known as *family group conferencing* (FGC). This model of restoring justice is an outgrowth of both aboriginal and feminist practice concerns stemming from the international women and children's rights movements of the late 1980s and beyond. Evoking the family group decision-making model in order to try to stop family violence, FGC made its mainstream criminal justice debut in New Zealand in 1989. It also made a stage appearance about the same time in England and Oregon. This model is currently being tested in Newfoundland and Labrador, as well as in other communities in New Zealand, Austria, England, Wales, Canada, and the United States (see Burford & Hudson, 2000). Currently FGC is used in many countries as a preferred sentencing and restorative justice forum for youthful offenders. Despite differences among jurisdictions, one common theme is overriding: FGC is more likely than traditional forms of dispute resolution to give effective voice to those who are traditionally disadvantaged.

In Child Welfare Practice

I have filtered out from the literature a number of characteristics of FGC relevant to child welfare practice. Compared to traditional practices in family work, the philosophy of FGC entails:

- The sharing of decision-making responsibilities with families.
- The social worker as partner/collaborator rather than expert.
- Decision-making by general consensus.
- Process and decision-making likely to reflect the culture, traditions, and needs of the participants.
- Stress on the *quality* of relationships, not family structures.
- A flexible definition of what constitutes a family.
- Acknowledgement of the value of kinship care over stranger care for children in need of care.
- A solution- rather than problem-focused framework.
- A proactive rather than investigative model for addressing child mistreatment.
- A focus on building up social networks while not being blind to the risks to children in an unhealthy social environment.

Social work educators Kemp, Whittaker, and Tracy (2000) have adapted a strengths-based *social network model* of FGC for child protection practice. Central to their model is network facilitation to tap into the real power of natural helping. Network meetings are conducted to prepare participants for extended family decision-making. The connection between the individual families and community resources is given special attention. For example, advocacy for kinship caregivers to become eligible for the same resources that are available to non-kin foster parents may be undertaken. Interlocking demands of previous poverty, social exclusion, weak community linkages, and troubled extended family relationships are typical challenges facing families seen in child welfare practice. Network facilitation is individually tailored, as Kemp and her colleagues indicate, based on an identification of existing and potential network members. Ideally, FGC will make creative use of network meetings for reconnecting estranged network members to the family circle.

In Juvenile Justice

Unlike FGC for decision-making concerning the welfare of an abused or neglected child, FGC for youthful offender situations involves a slightly different cast of characters and a focus on "deed not need." Here the focus is on the offense and the harm done. Compared to traditional forms of juvenile justice, FGC has the following characteristics (as described by Bazemore & Umbreit, 2001). Family group conferencing for youthful offenders:

- Entails an informal, "around the table," nonadversarial process.
- Includes a trained facilitator as discussion leader.
- Directly involves the victim and community affected by the wrongdoing in the discussion of the offense.
- Involves the victim and victim's family directly in decisions regarding appropriate sanctions.
- Stresses offender awareness of the human impact of his or her behavior.
- Provides the opportunity for the offender to take full responsibility for his or her behavior.
- Uses a narrative approach as each person involved tells how he or she is affected by the behavior in question.
- Engages the offender's family members and support system in the conference.
- Solicits the families' support in the process of the offender's making amends and repairing the harm.

The uniqueness of FGC for youth justice is that it enables the youth, the families involved, and any victims to produce collectively a plan of action that would be in the best interest of all (Masters, 2002). Following an apology by the offender and some discussion about making amends, private planning time is provided. Out of the hearing of the facilitator and others present, the youth and his or her supporters form a plan. The plan then is presented for approval to the victim(s) and the police. A latent goal of this process, as Masters indicates, is family empowerment.

Morris (2000) describes in detail the impact of FGC on the family members and others who attended the New Zealand gathering. This gathering of participants, seated in a circle, concerned Norman, a teenager who had robbed a store and then mugged a woman on the street:

> The conference opened in the usual New Zealand way: people introduced themselves, and a prayer was said. Then the facilitator explained the reasons for the Family Group Conference. The aims were to deal with past hurts, seek

any possible conciliation and reparation, and to make the offender accountable for his actions. The charges were read and Norman acknowledged he had done them....Norman's father spoke next. All those who report on FGCs say that one of the most powerful influences on offenders are the voices of those near and dear to them, speaking about how their behaviour has hurt them. Norman's father expressed sorrow to all the victims for his son's actions. (p. 129)

Events did not end there, however. Plans were made to help Norman get a job, to get re-involved with the church community, and to make arrangements to pay restitution for his crime.

The way it is presently practiced in the United States, FGC is criticized for its sometime failure to adequately prepare the victims and victim's family as well as the offender and his or her family. Umbreit (2000), for example, cautions FGC organizers against its offender-driven aspects, for example, letting the offender's group choose their seats first. Another idea that requires close monitoring, according to Umbreit, is the tendency to select probation officers and school officials as coordinators. Given the retributive climate of the American criminal justice system, conference coordinators may produce an atmosphere of shaming and blaming of the offender. The recommendation is for social workers or volunteers trained in conflict resolution skills to attend to the emotional needs of the diverse participants.

Community Conferencing and Circle Sentencing

The third of the restorative processes is that of community conferencing. Community conferences make it possible for victims, offenders, and community members to meet one another to resolve issues raised by the offenders' trespass (Swart, 2000). A particularly promising form of community conferencing is termed circle sentencing. Historically, sentencing circles were found in Canadian aboriginal and Native American cultures. These circles were adopted by the criminal justice system in the 1980s as First Nations peoples of the Yukon and local criminal justice officials endeavored to build more constructive ties between the criminal justice system and the grassroots community. In 1991, Judge Barry Stuart of the Yukon Territorial Court introduced circle sentencing in order to empower the community to participate in the justice process (Parker, 2001). One of the most effective developments in sentencing circles, as indicated by Parker, is the Hollow Water First Nations Community Holistic Healing Circle, which simultaneously addresses harm created by the offender, healing the victim, and restoring community goodwill. Circles have been developed most extensively in the Western provinces of Canada. They have also experienced a resurgence in modern times among American Indian tribes, for example, in the Navaho courts.

Sullivan and Tifft (2001) describe the "peacemaking circle" held by the Navaho court. This process involves all who have been harmed by an act of wrongdoing including members of their clans. At the beginning of the ceremony, the peacemaker will offer a prayer or ask an elder to do so, so that each person can seek guidance from the Great Spirit. Such a ritual, as Sullivan and Tifft indicate, helps each person transcend his or her own concerns. The talking process that ensues is not a matter of presenting legal evidence but of telling one's story within the context of one's own personal history.

Today circles increasingly may be found in more mainstream criminal justice settings. In Minnesota, circles fashioned after those traditionally used by First Nations People in the Canadian Yukon are used in a variety of ways for a variety of crimes and in varied settings including neighborhood disputes and problems at school (Bazemore & Umbreit, 2001). At St. Paul Transitional Housing Program, for example, to address concerns related to such issues as safety, self respect, race relations, and community building, a replica of an eagle feather is passed around a peacemaking circle (Chandler-Rhivers, 2001). Similarly, in a St. Paul suburban school district three restorative justice planners work in two elementary schools and one junior high school to conduct healing circles. Seated in a circle, students involved in conflict with other students communicate their feelings in the group. Students pass a feather back and forth; the holder of the feather is the only one allowed to speak. This process is often used in situations where racial slurs have been exchanged to promote understanding and empathy for members of other racial and ethnic groups (Riestenberg, 2001).

How does a sentencing circle work? The Yorkton Tribal Council Treaty Four Nations (1998) offer specific guidelines from a Native perspective on when to hold a sentencing or healing circle and procedures to follow. The process works as follows: participants typically speak out while passing around a "talking piece." Separate healing circles are initially held for the victim and the offender. After the healing circles meet, a sentencing circle (with feedback from family, community, and the justice system) determines a course of action. Other circles then follow up to monitor compliance, whether that involves, for example, restitution or community service (Bazemore & Umbreit, 2001; McCold, 2000). While few studies have been done on the effectiveness of sentencing circles, those studies do show generally positive results, despite some concerns over the duration of the process and the need to better prepare circle participants.

Community Reparation

At the Individual Level

Often referred to as the "Vermont model" of reparative probation, community reparation, or reparative probation, this form of restorative conferencing can be implemented more quickly within existing structures and processes of the criminal justice system. Vermont's radical restructuring of its corrections philosophy and practices stems from influences of the communitarian movement and to personalist philosophy generally (Hudson & Galaway, 1990; Thorvaldson, 1990).

In 1991, Vermont decided to overhaul its system, setting up reparative boards statewide to focus on repairing the damage to the victim and community. Composed of volunteers, the reparative group is charged with ensuring that low-risk nonviolent offenders are made aware of the impact of their behavior on members of the community. Vermont, in fact, is the first state to implement such conferencing on a statewide basis and the first to institutionalize the restorative justice philosophy.

The goal is to have all offenders pay back their victims even if they are in prison (van Wormer, 2001). Treatment is provided to meet the offender's needs as well. As with all restorative justice programs, the goal is to reduce the harm the offender has done to the victims and community and to reintegrate the offender into the community. Preliminary studies from Vermont show that more than 80% of the 4,000-plus offenders who entered the mediation process have completed it successfully, and that they are less likely to reoffend than those who enter probation (Bazemore & Umbreit, 1998).

This model involves a "reparative programs" track designed for offenders who commit nonviolent offenses and who are considered at low risk for reoffense. This track mandates that the offender make reparations to both the victim(s) and to the community. A reparative probation program such as Vermont's directly engages the community in sentencing and monitoring offenders, and depends heavily upon small-scale, community-based committees to deal with minor crimes (Sinkinson & Broderick, 1998). Reparative agreements are made between perpetrators and these community representatives, while citizen volunteers furnish social support in order to facilitate victim and community reparation.

This model involves members of the community in meting out justice. Unlike other forms of restorative justice, the process is more formal with the chairperson guiding participants through a questioning process. The victim's role has been minimal in the past although this may be strengthened in the future. To gain a sense of how the process works, read the following description from the U.S. Department of Justice bulletin written by Bazemore and Umbreit (2001):

The reparative board convened to consider the case of a 17-year-old who had been caught driving with an open can of beer in his father's pickup truck. The youth had been sentenced by a judge to reparative probation, and it was the board's responsibility to decide what form the probation should take. For about 30 minutes, the citizen members of the board asked the youth several simple, straightforward questions. The board members then went to another room to deliberate on an appropriate sanction for the youth. The youth awaited the board's decision nervously, because he did not know whether to expect something tougher or much easier than regular probation.

When the board returned, the chairperson explained the four conditions of the offender's probation contract: (1) Begin work to pay off his traffic tickets,

(2) complete a State Police defensive driving course, (3) undergo an alcohol assessment, and (4) write a three-page paper on how alcohol had negatively affected his life. The youth signed the contract, and the chairperson then adjourned the meeting. (p. 9)

The American public may be more familiar with this process today than formerly due to recent news accounts of the adjudication of presidential candidate Howard Dean's son who participated in a Vermont court diversion program for his role in the theft of alcoholic beverages from a country club. "In a few weeks," as stated in the ABC News report, "the younger Dean is to appear before a community board that will determine his punishment, which could include community service, writing a letter or apology or making restitution" (Associated Press, 2003, August 5). Lest the public think that the youth was receiving favored treatment, the article pointed out that for first-time offenders, this resolution was routine.

Societal Level Justice

Related to peacemaking on the small scale is conferencing at the societal level to right mass wrongs. Such wrongs generally consist of mistreatment and abuse of whole segments of the population based on differences in ethnicity, race, or creed. In contrast to the process we have explored thus far, this societal-level resolution often takes place years after the maltreatment, the victims may even be later generations, and the descendants of the original injured parties may be the actual complainants. The complaint is often filed in court through an attorney. The connection to restorative justice is in the aim of reparation or restoring what is due to victims, also the grassroots movement out of which the impetus for justice is derived.

When reparations were made in 1988 by the U.S. Congress to Japanese Americans for wrongs inflicted upon them after war was declared on Japan (including confiscation of their property and confinement in concentration camps), a precedent was set for other peoples to seek compensatory measures as, for example, Native Americans for treaties broken and brutal forced assimilation practices. In Australia, aboriginal peoples are currently organizing to receive reparations for their "stolen childhoods." The reference is to the forced removal of mixed race children from aboriginal mothers into orphanages or White homes. In the United States, the African American movement for reparations incurred by their ancestors through enslavement has been widely publicized.

How to obtain justice relevant to the priest sexual abuse scandal in the Catholic Church is a daunting problem to many communities in the United States and, to a lesser extent, Ireland. There is a lot at stake here because whole communities have suffered loss and disillusionment as a result of the scandal in perhaps the one institution they trusted. The church itself has been both victimizer and victim. Restorative justice principles, as opposed to seeking after retribution, therefore, are highly applicable to the kind of peacemaking that can benefit all parties.

Such principles are both meaningful within the Christian context and relevant to the needs of both the survivors and perpetrators of clergy sexual abuse. There is one relevant case on record to my knowledge. It sprang from the diocese of Providence, Rhode Island, and involved lawsuits by 36 people who were sexually abused as children by priests. Awards were provided in varying amounts proportionate to the severity of the abuse. What is remarkable about the case is that it was resolved not through adversarial means or impersonal plea bargaining, but through honest and open communication that took place in marathon mediation sessions. Survivors were treated with empathy by the church representatives; instead of attacking the victims' stories, compassion was shown and apologies offered. Consistent with the principles of restorative justice, the emphasis was on helping the victims, church, and community heal from the wrongs that had been done (Carroll, 2002).

In summary, the restorative process, with its peacemaking and reconciliatory attributes, is a powerful and highly effective means of handling conflict. Whether in a one-on-one situation or writ large, peacemaking is enhanced when amends can be made in a spirit of reconciliation.

For a comparative study of the four restorative conferencing models, refer to Table 8.1.

Evaluation Research

Restorative justice reform is an evolutionary process that begins with small pilot research projects in jurisdictions wishing to implement systemic change in juvenile and criminal justice (Bazemore & Umbreit, 1998). In order to ensure the continuation of such programs, it is important to examine the impact of initiatives on the participants, and to gauge the success of the interventions in achieving restorative justice goals; such goals include victim and offender progress toward rehabilitation. The evaluation research varies from general descriptions of particular interventions to more carefully conducted studies with comparison groups. For the form of intervention most often studied—victim–offender mediation—the evidence of program effectiveness has been consistently favorable. For example, in Vermont, the state that is at the forefront of the restorative justice movement, offenders who have successfully completed the requirements of the mediation process have been found to have lower recidivism rates than persons placed on probation (Bazemore and Umbreit, 1998).

In Winnipeg, Manitoba, in a diversionary project called the Restorative Resolutions Project, of 81 cases accepted into the program by officials, results were moderately successful. Over $130,000 in restitution was paid to victims. Many clients followed through with the community service work; one-quarter of the victims received written apologies from the offender; and clients demonstrated statistically significant lower recidivism rates as a result of participation in the program. One shortcoming of this project was the refusal of victims to meet offenders face

Table 8.1. Restorative Conferencing Models: Administration and Process

	Victim–Offender Mediation	Reparative Boards	Family Group Conferencing	Circle Sentencing
Origin	Since mid-1970s.	Since 1995 (similar youth panels, since 1920).	New Zealand, 1989; Australia, 1991.	Since approximately 1992.
Current Applications	Throughout North America and Europe.	Vermont; selected jurisdictions and neighborhoods in other states.	Australia; New Zealand; United States (since 1990s), in cities and towns in Montana, Minnesota, Pennsylvania, and other states.	Primarily the Yukon, sporadically in other parts of Canada, Minnesota, Colorado, and Massachusetts.
Referral Point in System	Mostly diversion and probation option. Some use in residential facilities for more serious cases.	One of several probation options (youth panels: almost exclusively diversion).	New Zealand: Throughout juvenile justice system. Australian Wagga Wagga model: Police diversion. United States: Mostly diversion, some use in schools and post-adjudication.	Various stages. May be diversion or alternative to formal court hearings and corrections process for indictable offenses.
Eligibility and target group	Varies. Primarily diversion cases and property offenders. In some locations, used with serious and violent offenders (at victim's request).	Target group is nonviolent offenders; eligibility limited to offenders given probation and assigned to the boards.	New Zealand: All juvenile offenders eligible except those charged with murder and manslaughter. Australian Wagga Wagga model: Determined by police discretion or diversion criteria.	Offenders who admit guilt and express willingness to change. Entire range of offenses and offenders eligible; chronic offenders targeted.

continues...

Staffing	Mediator. Other positions vary.	Reparative co-ordinator (probation staff).	Community justice coordinator.	Community justice coordinator.
Setting	Neutral setting (meeting room in library, church, community center); victim's home (occasionally, if all parties approve).	Public building or community center.	Social welfare office, school, community building, police facility (occasionally).	Community center, school, other public building, church.
Process and Protocols	Victim speaks first. Mediator facilitates but encourages victim and offender to speak, does not adhere to script.	Mostly private deliberation by board after questioning offender and hearing statements.	Australian Wagga Wagga model: Coordinator follows script in which offender speaks first, then victim and others. New Zealand: Model not scripted, allows consensus decision-making after private meeting of family members.	Keeper opens session and allows for comments from judge. Prosecutors and defense present legal facts of case (for more serious crimes). All participants allowed to speak when "talking piece" (feather or stick) is passed to them. Consensus decision making.
Managing Dialogue	Mediator manages.	Board chairperson manages. Participants speak when asked.	Coordinator manages.	After keeper initiates, dialogue managed by process of passing talking piece.

Source: Bazemore & Umbreit, 2001, pp. 8–9.

to face; instead, they submitted formal written statements. More educational counseling work presumably needed to be done to prepare victims for a personal encounter. (See Bonta, Wallace-Capretta, & Rooney, 1998).

Meta-analysis is a statistical technique that combines data from all the available empirical studies on a given intervention and provides a composite result. Meta-analysis is an analysis of analyses. To provide an aggregate measure of empirical findings on the effectiveness of restorative practices, Latimer, Dowden, and Muise (2001) have prepared a comprehensive report for the Department of Justice Canada. Studies selected for inclusion used a control of comparison groups and reported results on victim–offender satisfaction and/or recidivism rates. Curiously, few of the 22 studies that met the criteria were published in peer-reviewed journals. Most of the studies involved young males. Restorative programs were found to be significantly more effective on the basis of all criteria studied. Still offenders are more likely to adhere to restitution agreements and not to re-offend when they have gone through the conferencing ritual than are offenders processed through the standard format. Victim–offender mediation models had especially high victim and offender satisfaction results compared to family group conferencing. Recommendations are for more carefully randomly assigned pilot studies, long-term follow-up studies on victims, and effectiveness studies with female offenders.

An interview with Thomas Quinn (1998) of the National Institute of Justice provides the results of a survey developed by the University of Delaware and sent to a large sample including legislators, judges, and corrections officials. Findings revealed the respondents stressed several positive effects of the interactions—offenders were more likely to understand the impact of their crimes and to be forced to face the consequences of their acts, and the system worked more efficiently in diverting cases from the formal process and meeting the needs of victims. Concerns expressed about the program were vagueness of the term "restorative justice," due process issues—ensuring that participation was voluntary; the time-consuming nature of the preparatory work; and sentence disparities.

Perhaps more compelling than the survey findings on victim satisfaction are the personal stories collected by Morris (2000) in her world travels and Zehr (2001) in his interviews with crime victims years after their victimization. John Sage, for example, whose beloved sister was murdered, has found peace in speaking on a victim impact panel that visits prisons. "I'd never seen a group of people with less empathy in my life," he shares, "but I saw things happen. People's lives changed over a period of 90 days. I saw men admit to things they had never admitted to anybody" (p. 164).

Victim and Offender Healing

Where there has been victimization and possible trauma, rituals are needed to "heal the damaged souls of the people, to help them find ways to transform hatred into sorrow or forgiveness, to be able to move forward with hope rather than wallow in the evil of the past" (Braithwaite, 2002, p. 207). When the state is the culprit, restorative justice means reparations for the human rights violations that occurred. Reparations may take the form of governmental acceptance of responsibility for the wrongs done, often following a national inquiry.

On a global scale, the most astonishing example of public truth-telling and ca-
tharsis for crime has taken place in South Africa before the Truth and Reconciliation Commission. Victims of the old regime under apartheid testified, and former
officials who had committed unspeakable crimes in the name of apartheid were
forced to own up to these crimes.

"Without Memory, There Is No Healing. Without Forgiveness, There Is No
Future" is the title of an article by Green (1998) on how these Truth and Reconciliation Commission hearings on human rights abuses under apartheid attempted
to reconcile former victims and oppressors in that country. Cited in the article,
Archbishop Desmond Tutu declared:

> There's something in all of us that hungers after the good and true, and when
> we glimpse it in people, we applaud them for it. We long to be just a little like
> them. Restorative justice is focused on restoring the personhood that is dam-
> aged or lost. (pp. 5–6)

Forgiveness fosters healing, which in turn hastens forgiveness. The person who
stands to benefit the most from forgiving, or letting go of the hurt, is the person
who does the forgiving. Forgiveness is not forgetting or excusing the wrong. It
can be viewed as an unfolding process, a journey that involves working through
many issues. Forgiveness frees the self from the burden of hate and the right to
revenge. It involves rediscovering the humanity of the offender and surrendering
your right to get even and wishing your offender well (McCullough, Sandage, &
Worthington, 1997).

One of the most extraordinary accounts of forgiveness is provided by Morris
(1998), a survivor of rape and near-murder at the hands of the second of two vicious killers of *Dead Man Walking* fame. Morris's book is aptly titled *Forgiving the
Dead Man Walking*. In her words:

> Realizing I no longer "hated" Robert Willie freed me from some of the hold
> he'd had over me. If I didn't hate him, maybe I could actually forgive him. Not
> for his own sake: he would never know. But for my sake. Maybe then I would
> be free to get on with my life. (p. 173)

We talked about sentencing and peacemaking circles earlier, circles of justice
that connect everyone involved in the conflict or injury. The indigenous paradigm
that informs the circle of justice is based on a holistic worldview of the aboriginal
inhabitants of North America. Smith (2003) describes how the development of
healing circles helped guide a whole Indian community in which sexual abuse of
children had been rampant into a process of dealing with the harm created by the
offenders, of healing for the victims, and of restoring stability in the community.

Through embracing members of the extended family, restorative justice has
been found to be highly effective in work in minority communities. These minority communities, including Native, African American, and Latino traditions, are

collectively rather than individually focused. The spirituality components, non-bureaucratic processes, and reliance on mutual aid are compatible with the values and traditions of the Latino community (Gutiérrez & Suarez, 1999) as well as with African-centered principles (Carter, 1997). Indigenous populations such as North American Native tribes incorporate spiritual leaders into the healing process. In aboriginal culture, all life is viewed as sacred; disruptive acts typically are viewed as signals of relational disharmonies. The circles, as we have seen, often draw on spiritual powers to remedy the relational disharmonies (see Ross, 2000).

Social workers in Hawaii have been quietly incorporating Native Hawaiian culturally based tradition into their human service interventions. The impetus for introducing the culturally specific programming came in the 1970s when it was noted that Native children were not responding to the standard forms of psychotherapy provided. Hurdle (2002) chronicles how social workers in collaboration with Hawaiian elders worked to revitalize the use of *ho'oponopono*, an ancient Hawaiian conflict resolution process. This model is embedded in the traditional Hawaiian value of extended family, respect of elders, need for harmonious relationships, and restoration of good will or *aloha*. The process is highly ceremonial and follows a definite protocol. With the leader in tight control of communication, the opening prayer leads in to an open discussion of the problem at hand. The resolution phase begins with a confession of wrongdoing and the seeking of forgiveness. Uniquely, as Hurdle relates, all parties to the conflict ask forgiveness of each other; this equalizes the status of participants. Conducive to spiritual healing, this healing format can be applied in many contexts. In drawing on guidance of the Kupanas (or wise elders) and a reliance on the family as a natural resource in reliving social problems, social workers are tapping into the community's natural resources, a cardinal principle of the strengths perspective (Heffernan, Johnson, & Vakalahi, 2002).

Restorative Justice and the Core Social Work Values

Restorative justice is a model with special relevance to the field of social work because social workers, as stated previously, have caseloads that consist of persons who have been victimized by crime or who are court-ordered into treatment because of offending behavior. Such clients may or may not be entangled with the criminal justice system; social workers may be directly or indirectly involved in court proceedings, and they may even be in a position to influence legislation pertaining to correctional treatment. Restorative justice, similarly, is of relevance to social workers in the field of child welfare; family group conferencing is being used in some counties and states to arrive at decisions in cases of child abuse and neglect (see Burford & Hudson, 2000.)

In the United States, more than in countries where restorative principles are widely applied—for example, New Zealand, Britain, and even Canada—the teachings of social work, in many ways are out of sync with the dictates of criminal justice. Mainstream criminal justice and the punitive ethos that underlies it must be understood historically, as a carryover in the United States from our somber Puritan past. Whereas social work has had a commitment for over 100 years to the rehabilitation of youth offenders, the recent trend toward ever harsher punishment, even for minors who commit crimes, is all too typical (Roberts & Brownell, 1999). Children who have committed serious crimes are now being tried in adult courts as if they were adults. Increasingly, the focus is on the act itself, not on the age of the perpetrator or the individual circumstances. The treatment of drug offenders is downright criminal (van Wormer & Davis, 2003).

Criminal justice proceedings, moreover, often reinforce the negative view that somehow the victim is responsible for the occurrence of the crime (Van Ness & Strong, 2002). Although the primary victim today is encouraged to speak during the sentencing portion of the trial, the secondary victims of crime—families and neighbors in the local community—typically have no voice at all, no matter how great the impact of the crime (Bazemore, 1999).

Given the empowerment ethos of social work contrasted with the retributive thrust of criminal justice, one would expect to find the leadership positions in the field of restorative justice to be filled by members of the social work profession. This is indeed the case in Canada and New Zealand; in the United States, for the most part, the territory has been ceded to lawyers, judges, and correctional workers. Nevertheless, restorative justice is beginning to make inroads in social work both through the work of individual practitioners working with offenders in progressive states that are promoting this model and through treatment effectiveness research such as that conducted at the renowned Center for Restorative Justice and Peacemaking. In the future, as has happened in other countries, members of the social work profession, with its long history of advocacy for community-based treatment, its belief system that most human beings are redeemable, and the renewed stress on interdisciplinary team work, can expect to play an increasingly active role in facilitation of healing circles and other restorative processes.

A Strengths-Restorative Approach

Strengths-based practice asserts that the responsibility offenders owe to victims, the community, and even to themselves is realized from direct behavior change, not through passive acceptance of punishment for the crime (Clark, 1997). At its heart, restorative justice builds on such active involvement by offenders in their rehabilitation; this process of accepting responsibility for one's actions and making amends to the victim and the community can be empowering for all concerned. Restorative justice is a process designed to bring out the best in people, regardless of what they have done, or the worst they have done, and so is social work's strengths-based practice.

For community practice, social workers are trained in cultural sensitivity, to adapt treatment strategies to the communication styles of the clients and to help clients tap into their community resources. The restorative justice model is highly compatible with social work's strengths perspective in its ability to incorporate Native rituals in healing circles and in its inclusion of religious concepts that are culturally specific to the participants. The inclusion of input from extended family and community representatives further endears this approach to cultural minorities.

In *Counseling Female Offenders and Victims: A Strengths-Restorative Approach,* (van Wormer, 2001) I fused these two models into one for direct social work practice with victims and offenders. The paradigm that I presented incorporated the generally accepted principles of restorative justice with two modifications. The first is a formal recognition of the role of the state in overseeing that justice is done and protecting the rights of the victim—battered wife or rape victim, for example—and the second is an elimination of the concept of shaming, sometimes termed "integrative shaming"—a concept borrowed from New Zealand indigenous rituals. The concept of shaming, at least regarding the terminology, is incongruent with the strengths perspective.

In a nutshell, the basic assumptions of strengths-restorative justice from a strengths perspective are as follows:

The Strengths-Restorative Model

Victim

- Treated with utmost respect, victim blaming avoided, acknowledgement of harm done by all concerned.
- Directly involved in the entire process.
- Given strengths-based therapy for emotional impact of crime.
- Referred to support and victim advocacy groups to promote further healing; protected against further violation.
- Resources placed in women's shelters; long-term counseling to offset trauma.
- Victim's family involved in entire process if victim so wishes.

Offender

- Crime as an act against the victim, community, and state.
- Stress on prevention such as substance abuse treatment and gun control.
- Goal of criminal justice to restore harmony to society.
- Offender seen as a whole person, often redeemable and able to change.
- Emphasis on dialogue, consensus, truth-telling, and open communication after guilt is determined.
- Reintegration through work, victim empathy programs, and making amends in prison.

Community

- As a true partner in process of justice, assists victims and supports offenders in completing obligations.

- Community service to help repair the harm and strengthen community bonds.
- As one option, offender answers to community members; community policing encouraged.
- Reliance on community resources; extensive use of volunteers as mediators.

Summary and Conclusion

By way of summarizing the key concepts of this chapter, I have organized the main points to coincide with each of the core values of social work, values all six of which relate directly and indirectly to the overarching theme of this book—confronting injustice and restoring justice. We start with the social work emphasis on social justice. Because victims and offenders frequently are among the most oppressed groups in society, they typically lack access to essential social and economic resources. The alternative forms of justice (to standard criminal justice) described in the preceding pages give voice and personal power to such individuals. Each of the four principal models of restorative justice—victim–offender conferencing, reparation boards, family group conferencing, and circle sentencing—offers not only a model but also a method. *Listening* is the method—listening to the client's or participant's story, not passively, uncreatively, but with full attention to the person in his or her family network and social and cultural environment.

Social justice is provided to the victim in that effort is made to restore what the victim has lost, while at the same time requiring the offender to face the consequences of his or her acts and the personal pain caused to the victim, the victim's family, the offender's family, and the community. These strategies can be combined with those of community-based corrections to create multifaceted programs of benefit to all involved (Hahn, 1998). Rehabilitation, rather than retribution, is the thrust of this approach. Social justice is provided to the offender through this emphasis and encouragement toward corrective action. The offender thereby must willingly and actively participate in his or her own healing.

Through embracing members of the extended family, restorative justice also has been found to be highly effective in minority communities. These minority communities, including Native American, African American, and Latino traditions, are collectively rather than individually focused. The circle sentencing approach, as used in the Yukon of Canada, utilizes traditional justice processes of tribal communities to view crime holistically. Tapping into the strengths of community resources, the process develops sanctions based on consensus of community members. Often a strong, spiritual component is part of such sentencing and healing circles.

Forgiveness and healing can go hand in hand. Forgiveness, in the sense of an ability of the aggrieved party to let go, can never be forced. When it occurs, forgiveness can be a powerful force for both victim and offender. Through counseling preparatory to victim–offender–community conferencing, social workers can play a key role in helping participants deal with strong feelings connected to the offense.

Service, which, in the order provided by NASW, precedes the other core values, clearly relates to the requirement for social workers to volunteer their expertise and caring to persons in need. Community organizing to set up progressive programming to meet the needs of victims and offenders, advocacy with state legislators for restorative initiatives in the courts of law, volunteer work at local prisons in helping victims find solace in the aftermath of crime, participation in victim impact panels, membership in local restorative justice information-sharing groups, the conducting of workshops and trainings on principles of restorative justice—these are just a few examples of the kind of service that dedicated social workers are providing and can provide.

Dignity and worth of the person is the third core value of social work. Through restorative justice, the dignity of both the offender and victim are maintained through a process that is the opposite of customary criminal justice proceedings—the orange suit, publicity attached to the arrest and trial, and the indignities and accusations heaped upon witnesses by lawyers on the opposing side. The focus of restorative justice is on the offender's whole personality, not only on the acts that have caused the harm. Ideally, this informal but emotionally intense process will have a humanizing effect on all participants. Unique to this process is the emphasis on restoring the individual to the community rather than on temporarily removing him or her from the community. This aspect of restorative justice can produce a special benefit to women, minorities, and other vulnerable persons who often fail to receive individual attention through the adversarial process. In this framework, voice can be given to concerns, for example, those relating to his or her sense of safety.

Importance of human relationships is another theme of the restorative justice movement. Through community service projects and psychologically through the contrition and remorse shown toward persons who are injured by the wrongdoing, offenders help compensate for what they have done. Such a drawing together of offender and victim in a face-to-face meeting might be especially conducive to helping youth appreciate the impact of their behavior and begin to turn their lives around.

The core social work value of *integrity* is evidenced in a format built on truth and frank disclosure. In contrast to traditional forms of justice, in which the accused remains silent while his or her lawyer fights against disclosures of guilt being admitted into evidence and challenges the integrity of prosecuting witnesses, restorative justice encourages open sharing of information among involved parties. Related to integrity is the notion of accountability. For example, counselors subscribing to this model would encourage girls in trouble with the law to take an active role in the modification of their own behavior. Putting them in touch with their own victimization often is seen as a first step in helping them to empathize with persons they may have victimized. For these girls, as well as for men and women serving time in prison, victim-impact panels may be invited to speak of the suffering they and their families have endured as victims of crime.

Competence, the final core social work value, comes into play through social work education in the social aspects of human behavior, in their training and work with both victims and perpetrators, and in their development of that quality I call social work imagination. Through the School of Social Work at the University of Minnesota, St. Paul, the National Restorative Justice Training Institute trains social workers and others on mediation and conflict resolution in communities, schools, workplaces, and with the justice system. Support and technical assistance are provided by systemic change in the juvenile justice system (see http://ssw.che.umn.edu/rjp/Seminars.html).

As a paradigm that envisions systemic social change, as one that can be applied at the micro level to reach one youth in one community or at the macro level to help heal a nation's woundedness, restorative justice has the potential to be one of the most influential models of the 21st century. Worldwide, bolstered by endorsement from the United Nations, the European Union, and entire governments, the restorative justice concept has shifted from the periphery of justice discourse to the very center. The theme of restorative justice—violence wounds, justice heals—holds an important message for policymakers in search of a just society. It holds an important message for the social work profession as well, especially when we expand the definition of violence to include structural violence. Social work as the predominant helping profession seeks, to paraphrase Day (1952), to work toward the building of a society where it is easier for people to be good. To accomplish this, we need to confront oppression in the society and restore justice to persons who have been wronged. The use of restorative models and alternative economic and social models are proof that there are ways to get this done. We need to think globally in order to act locally. We need to draw on our own social work imaginations and diverse talents. Some will teach; some will speak; some will organize; and others will gather data to be used by the teachers, speakers, and organizers. In this volume, we have embarked on a journey from policy analysis to social action to radical social policy to social change. The real challenge lies ahead...

Appendix
U.N. Universal Declaration of Human Rights

United Nations Resolution 217A (III), 1948

Preamble

Whereas recognition of the inherent dignity and of the equal and inalienable rights of all members of the human family is the foundation of freedom, justice and peace in the world,

Whereas disregard and contempt for human rights have resulted in barbarous acts which have outraged the conscience of mankind, and the advent of a world in which human beings shall enjoy freedom of speech and belief and freedom from fear and want has been proclaimed as the highest aspiration of the common people,

Whereas it is essential, if man is not to be compelled to have recourse, as a last resort, to rebellion against tyranny and oppression, that human rights should be protected by the rule of law,

Whereas it is essential to promote the development of friendly relations between nations,

Whereas the peoples of the United Nations have in the Charter reaffirmed their faith in fundamental human rights, in the dignity and worth of the human person and in the equal rights of men and women and have determined to promote social progress and better standards of life in larger freedom,

Whereas Member States have pledged themselves to achieve, in cooperation with the United Nations, the promotion of universal respect for and observance of human rights and fundamental freedoms,

Whereas a common understanding of these rights and freedoms is of the greatest importance for the full realization of this pledge,

Now, therefore,

The General Assembly,

Proclaims this Universal Declaration of Human Rights as a common standard of achievement for all peoples and all nations, to the end that every individual and every organ of society, keeping this Declaration constantly in mind, shall strive by teaching and education to promote respect for these rights and freedoms and by progressive measures, national and international, to secure their universal and effective recognition and observance, both among the peoples of Member States themselves and among the peoples of territories under their jurisdiction.

Article 1

All human beings are born free and equal in dignity and rights. They are endowed with reason and conscience and should act towards one another in a spirit of brotherhood.

Article 2

Everyone is entitled to all the rights and freedoms set forth in this Declaration, without distinction of any kind, such as race, colour, sex, language, religion, political or other opinion, national or social origin, property, birth or other status.

Furthermore, no distinction shall be made on the basis of the political, jurisdictional or international status of the country or territory to which a person belongs, whether it be independent, trust, non-self-governing or under any other limitation of sovereignty.

Article 3

Everyone has the right to life, liberty and security of person.

Article 4

No one shall be held in slavery or servitude; slavery and the slave trade shall be prohibited in all their forms.

Article 5

No one shall be subjected to torture or to cruel, inhuman or degrading treatment or punishment.

Article 6

Everyone has the right to recognition everywhere as a person before the law.

Article 7

All are equal before the law and are entitled without any discrimination to equal protection of the law. All are entitled to equal protection against any discrimination in violation of this Declaration and against any incitement to such discrimination.

Article 8

Everyone has the right to an effective remedy by the competent national tribunals for acts violating the fundamental rights granted him by the constitution or by law.

Article 9

No one shall be subjected to arbitrary arrest, detention or exile.

Article 10

Everyone is entitled in full equality to a fair and public hearing by an independent and impartial tribunal, in the determination of his rights and obligations and of any criminal charge against him.

Article 11

1. Everyone charged with a penal offence has the right to be presumed innocent until proved guilty according to law in a public trial at which he has had all the guarantees necessary for his defence.
2. No one shall be held guilty of any penal offence on account of any act or omission which did not constitute a penal offence, under national or international law, at the time when it was committed. Nor shall a heavier penalty be imposed than the one that was applicable at the time the penal offence was committed.

Article 12

No one shall be subjected to arbitrary interference with his privacy, family, home or correspondence, nor to attacks upon his honour and reputation. Everyone has the right to the protection of the law against such interference or attacks.

Article 13

1. Everyone has the right to freedom of movement and residence within the borders of each State.
2. Everyone has the right to leave any country, including his own, and to return to his country.

Article 14

1. Everyone has the right to seek and to enjoy in other countries asylum from persecution.
2. This right may not be invoked in the case of prosecutions genuinely arising from non-political crimes or from acts contrary to the purposes and principles of the United Nations.

Article 15

1. Everyone has the right to a nationality.
2. No one shall be arbitrarily deprived of his nationality nor denied the right to change his nationality.

Article 16

1. Men and women of full age, without any limitation due to race, nationality or religion, have the right to marry and to found a family. They are entitled to equal rights as to marriage, during marriage and at its dissolution.
2. Marriage shall be entered into only with the free and full consent of the intending spouses.
3. The family is the natural and fundamental group unit of society and is entitled to protection by society and the State.

Article 17

1. Everyone has the right to own property alone as well as in association with others.
2. No one shall be arbitrarily deprived of his property.

Article 18

Everyone has the right to freedom of thought, conscience and religion; this right includes freedom to change his religion or belief, and freedom, either alone or in community with others and in public or private, to manifest his religion or belief in teaching, practice, worship and observance.

Article 19

Everyone has the right to freedom of opinion and expression; this right includes freedom to hold opinions without interference and to seek, receive and impart information and ideas through any media and regardless of frontiers.

Article 20

1. Everyone has the right to freedom of peaceful assembly and association.
2. No one may be compelled to belong to an association.

Article 21

1. Everyone has the right to take part in the government of his country, directly or through freely chosen representatives.
2. Everyone has the right to equal access to public service in his country.
3. The will of the people shall be the basis of the authority of government; this will shall be expressed in periodic and genuine elections which shall be by universal and equal suffrage and shall be held by secret vote or by equivalent free voting procedures.

Article 22

Everyone, as a member of society, has the right to social security and is entitled to realization, through national effort and international co-operation and in accordance with the organization and resources of each State, of the economic, social and cultural rights indispensable for his dignity and the free development of his personality.

Article 23

1. Everyone has the right to work, to free choice of employment, to just and favourable conditions of work and to protection against unemployment.
2. Everyone, without any discrimination, has the right to equal pay for equal work.
3. Everyone who works has the right to just and favourable remuneration ensuring for himself and his family an existence worthy of human dignity, and supplemented, if necessary, by other means of social protection.
4. Everyone has the right to form and to join trade unions for the protection of his interests.

Article 24

Everyone has the right to rest and leisure, including reasonable limitation of working hours and periodic holidays with pay.

Article 25

1. Everyone has the right to a standard of living adequate for the health and well-being of himself and of his family, including food, clothing, housing and medical care and necessary social services, and the right to security in the event of unemployment, sickness, disability, widowhood, old age or other lack of livelihood in circumstances beyond his control.
2. Motherhood and childhood are entitled to special care and assistance. All children, whether born in or out of wedlock, shall enjoy the same social protection.

Article 26

1. Everyone has the right to education. Education shall be free, at least in the elementary and fundamental stages. Elementary education shall be compulsory. Technical and professional education shall be made generally available and higher education shall be equally accessible to all on the basis of merit.
2. Education shall be directed to the full development of the human personality and to the strengthening of respect for human rights and fundamental freedoms. It shall promote understanding, tolerance and friendship among all nations, racial or religious groups, and shall further the activities of the United Nations for the maintenance of peace.
3. Parents have a prior right to choose the kind of education that shall be given to their children.

Article 27

1. Everyone has the right freely to participate in the cultural life of the community, to enjoy the arts and to share in scientific advancement and its benefits.
2. Everyone has the right to the protection of the moral and material interests resulting from any scientific, literary or artistic production of which he is the author.

Article 28

Everyone is entitled to a social and international order in which the rights and freedoms set forth in this Declaration can be fully realized.

Article 29

1. Everyone has duties to the community in which alone the free and full development of his personality is possible.

2. In the exercise of his rights and freedoms, everyone shall be subject only to such limitations as are determined by law solely for the purpose of securing due recognition and respect for the rights and freedoms of others and of meeting the just requirements of morality, public order and the general welfare in a democratic society.
3. These rights and freedoms may in no case be exercised contrary to the purposes and principles of the United Nations.

Article 30

Nothing in this Declaration may be interpreted as implying for any State, group or person any right to engage in any activity or to perform any act aimed at the destruction of any of the rights and freedoms set forth herein.

References

Abram, F., Schmitz, C. L., Taylor, S. A., Tebb, S. C., & Bartlett, M. C. (2001). Empowering students in a feminist social work practice course. *Journal of Teaching in Social Work, 21*(3/4), 139–158.

Abramovitz, M. (1999). *Regulating the lives of women: U.S. social policy from colonial times to the present* (2nd ed.). Boston: South End Press.

Aleman, M., & Susskind, Y. (2000). Beyond Beijing: Some priorities for the global women's movement. *Madre: An International Women's Human Rights Organization.* Retrieved from http://www.madre.org

Alford, C. F. (2002). *Whistleblowers: Broken lives and organizational power.* Ithaca, New York: Cornell University Press.

Al-Krenawi, A. & Graham, J. (Eds.). (2003). *Multicultural social work in Canada: Working with diverse ethno-racial communities.* Oxford, England: Oxford University Press.

Allport, G. (1988). *The nature of prejudice: 25th anniversary.* New York: Perseus Publishing. (Original work published 1954)

American Civil Liberties Union. (ACLU). (1997). The rights of immigrants. ACLU Briefing Paper. Retrieved from http://www.aclu.org

The American heritage dictionary of the English language (4th ed.). (2000). New York: Houghton Mifflin.

American Psychiatric Association (APA). (2000). *Diagnostic and statistical manual of mental disorders DSM-IV-TR* (Text revision). Arlington, VA: American Psychiatric Publishing.

Americans support drug treatment over jail. (2001, June 6). Television report. New York: ABC News.

Amnesty International. (1999). *Not a part of my sentence: Violations of the human rights of women in custody.* New York: Author.

Amnesty International. (2001a). *About AI.* Retrieved from http://web.amnesty.org

Amnesty International. (2001b). *Broken bodies, shattered minds: Torture and ill treatment of women.* New York: Author.

Amnesty International. (2002). *Worldwide executions doubled in 2001.* Retrieved from http://www.amnesty.ca/library/news

Andreas, J. (2002). *Addicted to war: Why the U.S. can't kick militarism.* Oakland, CA: AK Press.

Angelou, M. (1989, June 6). Interview: The Oprah Winfrey Show [Television broadcast]. Chicago, IL: American Broadcasting Company.

Appleby, G. A., Colon, E., & Hamilton, J. (2001), *Diversity, oppression, and social functioning: Person-in-environment assessment and intervention.* Boston: Allyn & Bacon.

Armstrong, K. (2001, October 1). The true, peaceful face of Islam. *Time,* 48.

Asamoah, Y., Healy, L., & Mayadas, N. (1997). Ending the international-domestic dichotomy: New approaches to a global curriculum for the millennium. *Journal of Social Work Education, 33,* 389–401.

Associated Press. (1999). Violence raises the idea of forced treatment of the mentally ill. In *Waterloo-Cedar Falls Courier,* A5.

Associated Press. (2001, April 25). Manufacturer agrees to settle PCB lawsuit. Retrieved from http://www.ejrc.cau.edu/monsantoap.htm

Associated Press (2001, May 8). Status of mothers in the U.S. out of top 10 in report. *Chicago Tribune.* Retrieved from http://sns.Chicagotribune.com

Associated Press. (2003, August 5). Dean son to join court diversion program. New York: ABC News.

Associated Press (2003, October 14). *Study shows depth of obesity stigma.* ABC News. Retrieved from http://www.ABCNEWS.com

Auld, A. (2002, August 29). Injured passengers confront boy who caused Nova Scotia derailment. Retrieved from http://www.canada.com

Ayto, J. (1990). *Dictionary of word origins.* New York: Arcade Publishing.

Ayvazian, A. (2001). Interrupting the cycle of oppression: The role of allies as agents of change. In P. S. Rothenberg, *Race, class, and gender in the United States: An integrated study* (pp. 609–615). New York: W.H. Freeman.

Back to Bedlam (1999, March 10). [Television broadcast.]   New York:MSNBC. Geraldo Rivera. Retrieved from www.msnbc.com/news/

Baptist, W., Bricker-Jenkins, M., & Dillon, M. (1999). Taking the struggle on the road: The new freedom bus—freedom from unemployment, hunger, and homelessness. *Journal of Progressive Human Services, 10*(2), 7–29.

Barajas, E. (1995). *Moving toward community justice: Topics in community corrections.* Washington, DC: U.S. Department of Justice.

Barker, R. L. (2003). *The social work dictionary* (5th ed.). Washington, DC: NASW Press.

Barnes, A., & Ephross, P. (1994). The impact of hate violence on victims: Emotional and behavioral responses to attacks. *Social Work, 39,* 247–251.

Barovick, H. (1999, December 27). Bad to the bone. *Time,* 130–131.

Barry, M., & Hallett, C. (Eds.). (1998). *Social exclusion and social work: Issues of theory, policy, and practice.* Lyme Regis, England: Russell House Publishing.

Bazemore,G. (1999). Crime victims, restorative justice and the juvenile court: Exploring victim needs and involvement in the response to youth crime. *International Review of Victimology, 6,* 295-320.

Bazemore, G, & Schiff, M. (2001). Understanding restorative community justice: What and why now? In G. Bazemore & M. Schiff (Eds.), *Restoring community justice: Repairing harm and transforming communities* (pp. 21–46). Cincinnati, OH: Anderson.

Bazemore, G., & Umbreit, M. (1998). Balancing the response to youth crime: Prospects for a restorative juvenile justice and the juvenile court: Exploring victim needs and involvement in the response to youth crime. *International Review of Victimology, 6,* 295–320.

Bazemore, G., & Umbreit, M. (2001). *A comparison of four restorative conferencing models.* Washington, DC: U.S. Department of Justice.

Beechem, M. (2002). *Elderly alcoholism: Intervention strategies.* Springfield, IL: Charles C. Thomas.

Berzon, B. (1996). *Setting them straight: You can do something about bigotry and homophobia in your life.* New York: Plume.

Bibus, A., & Link, R. J. (1999). Global approaches to learning social welfare policy. In C. S. Ramanathan & R. J. Link (Eds.), *All our futures: Principles and resources for social work practice in a global era* (pp. 94–120). Belmont, CA: Wadsworth.

Bishop, A. (1994). *Becoming an ally: Breaking the cycle of oppression.* Halifax, Nova Scotia: Fernwood Publishing.

Black, D. W. (1999). *Bad boys, bad men: Confronting personality disorder.* New York: Oxford University Press.

Blue, A. W., & Blue, M.A.R. (2001). The case for aboriginal justice and healing: The self perceived through a broken mirror. In M. Hadley (Ed.), *The spiritual roots of restorative justice* (pp. 57–80). Albany, NY: State University of New York Press.

Bonta, J., Wallace-Capretta, S., & Rooney, J. (1998, October). *Restorative justice: An evaluation of the restorative resolutions project* (Report No. 1998-05). Ottawa, Canada: Office of the Solicitor General of Canada.

Boser, U. (2001, June 18). The unsparing rod. *U.S. News & World Report*, 43.

Braithwaite, J. (2002). *Restorative justice and responsive regulation.* Oxford, England: Oxford University Press.

Brasswell, M., Fuller, J., & Lozoff, B.(2001). *Corrections, peacemaking, and restorative justice.* Cincinnati, OH: Anderson.

Brenner, C. (1995). *Eight bullets: One woman's story of surviving anti-gay violence.* Ithaca, NY: Firebrand Books.

Bricker-Jenkins, M. (1991). The propositions and assumptions of feminist social work practice. In M. Bricker-Jenkins, N. Hooyman, & N. Gottlieb (Eds.), *Feminist social work practice in clinical settings* (pp. 271–303). Newbury Park, CA: Sage.

Bricker-Jenkins, M. (2001). Review of the book *Social work with lesbians, gays, and bisexuals. Journal of School Social Work, 11*(2), 93–95.

Bricker-Jenkins, M. (2002). Feminist issues and practice in social work. In A. Roberts & G. Greens (Eds.), *Social worker's desk reference* (pp. 131–136). New York: Oxford University Press.

British Association of Social Workers. (2002). Code of ethics for social work. Retrieved from http://www.basw.co.uk/articles.php?articleId=2

British Columbia Teachers Federation. (1999, December 1). *BCTF News.* Retrieved from http://www.bctf.ca/bctf-news

Brownell, P., & Moch, M. (2001). A society for all ages: Older adults and the social contract. In R. Perez-Koenig & B. Rock (2001), *Social work in the age of devolution: Toward a just practice* (pp. 55–68). New York: Fordham University Press.

Bulhan, H. A. (1985). *Franz Fanon and the psychology of oppression.* New York: Plenum Press.

Bullard, R. (1994). *Unequal protection: Environmental justice and communities of color.* San Francisco: Sierra Club Books.

Bullard, R. D. (2001). It's not just, pollution. Retrieved from http://www.ourplanet.com

Bureau of Justice Statistics. (1994). *State prison expenditures.* Washington, DC: U.S. Department of Justice.

Bureau of Justice Statistics. (1999a). *Prisoners in 1998.* Washington, DC: U.S. Department of Justice.

Bureau of Justice Statistics (1999b). *Women offenders.* Washington, DC: U.S. Department of Justice.

Bureau of Justice Statistics. (2000). *Prison and jail inmates at mid-year 1999.* Washington, DC: U.S. Department of Justice.

Bureau of Justice Statistics. (2002a). Prison and jail inmates at midyear 2001. Washington, DC: U.S. Department of Justice.

Bureau of Justice Statistics. (2002b). *Prisoners in 2001.* Washington, DC: U.S. Department of Justice.

Bureau of Justice Statistics (2003a). Capital Punishment Statistics. U.S. Department of Justice. Retrieved from www.ojp.usdoj.gov/bjs/cp.htm

Bureau of Justice Statistics(2003b). Prison and jail statistics at midyear 2002. U.S. Department of Justice. Retrieved from www.ojp.usdoj.gov/bjs

Burford, G., & Hudson, J. (Eds.). (2000). *Family group conferencing: New directions in community centered child and family practice.* New York: Aldine de Gruyter.

Burns, R. (1985). To a mouse. In J. Kinsley (Ed.), *Burns: Poems and songs.* Oxford: Oxford University Press. (Original work published 1785)

Burns, R. (1983). To a louse. In A. Partington (Ed.), *Oxford dictionary of quotations* (3rd ed.). Oxford: Oxford University Press. (Original work published 1786)

"Burst of milestones for gays is really a long-term trend." (2003, July 16). *Waterloo-Cedar Falls Courier*, p. C8.

Bush-Baskette, S. (1998). The war on drugs as a war against black women. In S. L. Miller (Ed.), *Crime control and women: Feminist implications of criminal justice policy* (pp. 113–129). Thousand Oaks, CA: Sage.

Byrne, D. (1999). *Social exclusion*. Buckingham, England: Open University Press.

Canadian Association of Schools of Social Workers (2000). *Education policy statements: Board of accreditation manual*. Ottawa: Author.

Canadian Association of Social Workers (1994). *Code of ethics*. Ottawa: CASW.

Carroll, M. (2002, September 10). $13.5 million settlement in Rhode Island clergy abuse. *The Boston Globe*. Retrieved from http://www.boston.com/globe/spotlight/abuse

Carter, C. (1997, September/October). Using African-centered principles in family preservation services. *Family in Society, 78*, 531–538.

Carter, J. (2002). The troubling new face of America. *The Washington Post*, p. A31.

Cattell-Gordon, D. (1990). The Appalachian inheritance: A culturally transmitted traumatic stress syndrome. *Journal of Progressive Human Services, 1*(1), 41–57.

Cemlyn, S., & Briskman, L. (2002, February 1). Social (dys)welfare within a hostile state. *Social Work Education, 21*, 49–60.

Center for Substance Abuse Treatment. (1999, January). *Substance abuse treatment planning guide and checklist for treatment-based drug courts*. Rockville, MD: Substance Abuse and Mental Health Services Administration.

Chambers, D. (2000). *Social policy and social programs: A method for the practical public policy analyst*. Boston: Allyn & Bacon.

Chandler-Rhivers, G. (2001). Circles—"A way to be." *Newsletter of the Minnesota Restorative Justice Initiative*, 2–3.

Chao, C. (1995). A bridge over troubled waters. In J. Adleman & G. Enguidanos (Eds.), *Racism in the lives of women: Testimony, theory, and guides to antiracist practice* (pp. 33–43). New York: Harrington.

Chapin, R. K. (1995). Social policy development: The strengths perspective. *Social Work, 40*, 506–514.

Charlton, J.I. (1998). *Nothing about us without us: Disability oppression and empowerment*. Berkeley, CA: University of California Press.

Chen-Hayes, S. (2001). Social justice advocacy readiness questionnaire. *Journal of Gay and Lesbian Social Services, 13*(1/2), 191–203.

Chesler, E., & Dunlop, J. (1995, September 25). Consensus on women's rights cleared the skies in China. *Christian Science Monitor*, 18.

Chesney-Lind, M. (1999). Review of the book *When she was bad: Violent women and the myth of innocence*. *Women and Criminal Justice, 10*(4), 113–118.

Chesney-Lind, M., & Pasko, L. (2003). *The female offender: Girls, women and crime* (2nd ed.). Thousand Oaks, CA: Sage.

Chesney-Lind, M., & Pollock, J. (1994). *Women's prisons: Equality with a vengeance*. In A. Merlo & J. Pollock (Eds.), *Women, law, and social control* (pp. 155–177). Boston: Allyn & Bacon.

Children are collateral casualties of N.Y. drug laws. (2002, June 18). Human Rights Watch. Retrieved from http://www.hrw.org/press

Christodoulou, C. (1991). Racism—A challenge to social work education and practice: The British experience. *Journal of Multicultural Social Work, 1*(2), 99–106.

Clark, M. (1997). Strengths-based practice: The ABCs of working with adolescents. *Federal Probation, 62*(2), 46–53.

Cohen, S. (2001, April). Denial: The enemy of peace. Interviewed in Pagina 12, Buenos Aires. Reprinted in *World Press Review, 47*.

Cohn, D., & Fears, D. (2001, March 13). Seven million say they're multiracial: Official census results show more diverse nation in 2000. *Washington Post*, p. A1.

The Commonwealth Fund. (2003). Percentage of GDP spent on health care. Retrieved from http://www.cmwf.org

Congress, E., & Sealy, Y. (2001). The role of social work ethics in empowering clients and communities. In R. Perez-Koenig & B. Rock (Eds.), *Social work in the era of devolution* (pp. 305–330). New York: Fordham University Press.

Cook, B. W. (2001, June 3). Putting people first: A world made new. *Los Angeles Times*.

Cooper, G. (2001, July 19). Child welfare improving, study says. *Washington Post*, p. A3.

Corrin, C. (1996). Conclusion. In C. Corrin (Ed.), *Women in a violent world* (pp. vii–26). Edinburgh, Scotland: Edinburgh University Press.

Council of Europe (2001, February 14). Council endorses common position on social exclusion action plan. *European Report*, 490.

Council on Social Work Education. (2001) *Educational policy and accreditation standards*. Retrieved from http://www.cswe.org/accreditation/EPAS/epas.pdf

Council on Social Work Education. (2003). *Handbook of accreditation standards and procedures* (5th ed.). Alexandria, VA: Author.

Coursen-Neff, Z., & Sifton, J. (2003, January 21). Falling back to Taliban ways with women. *International Herald Tribune*. Retrieved from http://www.hrw.org

Cowger, C. D. (1994). Assessing client strengths: Clinical assessment for client empowerment. *Social Work, 39*(3), 262–268.

Cowger, C. D. (1998). Assessing client strengths: Critical assessment for client empowerment. *Social Work, 39*(3), 262.

Coyle, E. A., Campbell, A., & Neufeld, R. (Eds.). (2003). *Capitalist punishment: Prison privatization and human and human rights*. London: Zed Books.

Cramer, E. P., Oles, T. P., & Black, B. (1997). Reducing social work student's homophobia: An evaluation of teaching strategies. *Arete, 21*(2), 36–49.

CreditCareCenter.com. (2003). "Women, Work and Wages." Retrieved from http://www.creditcarecenter.com/women/wage_gap_between_women_and_men.htm

Crime control and women: Feminist implications of criminal justice policy (pp. 113–129). Thousand Oaks, CA: Sage.

Criminal Justice Collective of Northern Arizona University. (2000). *Investigating difference: Human and cultural relations in criminal justice*. Boston: Allyn & Bacon.

Crittenden, A. (2001). *The price of motherhood: Why the most important job in the world is still the least valued*. New York: Metropolitan Books.

Curley, B. (2002). Wyoming launches most comprehensive anti-drug plan in U.S. *Join Together Report*. Retrieved from http://www.jointogether.org

Daalder, I. (2002, June 1). The anti-immigrant parties are racist, xenophobic and intolerant and could undermine the European Union. *Insight Magazine*. Retrieved from http://www.brook.edu/views/articles/daalder

Dabbs, J. M., & Dabbs, M. G. (2000). *Heroes, rogues and lovers: Testosterone and behavior*. Hightstown, NJ: McGraw-Hill.

Dalrymple, J., & Burke, B. (1995). *Anti-oppressive practice: Social care and the law*. Buckingham, England: Open University Press.

Daly, A., Jennings, J., Beckett, J., & Leashore, B. (1996). Effective coping strategies of African Americans. In P. Ewalt, E. Freeman, S. Kirk, & D. Poole, *Multicultural issues in social work* (pp. 189–203). Washington, DC: NASW Press.

Davis, A. Y. (2000). Foreword. In A. K. Wing (Ed.), *Global critical race feminism: An international reader* (pp. xi–xiii). New York: New York University Press.

Davis A. (1974). *With my mind on freedom: An autobiography*. New York: Bantam Books.

Davis, L. E. (1993). *Black and single: Meeting and choosing a partner who's right for you*. Chicago: Noble Press.

Day, D. (1952). *The long loneliness*. San Francisco: Harper.

DeWees, M., & Roche, S. (2001). Teaching about human rights. *Journal of Teaching in Social Work, 21*(1/2), 137–155.

Dinerman, M. (2002). Time for reform? *Affilia, 17*(3), 274–278.

Dobelstein, A. W. (2003). *Social welfare: Policy and analysis*. Belmont, CA: Brooks/Cole.

Dollard, J. (1998). *Caste and class in a southern town*. New York: Routledge. (Original work published 1957)

Dominelli, L. (2002a). *Anti-oppressive social work theory and practice*. New York: Palgrave.

Dominelli, L. (2002b). *Feminist social work: Theory and practice*. Hampshire, England: Palgrave.

Douglas-Brown, L. (2002, April 26). Fewer anti-gay hate crimes reported in 2001. Retrieved from http://www.washingtonblade.com

Downey, E., & Romano, M. (2001, November 3). Cross-cultural research on human rights: Knowledge and attitudes. Paper presented at the 19th Annual Baccalaureate Program Directors (BPD) Conference, Denver, CO.

Dr. Seuss. (1971). *The Lorax*. New York: Random House.

Drug Strategies. (2001). Critical choices: Making drug policy at the state level. Retrieved from http://www.drugstrategies.org/criticalchoices

Dubois, B., & Miley, K. K. (2002). *Social work: An empowering profession* (4th ed.). Boston: Allyn & Bacon.

Dyer, C. (1999, July 3). UK introduces far-reaching law to protect whistleblowers. *British Medical Journal*. Retrieved from http://www.findarticles.com

East, J. (1999). An empowerment practice model for low-income women. In W. Shera & L. Wells (Eds.), *Empowerment practice in social work: Developing wider conceptual foundations* (pp. 142–158). Toronto: Canadian Scholars Press.

"Editorial: The reluctant quitters." (2002, April 19). *The Des Moines Register*. Retrieved from http://miva.dmregister.com

Edwards, R. L. (Ed.-in-Chief). *Encyclopedia of social work* (19th ed.). Washington, DC: NASW Press.

Ehrenreich, B. (2001). *Nickel and dimed: Getting by in America*. New York: Metropolitan Books.

Einbinder, S. (1995). Policy analysis. In R. L. Edwards (Ed.-in-Chief), *Encyclopedia of social work* (19th ed., pp. 1849–1854). Washington, DC: NASW Press.

Elliott, D., & Mayadas, N. (1999). Infusing global perspective into social work practice. In C. S. Ramanathan & R. J. Link, *All our futures: Principles and resources for social work practice in a global era* (pp. 52–68). Belmont, CA: Brooks/Cole.

Elliott, K., & Denny, C. (2002, January 18). Top 1% earn as much as poorest 57%. *Guardian*. Retrieved from http://www.guardian.co.uk/Archive

Environmental Justice Resource Center. (August 31, 2001). Proposed NGO language on environmental racism, World Conference Against Racism. Retrieved from http://www.ejrc.cau.edu/NGOEJ.htm

Excerpts from the United Nations Declaration on Children (1990, October 2). *New York Times*, p. A1.

Faith, K. (2000). Reflections on inside/out organizing. *Social Justice, 27*(3), 158–168.

Faludi, S. (1991). *Backlash: The undeclared war against American women*. New York: Doubleday.

Farrell, J. (1967). *Beloved lady: A history of Jane Addams' ideas on reform and peace*. Baltimore: John Hopkins University Press.

Faulkner, W. (1950, December 10). Speech upon receiving the Nobel Prize, Oslo, Norway. In W. Faulkner, *The Faulkner reader: Selections from the works of William Faulkner* (p. 4). New York: Random House.

Femi, I. (1997). Interviewed by D. Rothberg, Unlearning oppression: Healing racism, healing violence. *ReVision, 20*(2), 18–25.

Figueira-McDonough, J. (1993). Policy practice: The neglected side of social work intervention. *Social Work, 38*, 179–188.

Finn, J. L., & Jacobson, M. (2003). Just practice: Steps toward a new social work paradigm. *Journal of Social Work Education, 39*, 57–78.

Firshein, J. (1998). Does treatment work? Washington, DC: Public Broadcasting Service. Retrieved from http://www.pbs.org/wne/closetohome

Fiske, H. (2002, July 22). Obesity prejudice: Stemming the tide of a tolerated injustice. *Social Work Today*, 14-17.

Flagg, F. (1987). *Fried green tomatoes at the whistle stop café.* New York: Ballantine Books.

Fleming, J., & Ward, D. (1999). Research as empowerment: The social action approach. In W. Shera & L. Wells (Eds.), *Empowerment practice in social work: Developing richer conceptual foundations* (pp. 370–389). Toronto: Canadian Scholars Press.

Flynn, J. P. (1995). Social justice in social agencies. In R. L. Edwards (Ed.-in-Chief), *Encyclopedia of social work* (19th ed.). (pp. 2173–2179). Washington, DC: NASW Press.

Food First (2002). Food first fact sheet: Hunger, a growing epidemic in America. Retrieved from http://www.FoodFirst.org

Franklin, D. (1990). The cycles of social work practice: Social action vs. individual interest. *Journal of Progressive Human Services, 1*(2), 59–80.

Freire, P. (1973). *Education for critical consciousness.* New York: The Seabury Press.

Fried, S. T (1997, Summer). Accountability and action: Monitoring U.N. commitments to the human rights of women. *Global Center News 4*, 4.

Fulbright, W. (1966). *The arrogance of power.* New York: Vintage.

Gambrill, E. (1997). *Social work practice: A critical thinker's guide.* New York: Oxford University Press.

Gambrill, E. D. (2001). Evaluating the quality of social work education: Options galore. *Journal of Social Work Education, 37*(3), 418–429.

Gambrill, E. D. (2002, Spring-Summer). Encouraging transparency (from the editor). *Journal of Social Work Education, 38*(2), 211–216.

Gans, H. (1976). The positive functions of poverty. *American Journal of Sociology, 78*(2), 275–289.

Gardner, M. (2001, November 28). Lifting the veil on women's subjugation. *Christian Science Monitor*, 15.

"Gays comprise 5 percent of electorate in 2002, new poll finds." (2002, November 21). Human Rights Campaign. Retrieved from http://www.hrc.org

George, J. (2002). Immigrants' rights stressed following September 11 attacks. *The Daily Camera.* Retrieved from http://www.thedailycamera.com

Geer, N. (2000) Human rights and wrongs in our own backyard: A case study of women in U.S. prisons. *The Harvard Environmental Law Review, 13.* Retrieved from http://www.lexis-nexis.com/universe/doc

Gil, D. (1998). *Confronting injustice and oppression: Concepts and strategies for social workers.* New York: Columbia University Press.

Gil, D. (2001). Challenging injustice and oppression. In M.O'Melia and K. K. Miley (Eds.), *Pathways to power: Readings in contextual social work practice* (pp. 35–44). Boston: Allyn & Bacon.

Gillespie, M. A. (2002, December). Turning point, *World Press*, 1.

Gillon, S. M. (2000). *That's not what we meant to do: Reform and its unintended consequences in twentieth-century America.* New York: W.W. Norton.

Glanton, D. (2001, April 4). More seek recognition as Indian. *Chicago Tribune*, 1A.

Glazer, M.P., & Glazer, P.M. (1991). *The whistleblower: Exposing corruption in government and industry.* New York: Basic Books.

Glazer, N. (1998, April 6). In defense of preference. *New Republic, 20.*

GlenMaye, L. (1997). Empowerment of women. In L. M. Gutiérrez, R .J. Parsons, & E. O. Cox (Eds.), *Empowerment in social work practice* (pp. 29–51). Pacific Grove, CA: Brooks/Cole.

Goodenough, K. (2000). AMICUS: Restorative justice for girls. Unpublished manuscript.

Goodman, E. (2002, July 12). Surely this country can sign a women's rights treaty. *Des Moines Register, 6A.*

Goodson, D. (2003). Quote cited in K. van Wormer, *Counseling female offenders and victims: A strengths-restorative approach.* New York: Springer.

Goodwin, J. (1994). *Price of honor: Muslim women lift the veil of silence in the Islamic world.* New York: Little, Brown.

Gould, A. (2001). *Developments in Swedish social policy: Resisting Dionysus.* London: Palgrave.

Graham, J. R., Swift, K. J., & Delaney, R. (2000). *Canadian social policy: An introduction.* Scarborough, Ontario: Allyn & Bacon Canada.

Green, C. (1998, January 11). Without memory, there is not healing: Without forgiveness, there is no future. *Parade, 5–7.*

Green, J. (1995). *Cultural awareness in the human services: A multi-ethnic approach* (2nd ed.). Englewood Cliffs, NJ: Prentice-Hall.

Greene, B. (1995). Institutional racism in the mental health profession. In J. Adleman & G. Enguidanos (Eds.), *Racism in the lives of women: Testimony, theory, and guides to antiracist practice* (pp. 113–125). New York: Harrington.

Gutiérrez, L. (1991). Empowering women of color: A feminist model. In M. Bricker-Jenkins, N. Hooyman, & N. Gottlieb (Eds.), *Feminist social work practice in clinical settings* (pp. 119–211). Newbury Park: Sage.

Gutiérrez, L., Fredricksen, K., & Soifer, S. (1999). Perspectives of social work faculty on diversity and societal oppression content: Results of a national survey. *Journal of Social Work Education, 35,* 409–419.

Gutiérrez, L., & Lewis, E. A. (1999a). *Empowering women of color.* New York: Columbia University Press.

Gutiérrez, L. M., & Lewis, E. A. (1999b). Preface. In L.M. Gutiérrez & E.A. Lewis (Eds.), *Empowering women of color* (pp. xi–xix). New York: Columbia University Press.

Gutiérrez, L. M., & Suarez, Z. (1999). Empowerment with Latinas. In L. M. Gutiérrez & E. A. Lewis (Eds.), *Empowering women of color* (pp. 167–186). New York: Columbia University Press.

Hahn, P. (1998). *Emerging criminal justice: Three pillars for a proactive justice system.* Thousand Oaks, CA: Sage.

Hanson, L. (2001, September 9). Racism world conference [Radio broadcast], Weekend Edition. Washington, DC: National Public Radio.

Harrington, N. (1962). *The other American: Poverty in the United States.* Baltimore, MD: Penguin Books.

Haynes, K. S., & Mickelson, J. S. (2000). *Affecting change: Social workers in the political arena* (4th ed.). Boston: Allyn & Bacon.

Healing circle shows offenders their human toll. (2001). *Toronto Star, NE4.*

Healy, L. (2001). *International social work: Professional action in an interdependent world.* New York: Oxford University Press.

Heffernan, K., Johnson, R., & Vakalahi, H. (2002, October 23–25). Ho'okele: A Pacific Island approach to aging. Paper presented at the Baccalaureate Program Directors Conference, Pittsburgh, PA.

Herrnstein, R., & Murray, C. (1994). *The bell curve.* New York: Free Press.

Hill, M., & Ballou, M. (1998). Making therapy feminist: A practice survey. In M. Hill (Ed.), *Feminist therapy as a political act* (pp. 1–16). New York: Haworth.

Hispanics now largest U.S. minority. (2003, January 21). Television broadcast, CBS News. New York: CBS Broadcasting. Retrieved from http://www.cbsnews.com

hooks, b. (1993). *Sisters of the yam: Black women and self-recovery.* Boston: South End Press.

hooks, b. (1994). *Teaching to transgress: Education as the practice of freedom.* New York: Routledge.

hooks, b. (2000). *Where we stand: Class patterns.* New York: Routledge.

Hooper, R. M. (1997, November/December). Attacking prison-based substance abuse. *Behavioral Health Management, 28–29.*

Houston, S., & Campbell, J. (2001). Using critical social theory to develop a conceptual framework for comparative social work. *International Journal of Social Welfare, 10,* 66–73.

Hudson, J., & Galaway, B. (1990). Community service: Toward program definition. *Federation Probation, 54*(2), 3–9.

Human Rights in the USA (1995). *Progressive, 59* (5), 15.

Human Rights Watch. (2001a). Children's rights. Retrieved from http://www.hrw.org/wr2k1/children

Human Rights Watch. (2001b). Hatred in the hallways: Violence and discrimination against lesbians, gay, bisexual, and transgender youth in U.S. schools. Retrieved from http://www.hrw.org/reports/2001/uslgbt

Human Rights Watch. (2002). Human Rights watch world report: United States. Retrieved from http://www.hrw.org/wr2k2/us.html

Human Rights Watch World Report. (2001). *Events of 2000.* New York: Human Rights Watch.

Hunt, G. (1998). *Whistleblowing in the social sciences.* London: Arnold.

Hurdle, D. (2002). Native Hawaiian traditional healing: Culturally based interventions for social work practice. *Social Work, 47,* 183–192.

Iatridis, D. S. (1995). Policy practice. In R. L. Edwards (Ed.-in-Chief), *Encyclopedia of social work* (19th ed.). (pp. 1855–1866). Washington, DC: NASW Press.

Icard, L., Jones, T., & Wahab, S. (1999). Empowering lesbian and bisexual women of color: Overcoming three forms of oppression. In L. M. Gutiérrez & E.A. Lewis, *Empowering women of color* (pp. 208–225). New York: Columbia University Press.

Ife, J. (2001). *Human rights and social work: Towards rights-based practice.* Cambridge, England: Cambridge University Press.

Jansson, B. (2001). *The reluctant welfare state: American social welfare policies-past, present, and future.* Belmont, CA: Brooks/Cole.

Jansson, B. S. (2003). *Becoming an effective policy advocate: From policy practice to social justice* (4th ed.). Pacific Grove, CA: Brooks/Cole.

Jimenez, M.A. (1999). A feminist analysis of welfare reforms: The Personal Responsibility Act of 1996. *Affilia, 14*(3), 278–293.

Johannesen, T. (1997). Social work as an international profession. In M.C. Hokenstad & J. Midgley, *Issues in International Social Work* (pp. 146–158). Washington, DC: NASW Press.

Johnson, C. (2003). *Blowback: The costs and consequences of American empire.* Berkeley, CA: Owl Books.

Johnson, K. (1998, May 15). Drug courts help addicts find way back. *USA Today,* 12A.

Johnson, K., & Locy, T. (2001, November 1). Terror-related arrests soar. *USA Today,* 1A.

Join Together Online (2002, July 26). *Study confirms effectiveness of drug courts.* Retrieved from www.jointogether.org

Jones, J. C., Bricker-Jenkins, M., & Members of the Kensington Welfare Rights Union (2002). Creating strengths-based alliances to end poverty. In D. Saleebey, *The strengths perspective in social work practice* (3rd ed., pp. 186–212). Boston: Allyn & Bacon.

Jost, K. (1993, January 8). Hate crimes. *CQ Researcher* 3(1), 3–14.

Kanenberg, H. (2003). Is managed care improving access to health care? No. In H. J. Karger, H. J. Midgley, & C. B. Brown, *Controversial issues in social policy* (2nd ed.) (pp. 212–219). Boston: Allyn & Bacon.

Kapur, R., & Campbell, J. (2002). The troubled mind of Northern Ireland: Social care object relations theory and political conflict. *Journal of Social Work Practice, 16*(1), 67–76.

Kaplan, E. (2001, July-August). Blue like me. *Utne Reader*, 85–93.

Karger, H. J. Midgley, & C. B. Brown. *Controversial issues in social policy* (2nd ed., pp. 212–219). Boston: Allyn & Bacon.

Karger, H. J., & Stoesz, D. (2002). *American social welfare policy: A pluralist approach.* Boston: Allyn & Bacon.

Kassebaum, P. A. (1999). *Substance abuse treatment for women offenders: Guide to promising practices.* Rockville, MD: U.S. Department of Health and Human Services.

Keefe, T. (2003). The bio-psycho-social-spiritual origins of environmental justice. *Critical Social Work, 3*(1), 1–17.

Kelley, P. (1996). Narrative theory and social work treatment. In F. Turner (Ed.), *Social work treatment: Interlocking theoretical approaches* (pp. 461–479). New York: Free Press.

Kemp, S., Whittaker, J. K., & Tracy, E. (2000). Family group conferencing as person-environment practice. In G. Burford & J. Hudson (Eds.), *Family group conferencing: New directions in community-centered child and family practice* (pp. 72–85). New York: Aldine de Gruyter.

Kendall, K. (1989). Women at the helm: Three extraordinary leaders. *Affilia, 4*(1), 23–32.

Kenyon, P. (1999). *What would you do?: An ethical case workbook for human service professionals.* Pacific Grove: Brooks/Cole.

King, M. L. (1963, August 28). I have a dream. Speech given on the steps at the Lincoln Memorial, Washington, DC.

King, M. L. (1967). *Where do we go from here: Chaos or community?.* New York: Harper & Row.

King, M. (1996, November 12). Suicide watch. *The Advocate*, 41–44.

Kirst-Ashman, K. K. (2003). *Introduction to social work and social welfare: Critical thinking perspectives.* Belmont, CA: Brooks/Cole.

Kirst-Ashman, K., & Hull, G. (1997). *Generalist practice with organizations and communities.* Chicago: Nelson-Hall.

Knapp, K. (1999). *An evaluation of community conferencing: The Central City Neighborhoods Justice Program.* Minneapolis: Central City Neighborhoods Partnership. Retrieved from http://www.crosswinds.net

Knickerbocker, B. (1999, July 30). Connections between hate crimes and churches. *Christian Science Monitor*, 3.

Kurzban, R., & Leary, M.R. (2001). Evolutionary origins of stigmatization: The functions of social exclusion. *Psychological Bulletin,*127(2), 187–209.

Kurzman, P. (1983). Ethical issues in industrial social work practice. *Social Casework, 64,* 105–112.

Lacayo, R., & Ripley, A. (2002, December 30), Persons of the year. *Time*, 32–50.

Laird, J. (2000). Family-centered practice with lesbian and gay families. In J. M. Mandiberg (Ed.), *Stand! An introduction to social work* (pp. 266–275). Madison, WI: Coursewise Publishing.

Larochelle, C., & Campfens, H. (1992). The structure of poverty: A challenge for the training of social workers in the North and South. *International Social Work, 35,* 105–119.

Latimer, J., Dowden, C., & Muise, D. (2001). *The effectiveness of restorative justice practices: A meta-analysis.* Ottawa, Canada: Research and Statistics Division, Department of Justice Canada.

Lee, J. A. (2001). *The empowerment approach in social work practice: Building the beloved community* (2nd ed.). New York: Columbia University Press.

Leland, J. (1995, July 17). Bisexuality. *Newsweek*, 44–50.

Lerner, M. (1971, January). All the world loathes a loser. *Psychology Today*, 5(1), 54–56, 66.

Leshner, A. (1998, October). Addiction is a brain disease—and it matters. *National Institute of Justice Journal*, 2–6.

Levi, P. (1991). Social work roles in law reform litigation. *Social Work, 36*, 434–439.

Levy, C. (1976). *Social work ethics*. New York: Human Services Press.

Lewis, R. (1995). American Indians. In *Encyclopedia of social work*: (pp. 216–225) Washington, DC: NASW Press.

Leyva, Y. (2001, November 28). Attacks have Mexicans heading south of the border. The Progressive Media Project. Retrieved from http://www.progressive.org

Link, R. (2002). Can re-authorization revitalize children's lives? Welfare reform through an international lens. *Electronic Journal of Social Work, 1*(1). Retrieved from http://www.ejsw.net

Lite, J. (2002, July 2). Staggering AIDS report from U.N. Retrieved from http://www.wired.com

Longres, J. (1995). Hispanics overview. In R. L. Edwards (Ed.-in-Chief), *Encyclopedia of social work* (19th ed., pp. 1214–1222). Washington, DC: NASW Press.

Lorde, A. (1984). *Sister outsider: Essays and speeches*. Trumansburg, NY: Crossing Press.

Lorenz, W. (1994). *Social work in a changing Europe*. London: Routledge.

Mackelprang, R. (2003, April). Interviewed by L. Stoesen, Rearranging the perception of disability. *NASW News*, 4.

Mandel, D. (2002). Instigators of Genocide: Examining Hitler from a social psychological perspective. In L. Newman & R. Erber (Eds.), Wh*at social psychology can tell us about the Holocaust* (pp. 259–284). Oxford: Oxford University Press.

Manning, S. (1997). The social worker as moral citizen: Ethics in action. *Social Work, 42*(3), 223–230.

Marano, H. (1993, November/December). Inside the heart of marital violence. *Psychology Today*, 50–53, 76–78, 91.

Markowitz, L. (1994, July/August). The cross-currents of multiculturalism. *The Family Therapy Networker*, 18–69.

Martinez, E. (1994). Seeing more than black and white. *Z Magazine*. Retrieved from http://www.zmag.org/zmag/articles/may94martinez.htm

Mason, R. (1995, June 1–4). An agenda for women's empowerment. *Quaker United Nations Office Briefing Paper*, 1.

Masters, G. (2002). Family group conferencing: A victim perspective. In B. Williams (Ed.), *Reparation and victim focused social work* (pp. 45–65). London: Jessica Kingsley Publications.

Matlovich, L. (2000). Words on his tombstone. Cited in K. van Wormer, J. Wells, & M. Boes, *Social work with lesbians, gays, and bisexuals: A strengths perspective* (p. 29). Boston: Allyn & Bacon.

Mattaini, M. (2001*). Peace power for adolescents: Strategies for a culture of nonviolent behavior for schools, home, and community*. Washington, DC: NASW Press.

Mawhiney, A. (1995). The First Nations in Canada. In J. Turner & F. Turner (Eds.), *Canadian social welfare* (3rd ed., pp. 213–230). Scarborough, Ontario: Allyn & Bacon.

Mayfield, E., Valentine, P., & McNeece, C. A. (1998, March 5–8). *Evaluating drug courts: An alternative to incarceration*. Paper presented at the Council on Social Work Education Annual Program Meeting, Orlando, FL.

McCold, P. (2000, April 10–17). Overview of mediation, conferencing and circles. Paper presented to the 10th United Nations Congress on Crime Prevention and Treatment of Offenders. International Institute for Restorative Practices, Vienna.

McCourt, F. (1996). *Angela's ashes: A memoir*. New York: Scribner.

McCullough, M. E., Sandage, S. J., & Worthington, E. L. (1997). *To forgive is human: How to put your past in the past.* Downers Grove, IL: Intervarsity Press.

McGirk, T., & Plain, S. (2002, February 18). Lifting the veil on sex slavery, *Time*, 8.

McMahon, M. O. (1994). *Advanced generalist practice with an international perspective.* Englewood Cliffs, NJ: Prentice Hall.

McRoy, R. G. (1995). Lower barriers to black adoptive families (Editorial). *Insight on the News, 11*(22), 19–21.

McWhirter, E. H.(1991). Empowerment in counseling. *Journal of Counseling and Development, 69*(3), 222–227.

Member blows whistle on Rx refills. (1990, June). *NASW News*, p. 3.

Menninger, K. (1966). *The crime of punishment.* New York: Viking Press.

Miley, K. K., O'Melia, M., & DuBois, B. (1998). *Generalist social work practice: An empowering approach.* Boston: Allyn & Bacon.

Miller, D. (2000). *Principles of social justice.* Cambridge, MA: Harvard University Press.

Miller, J., & Schamess, G. (2000). The discourse of denigration and the creation of "other." *Journal of Sociology and Social Welfare, 27*(3), 39–62.

Mills, C.W. (1956). *The power elite.* New York: Oxford University Press.

Mills, C. W. (1959). *The sociological imagination.* New York: Oxford University Press.

Mindell, C. (2001). Religious bigotry and religious minorities. In G. A. Appleby, E. Colon, & J. Hamilton (Eds.), *Diversity, oppression and social functioning: Person-in-environment assessment and intervention* (pp. 196–216). Boston: Allyn & Bacon.

Mitchell, A. (2000). [Review of the book *Social exclusion: An ILO perspective*]. *Industrial Relations*, 55(2), 357.

"Montreal civil union is Canada's first." (2002, July 22). *The Data Lounge*. Retrieved from http://www.datalounge.com

Morales, A., & B. Sheafor. (1995). *Social work: A profession of many faces* (7th ed.). Boston: Allyn & Bacon.

Morin, R., & Cottman, M. (2001, July 2–8). The invisible slap. *Washington Post National Weekly Edition*, p. 6.

Morris, D. (1998). *Forgiving the dead man walking.* Grand Rapids, MI: Zondervan.

Morris, R. (2000). *Stories of transformative justice.* Toronto: Canadian Scholars Press.

Moyers, B. (2002, February 2). Bill Moyers reports: Trading democracy [Television broadcast]. New York and Washington, DC: Public Broadcasting Service.

Moyers, B. (2002, October). The costs of war [Television broadcast]. Washington, DC: Public Broadcasting Service. Retrieved from http://www.pbs.org

Mullaly, B. (1997). *Structural social work: Ideology, theory, and practice* (2nd ed.). Toronto: Oxford University Press.

Murray, C. (1984). *Losing ground: American social policy, 1950–1980.* New York: Basic Books.

Murray, C. (1993, October). The coming white underclass. *The Wall Street Journal*, A14.

Nagda, B. A., Spearmon, M. L., Holley, L. C., Harding, S., Ballassone, M. L., Moise-Swanson, D., & de Mello, S. (1999). Intergroup dialogues: An innovative approach to teaching about diversity and justice in social work programs. *Journal of Social Work Education, 35*, 433–449.

Nakanishi, M., & Rittner, B. (1992). The inclusionary cultural model. *Journal of Social Work Education, 28*, 27–35.

Nash, M. (1999, November 1). Telling right from wrong. *Time*, 84.

National Association of Social Workers. (1996). *Code of ethics.* Washington, DC: Author. (Revised 1999)

National Association of Social Workers. (2000a). Electoral politics. In *Social work speaks* (pp. 96–100). Washington, DC: NASW Press.

National Association of Social Workers. (2000b). International policy on human rights. In *Social work speaks* (pp. 178–182). Washington, DC: NASW Press.

National Association of Social Workers. (2000c). *Social work speaks: National Association of Social Workers policy statements 2000–2003*. Washington, DC: NASW Press.

National Association of Social Workers. (2003). *Social work speaks: National association of social workers policy statements 2003–2006* (6th ed.). Washington, DC: NASW Press.

National Association of Social Workers, New York City Chapter. (1996, October). Historic delegate assembly revises the Code of Ethics. Retrieved at http://www.naswnyc.org/e10.html

Nelson, S. (2001, July 2-8). We must never forget. *Washington Post Weekly Edition*, p. 22.

Nonviolent solution backed on Iraq. (2002, November). *NASW News*, 6.

Office of Justice Programs (1998). *Victim impact panels*. Office of Justice Programs. Retrieved on October 26, 2003, from www.ojp.usdoj.gov

Ogletree, C. J. (2002, August 16–18). The case for reparations. *USA Weekend*, 6–7.

Oliphant, T. (2001, May 7). Poverty is a national disgrace. *Des Moines Register*, 7A.

O'Neill, J. V. (2000). Practice-research sync "crucial for survival." *NASW News*. Washington, DC: NASW Press.

Orwell, G. (1949). *1984*. New York: Harcourt, Brace, Jovanovich.

Otis, G. (2001, June/July). The global gag. *MS*, 17–20.

Palmer, P. J. (1998). *The courage to teach: Exploring the inner landscape of a teacher's life*. San Francisco: Jossey-Bass.

Parenti, M. (2002, February 10). Globalization and imperialism [Radio broadcast]. Boulder, CO: Alternative Radio.

Parker, L. (2001). *Circles*. Retrieved from http://www.restorativejustice.org

Parsons, R. (2002). Guidelines for empowerment-based social work practice. In A. Roberts & G. Greene (Eds.), *Social workers' desk reference* (pp. 396–401). New York: Oxford University Press.

Pawlak, E. (1976). Organizational tinkering. *Social Work 21*, 373–380.

Payne, M. (1997) *Modern social work theory: A critical introduction* (2nd ed.). Chicago: Lyceum Books.

Pearce, D. (2000). Rights and wrongs of welfare reform: A feminist approach. *Affilia, 15*(2), 133–152.

Pearsall, J. (Ed.) (1998). *New Oxford dictionary of English*. Oxford: Oxford University Press.

Pearson, P. (1997). *When she was bad: Violent women and the myth of innocence*. New York: Viking.

Pelton, L. H. (2001). Social justice and social work. *Journal of Social Work Education, 37*, 433–444.

Perez-Koenig, R. (2001). Actualizing social justice within the client/social worker relationship. In R. Perez-Koenig & B. Rock, *Social work in the era of devolution* (pp. 3–16). New York: Fordham University Press.

Petchesky, R. (2002, January). Phantom towers. *MS*, 8–13.

Peterson, K. S. (2001, September 19). Do we seek vengeance or justice? *USA Today*, 3D–4D.

"Petition Asks U.N. Racism Conference to Take Up U.S. War on Drugs." (2001, August 22). Retrieved from http://www.drugwarinjustice.org

Pfalzgraf, E. (2001, February 12). Sexual orientation motion, presented before the Cedar Falls, Iowa, City Council.

PFI Center for Justice and Reconciliation. (2002, October). New Zealand expands official recognition of restorative justice. *Restorative Justice Online*. Retrieved from http://www.restorativejustice.org/rj3/Feature/October02/NewZealand.htm

Pharr, S. (2001). Homophobia as a weapon of sexism. In P. Rothenberg (Ed.), *Race, class, and gender in the United States* (5th ed., pp. 143–152). New York: Worth Publishing Company.

Pinto, R. M. (2002). Social work values, welfare reform, and immigrant citizenship conflicts. *Families in Society, 83*(1), 85–92.

Piven, F. F., & Cloward, R. A. (1993). *Regulating the poor: The functions of public welfare* (updated edition). New York: Random House.

Pohiewozik, J. (2001, May 28). What's wrong with this picture? *Time,* 80.

Polansky, N. (1986). "There is nothing so practical as a good theory." *Child Welfare, 65*(1), 3–15.

Political Research Associates. (1999, August 6). What are the aggregate patterns of hate crime in the U.S.?. Retrieved from http://www.publiceye.org/

Pollard, C. (2000). Victims and the criminal justice system: A new vision. *Criminal Law Review, 5,* 13–17.

Popple, P. R., & Leighninger, L. (2001). *The policy-based profession: An introduction to social welfare policy analysis for social workers* (2nd ed.). Boston: Allyn & Bacon.

Pranis, K. (1999, May). Restorative justice: Reflections on national and international developments. Restorative Justice Online. Retrieved from http://www.restorativejustice.org

Presser, L., & Gaarder, E. (2000). Can restorative justice reduce battering?: Some preliminary considerations. *Social Justice, 27,* 175–187.

Presser, L., & Van Voorhis, P. (2002). Values and evaluation: Assessing processes and outcomes of restorative justice programs. *Crime and Delinquency, 48*(1), 162–187.

Prigoff, A. (2000). *Economics for social workers: Social outcomes of economic globalization.* Belmont, CA: Wadsworth.

Public Policy Institute of California. (2001, March 1). *Just the facts.* Retrieved from http://www.ppic.org/main/series.asp?i=14

Quinn, T. (1998, March). Interview. *The National Institute of Justice Journal,* 10–17.

Ramanathan, C., & Link, R. (1999). *All our futures: Principles and resources for social work practice in a global era.* Belmont, CA: Wadsworth.

Rapp, C. A. (1998). *The strengths model: Case management with people suffering from severe and persistent mental illness.* New York: Oxford University Press.

Reasons, C.E. and Hughson, Q. (1999). Violence against gays and lesbians. *Journal of Offender Rehabilitation, 30*(1–2), 137–150.

Reichert, E. (2003). *Social work and human rights: A foundation for policy and practice.* New York: Columbia University Press.

Reiman, J. (2000). *The rich get richer and the poor get prison: Ideology, class, and criminal justice* (6th ed.). Boston: Allyn & Bacon.

Reisch, M., & Andrews, J. (2001). *The road not taken: A history of radical social work in the United States.* Philadelphia: Brunner-Routledge.

Remafedi, G., French, S., Story, M., Resnick, M., & Blum, R. (1998, January). The relationship between suicide risk and sexual orientation. *American Journal of Public Health, 88,* 57–60.

Riestenberg, N. (2001, Winter/Spring). Restorative justice circles in Minnesota schools. *Newsletter of the Minnesota Restorative Justice Initiative,* p. 6.

Roach, K. (2000). Changing punishment at the turn of the century: Restorative justice on the rise. *Canadian Journal of Criminology, 42*(3), 249–282.

Robbins, S.P., Chatterjee, P., & Canda, E.R. (1998). *Contemporary human behavior theory: A critical perspective for social work.* Boston: Allyn & Bacon.

Roberts, D. (1996). *The color of welfare: How racism undermined the war on poverty.* New Haven, CT: Yale Law Journal Company.

Roberts, A., & Brownell, P. (1999). A century of forensic social work: Bridging the past to the present. *Social Work, 44*(4), 359–369.

Roche, M. (2001, November 11). Restorative justice. Presentation before a graduate social work class. Cedar Falls: University of Northern Iowa.

Rochlin, M. (2000). Heterosexual questionnaire. In K. van Wormer, J. Wells, & M. Boes, *Social work with lesbians, gays, and bisexuals: A strengths perspective* (p. 50). Boston: Allyn & Bacon.

Rogers, P. (2002). Latinos take lead on environmental issues. *Mercury News*. Retrieved from http://www.ejrc.can.edu/latinosej.html

Ronnau, J. (1994). Teaching cultural competence: Practical ideas for social work education. *Journal of Multicultural Social Work, 3*(1), 29–42.

Roosevelt, E. (1958). Remarks at the United Nations, March 27, 1953. In J. Lash, *Eleanor: The years alone* (p. 81). New York: W.W. Norton.

Ross, R. (2000). Searching for the roots of conferencing. In G. Burford & J. Hudson (Eds.), *Family group conferencing: New directions in community centered child and family practice* (pp. 5–14). New York: Aldine de Gruyter.

Roth, W. (1987). Disabilities, physical. In A. Minahan (Ed.-in-Chief), *Encyclopedia of social work* (18th ed., p. 86). Washington, DC: NASW Press.

Ryan, W. (1976). *Blaming the victim*. New York: Random House.

Sackett, D., Straus, S., Richardson, W., & Haynes, R. B. (2000). *Evidence-based medicine: How to practice and teach EBM* (2nd ed.). New York: Churchill Livingston.

Saleebey, D. (2001). *Human behavior and social environments: A biopsychosocial approach*. New York: Columbia University Press.

Saleebey, D. (Ed.). (2002). *The strengths perspective in social work practice* (3rd ed.). Boston: Allyn & Bacon.

Schechter, S. (1982). *Women and male violence: The visions and struggles of the battered women's movement*. Boston: South End Press.

Schechter, S. (2002, September 21). Presentation at The Effects of Domestic Violence on Children Conference, Cedar Falls, IA, University of Northern Iowa.

Scherrer, P. (2000). One third of Milwaukee, Wisconsin children growing up in working poor families. *World Socialist Web-Site*. Retrieved from http://www.wsws.org

Schneider, R. L., & Lester, L. (2001). *Social work advocacy: A new framework for action*. Pacific Grove, CA: Brooks/Cole.

Schor, J. (1991). *The overworked American: The unexpected decline of leisure*. New York: Basic Books.

Schwartz, M., & DeKeseredy, W. (1997). *Sexual assault on the college campus: The role of male peer support*. Thousand Oaks, CA: Sage.

Seccombe, K. (1999). *"So you think I drive a Cadillac?" Welfare recipients' perspectives on the system and its reform*. Boston: Allyn & Bacon.

Sharpe, R. (2001, May 28). What exactly is a "living wage"? *BusinessWeek Online*. Retrieved from http://www.businessweek.com

Shera, W., & Wells, L. M. (1999). *Empowerment practice in social work: Developing richer conceptual foundations*. Toronto: Canadian Scholars Press.

Sherraden, M. S., Slosar, B., & Sherraden, M. (2002). Innovation in social policy: Collaborative policy advocacy. *Social Work, 47*(3), 209–221.

Shulman, L. (1999). *Skills of helping individuals, families, groups, and communities* (4th ed.). Itasca, IL: Peacock Publishers.

Simon, B. (1994). *The empowerment tradition in American social work: A history*. New York: Columbia University Press.

Sinkinson, H. D., & Broderick, J. J. (1998). A case study of restorative justice: The Vermont Reparative Probation Program. In L. Walgrave (Ed.), *Restorative justice for juveniles: Potentialities, risks and problems*. Leuven, Belgium: Leuven University Press.

Smith, F. (2003). Incarceration of Native Americans and private prisons. In A. Coyle, A. Campbell, & R. Neufeld (Eds.), *Capitalist punishment: Prison privatization and human rights* (pp. 114–126). London: Zed Books.

Spitz, R. (1945). Hospitalization: Genesis of psychiatric conditions in early childhood. *Psychoanalytical Study of the Child, 1*, 53.

Steinberger, R. (2000). Incarcerated Indians. *Native Times*. Retrieved from http://www.okit. com

Stevenson, R., & Elder, J. (2002, July 18). Poll finds concern that Bush is overly influenced by business. *New York Times*. Retrieved from http://www.nytimes.com

Stiglitz,, J.E. (2003). Globalization and its discontents. New York: W.W. Norton.

Stoesen, L. (2002, October). Human rights measure passes in Pennsylvania House. *NASW News*, 10.

Stoesen, L. (2003, January). NASW, Canadians bolster relationship. *NASW News*, 6.

Stone, L., & C. James. (1995). Dowry, bride-burning, and female power in India. *Women's Studies International Forum, 18*(2), 125–134.

"Study: Spanking is a no-no." (2002, June 25). *Associated Press*. Retrieved from http://www. nospank.net/news3.htm

Substance Abuse and Mental Health Services Administration. (1999). Summary of outcomes in the National Treatment Improvement Evaluation Study, NEDS Fact Sheet 4, 1997. Rockville, MD: Author.

Sullivan, D., & Tifft, L. (2001). *Restorative justice: Healing the foundations of our everyday lives*. Monsey, NY: Willow Tree Press.

Sun, A-P. (2002). Homophobia among social work and non-social work students. *The Journal of Baccalaureate Social Work, 7*(2), 15–32.

Swan, N. (1995). California study finds $1 spent on treatment saves taxpayers $7. *NIDA Notes, 10* (2). Retrieved from www.drugabuse.gov/NIDA

Swart, S. (2000). Restorative processes: Mediation, conferencing and circles. Restorative Justice Online. Retrieved from http://www.restorativejustice.org

Swenson, C. R. (1998). Clinical social work's contribution to a social justice perspective. *Social Work, 43*, 527–537.

Swift, J. (1905). Thoughts on various subjects. In T. Scott (Ed.), *The prose works of Jonathan Swift*, Vol. 1, 273. London: George Bell and Sons. (Original work published 1706)

Talmage, E. (2001, January). "The dark past." Unpublished poem.

Tereshkova, Z. (2000, March 15). A chance to find peace. *Lexington Herald*, 1A.

Thorvaldson, S. (1990). Restitution and victim participation in sentencing: A comparison of two models. In B. Galaway & J. Hudson (Eds.), *Criminal justice, restitution, and reconciliation* (pp. 23–36). Monsey, NY: Criminal Justice Press.

Tice, C. J., & Perkins, K. (2002). *The faces of social policy: A strengths perspective*. Pacific Grove, CA: Brooks/Cole.

Torczyner, J. (2000). Globalization, inequality and peace building: What social work can do. In Canadian Association of Social Workers, *Social work and globalization* (pp. 123–145).. St. Joseph, Ontario: MOM Printing.

Tropman, J. (1989). *American values and social welfare: Cultural contradictions in the welfare state*. Englewood Cliffs, NJ: Prentice Hall.

Turner, F. (1996). An interlocking perspective for treatment. In F. Turner (Ed.), *Social work treatment: Interlocking theoretical approaches* (pp. 699–706). New York: Free Press.

Turner, D., & Cheboud, E. (2000). Advocacy and conflict resolution in social work: Can they really promote justice? An anti-oppressive approach. Paper presented at the Joint Conference of the International Federation of Social Workers and the International Association of Schools of Social Work, Montreal, Canada, July 29–August 2.

Umbreit, M. (1993). Crime victims and offenders in mediation: An emerging area of social work practice. *Social Work, 38*, 69–73.

Umbreit, M. (1999). Victim–offender mediation in Canada: The impact of an emerging social work intervention. *International Social Work, 42*(2), 215–227.

Umbreit, M. (2000). *Family group conferencing: Implications for crime victims.* Office for Victims of Crime. Washington, DC: U.S. Department of Justice.

Umbreit, M. (2001). *The handbook of victim offender mediation: An essential guide to practice and research.* San Francisco: Jossey-Bass.

Umbreit, M., Coates, R., & Roberts, A.W. (2000). The impact of victim–offender mediation: A cross-national perspective. *Mediation Quarterly, 17*(3), 215–229.

United Nations. (1948). *Universal declaration of human rights,* Resolution 217A (III). New York: United Nations.

United Nations. (1989). *Convention on the rights of the child.* (U.N. Document A/res/44/23). New York: United Nations. Retrieved from http://www.hrweb.org/legal/child.html

United Nations Children's Fund. (2000). UNICEF executive director targets violence against women. Retrieved from http://www.unicef.org

United Nations Children's Fund. (2001). *The state of the world's children 2001.* New York: Author.

U.N. Crime Commission acts on basic principles. (2002). Retrieved from http://www.restorativejustice.org

U.S. Census Bureau. (2000). Census 2000. Washington, DC: Author. Retrieved from http://www.census.gov

U.S. Centers for Disease Control and Prevention. (2002, January). *Trends in racial and ethnic specific rates for the health status indicators. Healthy People 2000.* No. 23. Retrieved from www.cdc.gov/nchs/data

University of Victoria School of Social Work. (2003). *Mission statement.* Retrieved from http://web.uvic.ca/socw/home.htm

Van Den Bergh, N. (Ed.). (1995). Introduction. In N. Van Den Bergh, *Feminist practice in the 21st century* (p. xix). Washington, DC: NASW Press.

Van Ness, D., & Strong, K. H. (2002). *Restoring justice* (2nd ed.). Cincinnati, OH: Anderson.

Van Soest, D. (1995). Peace and social justice. In *Encyclopedia of Social Work* (19th ed., pp. 95–100). Washington, DC: NASW Press.

Van Soest, D., Canon, R., & Grant, D. (2000). Using an interactive website to educate about cultural diversity and societal oppression. *Journal of Social Work Education, 36*(3), 463–479.

van Wormer, K. (1995a). *Alcoholism treatment: A social work perspective.* Belmont, CA: Wadsworth.

van Wormer, K. (1995b). Whistleblowing against the company: A case of ethical violations at a Norwegian treatment center. *The International Journal of Drug Policy, 6*(1), 8–15.

van Wormer, K. (1997). *Social welfare: A world view.* Belmont, CA: Wadsworth.

van Wormer, K. (1997, Summer). Doing alcoholism treatment in Norway: A personal reminiscence. *Reflections, 3*(3), 67–71.

van Wormer, K. (2001). *Counseling female offenders and victims: A strengths-restorative approach.* New York: Springer.

van Wormer, K., & Davis, D. R. (2003). *Addiction treatment: A strengths perspective.* Belmont, CA: Brooks/Cole.

van Wormer, K., Wells, J., & Boes, M. (2000). *Social work with lesbians, gays and bisexuals.* Boston: Allyn & Bacon.

Vermont Reparative Probation Program. In L. Walgrave (Ed.), *Restorative justice for juveniles: Potentialities, risks and problems.* Leuven, Belgium: Leuven University Press.

Verschelden, C. (1993). Social work values and pacifism: Opposition to war as a professional responsibility. *Social Work, 38,* 765–769.

Viano, E. (2000). Restorative justice for victims and offenders: A return to American tradition. *Corrections Today, 62*(4), 132–136.

Vines, G. (1999, November 29). The gene in the bottle. *New Scientist,* 29–43.

Wagner, D. (2001). *What's love got to do with it?: A critical look at American charity*. New York: The New Press.

War Resisters League. (2002). Where your income tax money really goes. Retrieved from http://www.warresisters.org/piechart.htm

Watkinson, A. M. (2001). Human rights laws: Advocacy tools for a global civil society. *Canadian Social Work Review, 18*(2), 267–286.

Weber, M. (1947). *The theory of social and economic organization*. New York: Oxford University Press.

Whitlock, K. (2001). *In a time of broken bones*. Philadelphia: American Friends Service Committee.

Wiesel, E. (1982). *Night*. New York: Bantam Books.

Williams, J. (2001). 1998 human rights act: Social work's new benchmark. *British Journal of Social Work, 31*, 831–844.

Williams, R. B. (2001, April 4). A blind eye toward racism. *The Denver Post*. Retrieved from http://www.collegefund.org/news

Wilson, J. C. (1997, November 3). No more music today. *Des Moines Register.*

Wilson, M. K., & Anderson, S. C. (1997). Empowering female offenders: Removing barriers to community. *Affilia: Journal of Women and Social Work, 12*, 342–369.

Wilson, M.G., & Whitmore, E. (2000). *Seeds of fire: Social development in an era of globalization*. Halifax, Nova Scotia: Fernwood Publications.

Wing, A. K. (2000). Global critical race feminism for the twenty-first century. In A. K. Wing (Ed.), *Global critical race feminism: An international reader* (pp.1–23). New York: New York University Press.

Wipf, J., & Wipf, P. (2001, September 13). Anti-immigration sentiments soar. Retrieved from http://immigration.about.com/library/weekly

Wood, P. (1992, Fall). Re-viewing the map: America's "empty wilderness." *Cultural Survival Quarterly*, 59–62.

Worldwatch Institute. (2002). Friday, March 8 is international women's day. Retrieved from http://www.worldwatch.org/press/news/2002/03/05

Wrangham, R., & Peterson, D. (1996). *Demonic males: Apes and the origins of human violence*. Boston: Houghton Mifflin.

Wronka, J. (1998). *Human rights and social policy in the 21st century*. Lanham, MD: University Press of America.

Yorkton Tribal Council Treaty Four Nations (1998). Sentencing circle: A general overview and guidelines. *Justice as healing, 3* (3). Retrieved from www.usask.ca/nativelaw/jah_circle.html

Young, I. M. (1990). *Justice and the politics of difference*. Princeton, NJ: Princeton University Press.

Zehr, H. (1995). *Changing lenses: A new focus for crime and justice*. Scottsdale, PA: Herald Press.

Zehr, H. (1997). Restorative justice: The concept. *Corrections Today, 59*(7), 68–71.

Zehr, H. (2001). *Transcending: Reflections of crime victims*. Intercourse, PA: Good Books.

Zeleny, J. (1997, October 19). Drug court: System's second chance. *Des Moines Register*, 1-2A.

Index